Icons *of* Hope

JOHN E. THIEL

Icons
of Hope

The "Last Things" in Catholic Imagination

University of Notre Dame Press · *Notre Dame, Indiana*

Sections of chapters 1 and 2 appeared originally as "For What
May We Hope? Thoughts on the Eschatological Imagination,"
Theological Studies 67 (September 2006): 517–41. © *Theological Studies.*

Chapter 3 appeared originally as "Time, Judgment, and Competitive
Spirituality: A Reading of the Development of the Doctrine of Purgatory,"
Theological Studies 69 (December 2008): 741–85. © *Theological Studies.*

Manufactured in the United States of America

Library of Congress Cataloging-in-Publication Data
Thiel, John E.
  Icons of hope : the "last things" in Catholic imagination / John E. Thiel.
    pages   cm
  Includes bibliographical references and index.
  ISBN 978-0-268-04239-4 (pbk. : alk. paper) — ISBN 0-268-04239-X
(pbk. : alk. paper)
  1. Eschatology.   2. Catholic Church—Doctrines.   I. Title.
  BT821.3.T44   2013
  236—dc23
                                                            2013022549

∞ *The paper in this book meets the guidelines for permanence and
durability of the Committee on Production Guidelines for Book Longevity
of the Council on Library Resources*

For

DOROTHEA

Ancora una volta

CONTENTS

ILLUSTRATIONS

Gallery of figures begins following page 106.

Figure 1. Christ in Majesty. *Last Judgment* mosaic (13th–14th c.). Baptistery of San Giovanni, Florence. Photo © DeA Picture Library/Art Resource, NY.

Figure 2. *Last Judgment* fresco, Giorgio Vasari (1511–74) and Federico Zuccari (ca. 1540/41–1609). Basilica di Santa Maria del Fiore, Florence. Photo: Scala/Art Resource, NY.

Figure 3. Detail of the Damned, *Last Judgment* fresco, Giorgio Vasari and Federico Zuccari. Basilica di Santa Maria del Fiore, Florence. Photo: Nicolo Orsi Battaglini/Art Resource, NY.

Figure 4. *Last Judgment* mosaic (11th c.). Cattedrale di Santa Maria Assunta, Torcello, Italy. Photo: Alinari/Art Resource, NY.

Figure 5. *Last Judgment* fresco, Giotto di Bondone (1266–1336). Scrovegni Chapel, Padua, Italy. Photo: Scala/Art Resource, NY.

Figure 6. *Last Judgment* fresco, 1538–41, Michelangelo Buonarrotti (1475–1564). Sistine Chapel, Vatican Museums and Galleries, Vatican City. Photo: Alinari/The Bridgeman Art Library.

ACKNOWLEDGMENTS

Once again, I have been fortunate to have the experience of just how communal a project writing a book is. So much of it seems to be a solitary exercise, and so much of it is. But all the hours of reading and writing alone would be so much less productive—if they could be productive at all—were they not informed by insights gained through scholarly discussion with friends, and by the unflagging support of a wider circle of friends and family. I have many to thank.

Fairfield University supported the writing of this book through a sabbatical in the spring of 2007, through a Board of the College of Arts and Sciences Research Grant in the summer of 2008, and through its Senior Summer Fellowship in 2011. I am grateful to the faculty members who served on the Research Committee and to the academic vice-presidents, Orin Grossman and Paul Fitzgerald, S.J., who approved my proposals. More gratitude still to Paul Fitzgerald for supporting the permissions for the artwork that appears in these pages.

I presented the ideas of this book in a number of fora in the last several years—as the 2007 Nostra Aetate Lecture at Fordham University, in the Iona College Lecture Series "Shared Roots: Meanings of the Afterlife for Christians and Jews" in 2008, as the 2011 Christopher F. Mooney, S.J., Lecture in Theology, Religion, and Society at Fairfield University, and as the 2011 inaugural Dolores L. Christie Lecture at John Carroll University, sponsored by John Carroll University and the Catholic Theological Society of America. I am grateful for the invitations for these presentations and to the audiences at these events for the good discussion.

I presented the subject matter of chapter 2 to the New Haven Theological Discussion Group in 2007, and, as always, my colleagues there helped me to think through any number of loose ends. I am especially grateful to the conveners of the New Haven Theological Discussion Group, Gene Outka and Christopher Morse, for encouraging me to consider the theology of Jonathan Edwards for my project. As I was writing this book, I profited as always from my theological conversations with David Kelsey and Cyril O'Regan. My friends in a local research subgroup of the Constructive Theology Working Group— Roger Haight, S.J., Elena Procario-Foley, Brad Hinze, Michele Saracino, Paul Lakeland, and Jeannine Hill-Fletcher—offered insightful criticism of chapters 3 and 4 at meetings in 2007 and 2010. Members of the Department of Religious Studies, Fairfield University, discussed a version of chapter 3 at our faculty's ongoing research seminar in 2008 and offered valuable feedback. I am especially grateful for conversations with my colleagues Al Benney and Ellen Umansky.

Earlier versions of chapters 2 and 3 appeared previously as articles in *Theological Studies*, and I am grateful to the journal's editor, David Schultenover, S.J., for his fine criticism that made my writing better. Jim Buckley, John Jones, Dennis Keenan, Bill McConville, O.F.M., Randy Sachs, S.J., and Kathy Tanner read pieces of this work in draft and helped me fine-tune my argument. Paul Lakeland generously read this entire book as it was being written, a favor he has done me many times throughout my career. I am extraordinarily grateful for this most recent gift. Hugh Humphrey helped me think through some taxonomy issues in New Testament styles of faith. Brian Daley, S.J., took the time to offer valuable advice on the historical trajectory of belief in the Last Judgment. Franklin Harkins assisted with a textual issue in the literary corpus of the Angelic Doctor.

I am grateful to Stephen Little of the University of Notre Dame Press for his work in bringing the manuscript to publication. Rebecca DeBoer and Wendy McMillen of the University of Notre Dame Press ably and graciously saw the manuscript to production, and Philip Holt - haus brought his fine critical eye to my words as copy editor. Berthold Kress of the Warburg Institute, University of London, reminded me of the kindness of strangers with his offer to provide an image of one of the woodcuts that appears in these pages.

My friends who happen not to be theologians supported the writing of this book in all sorts of ways of which they are probably unaware—Gregory Schopen, Susan Rakowitz, Beth Boquet, Brian Clements, Fred Roy, and Maria Roy. I am especially grateful for the emotional gift of constant support that I have received from Dorothea Cook Thiel, our sons David and Benjamin, and our daughter-in-law, Sara Ortiz Thiel.

Fairfield, Connecticut
March 11, 2013

CHAPTER 1

For What May We Hope?

Thoughts on the Eschatological Imagination

In an essay entitled "Last Things First? The Century of Eschatology in Retrospect," Christoph Schwöbel observes that the twentieth century "could correctly be called the century of eschatology."[1] In
the first years of the century, Albert Schweitzer's groundbreaking work
The Quest of the Historical Jesus (1906) highlighted the eschatological
character of Jesus' preaching in order to criticize the bourgeois understandings of Jesus' life and message so typical of nineteenth-century
interpretation.[2] Against the staid portrait of Jesus as a teacher of rational ethics sketched by Albrecht Ritschl and his followers, Schweitzer
stressed Jesus' apocalyptic hope in the power of God's kingdom breaking into history as an undeniable and, indeed, central theme of the
gospel. Schweitzer's influential reading of the New Testament reprised
the accent on early Christian apocalyptic offered by the German scholar
Johannes Weiss at the end of the nineteenth century[3] and set a direction for certain emphases in twentieth-century Christian thought.
Since Schweitzer's time, Christians from a range of confessions have
attended to eschatological themes in their efforts to grapple with the
meaning of the gospel, and in doing so the theologically minded have

taken advantage of an ever-burgeoning scholarship on apocalypticism in the fields of scriptural and historical studies.[4]

If, though, the last one hundred years can be called the century of eschatology, we should note that it largely has produced two very particular, and mutually opposed, styles of eschatological reflection. The first style is represented by fundamentalist readings of the Bible that find expression in sermons, prophecies, and faith-filled discourses; the second style is represented by modern theologies that measure valid interpretation by the standard of the historical-critical method. Modern theologians tend to overlook the rise of apocalypticism in fundamentalist Christian traditions as a powerful current in contemporary eschatology, if only because it does not typically appear as an identifiable theological genre. Like all religious movements, Christian fundamentalism unfolds in a pluralism of forms, though many of these are keen to make the biblical book of Revelation a template for interpreting the present moment and the imminent future. A particular style of eschatological faith has figured prominently in the belief of fundamentalist Christians, who eagerly anticipate the end of the world to materialize soon in history with the same literal clarity they expect of God's word on the biblical page. Modern theologians often overlook fundamentalist apocalyptic too because they judge its literalist commitments to be naïve at best and intellectually scandalous at worst, rightly judging its religious worldview to be a repudiation of the modern culture in which contemporary belief and practice flourish. Modern theologians have judged fundamentalist literalism to be a failure in religious imagination, since such literalism undervalues the rich meaning latent in religious symbolism, and particularly in the symbolism of Christian eschatology.

Yet, this second style of eschatology—modern, critical theology—may be judged guilty of another kind of imaginative reductionism in its approach to eschatology. In their eagerness to reconcile their faith with modernity's commitment to reason and scientific standards for knowledge, critical theologians have often been inclined to regard ancient doctrines only as tropes for personal, political, or historical circumstances, as though the doctrines could not possibly mean what they say were they to be intelligible. Their interpretive approach requires the imagination to find existentially meaningful images for eschatological events, presumably because such events are epistemically inaccessible at best or outlandish claims for reality at worst. Modern theology has contributed to this second kind of imaginative reduction, largely because it has conducted its affairs in light of the Kantian critique of traditional metaphysics.

Near the end of the *Critique of Pure Reason* (1781), Kant took stock of his philosophical project by observing that all the interests of speculative and practical reason come together in three questions: "What can I know?" "What ought I to do?" "What may I hope?"[5] Kant had already addressed and answered the first question earlier in the work, and in a way that undermined the very possibility of traditional metaphysics. I may know worldly appearances presented in the manifold of sense experience as ordered by the a priori categories of the understanding. There is no knowledge, he claims, without sensibility shaped by the intellect. The second question would be addressed and answered in the *Critique of Practical Reason* (1788). I ought to act on the basis of the moral imperative constructed a priori by practical reason.

Although addressed in the First and Second Critiques, the third question was not itself the subject of a book-length writing, undoubtedly because it only functioned as a heuristic for the second question. I may hope for a final happiness in God and a future life beyond death, "two postulates," Kant states, "which, according to the principles of pure reason, are inseparable from the [moral] obligation which that same [practical] reason imposes on us."[6] God and life after death are hypotheses required by pure practical reason to ensure that morality finally will be its own reward, even if happiness proves elusive in this life. Hope in this Kantian key is dispassionate. It is not the emotional companion of an ardent faith. As mere postulates, the objects of Kantian hope do not evoke ardor, and hope, for Kant, is not the sister of faith, as Charles Péguy insisted it was.[7] Rather, Kantian hope in the life to come is only a guiding principle that offers the possibility of rational consistency and purposiveness to one's moral life here and now.

It is with some irony that I have chosen a variant of Kant's well-known question for the title of the first, introductory chapter of a book on the eschatological imagination. As his answer to the third question attests, Kant had no eschatological imagination. Kant, of course, would not have been offended by this judgment. For Kant, the faculty of imagination is incapable of eschatological employment since it requires the concreteness of sensibility to go about its business, and God and the afterlife are not possible objects of sensible experience. In the short essay that Kant did devote to eschatology, he makes this point clearly:

> The speculative man [*sic*] becomes entangled in mysticism where his reason does not understand itself and what it wants, and rather prefers to dote on the beyond than to confine itself within the bounds of this world, as is fitting for an intellectual inhabitant of a sensible world; for reason, because it is not easily satisfied with its immanent, that is, its practical use but likes to attempt something in the transcendent, also has its mysteries.[8]

And these mysteries, Kant continues, are the pseudoconcepts of "eternal repose" served up by the various religions, concepts "in company with which . . . understanding disintegrates and all thinking itself comes to an end."[9]

It is both expected and surprising that modern theologians have followed Kant's lead in their attention to eschatology. On the one hand, Kant's position on the limitations of knowledge has become axiomatic in modern theories of interpretation. Embraced theologically, it issues in the expected refusal of theologians to speak flourishingly about the *eschata* or the "last things"—death as a cusp to the afterlife, judgment, heaven, and hell, and a host of ancillary topics such as purgatory, the communion of the saints, and the eschatological forgiveness of sins. On the other hand, this epistemological modesty is somewhat surprising when one recalls that assertions about the eschata are not claims for knowledge but claims made in faith. It is surprising that many modern theologians have chosen to observe the Kantian strictures on knowledge as a matter of principle, since the understanding they construct is measured (or should be!) by faith in the Christ event as revealed in Scripture and tradition. The apologetic interests of modern theologians do much to explain this anomaly. Concerned to justify their discipline before the canons of critical thinking, many theologians have been willing to embrace historicist assumptions in order to play by the same epistemic rules as fellow travelers in the academy. Or, better put, apologetic theologians make some interpretive negotiation between the value of critical knowing and the claims of revelation, since, they assume, neither can be strictly reconciled with the other on its own terms.

This negotiation is more accomplishable for theological loci that address Christian realities within the scope of history. A theology of tradition or a theology of the Church or a theological anthropology all interpret a possible object of experience, even if they claim that the sensible object has a supernatural orientation. Eschatology will have a much more difficult time satisfying apologetic interests. The last things are not possible objects of sensible experience but instead are objects of a hope inextricably tied to faith. For believers, the last things are not mere postulates but realities and events having to do with the very meaning of life and the final destiny of the human person. The subject matter of eschatology may have flourished in the last century, at least in comparison to previous times in the history of theology. And yet, by comparison with other theological loci with historical orientations, there still has been far less writing on this topic.

Even when theologians take up eschatological themes, it is interesting to see how much their work transpires as though Kant were looking over their shoulders. Abiding by Kant's own critical strictures, theologians who write today on eschatology often focus their efforts on the existential dimensions of Christian hoping, and are decidedly reluctant to speculate about the objects of hope professed in faith.[10] This version of the reduction seems to rest on the judgment that an imagination more artistic than theological is especially suited to the sort of speculation that eschatological description would require. Perhaps a poetic imagination like Dante's in the *Divine Comedy* or a painterly imagination like Fra Angelico's in his *Last Judgment* might speculate effectively on the eschata, but the speculative capacities of the artistic imagination seem to elude the forensic, argumentive style of modern theology. In the trajectory of this kind of imaginative reduction, eschatology becomes an "immanentology" in which talk about the life to come is really taken to be talk about life in the present.

In opposition to this view, I will argue that theology should not be resigned to the Kantian despair in the eschatological imagination. Theology on this side of the Enlightenment need not be embarrassed by speculative accounts of the afterlife, for such accounts can be powerful expressions of faith and hope. In the following chapters, I will attempt an eschatology that regards the last things as real events that Christians are theologically obliged to imagine seriously and to describe with some measure of coherence. This task requires the retrieval of a speculative approach to interpretation that seems far more in tune with premodern than with modern theological sensibilities. Such a speculative approach may seem odd or antiquated when judged by the Kantian standards of modern, apologetical theologies. From another perspective, however, our own moment in the history of theology may offer surprising opportunities for the wisdom of the past to reappear in unexpected ways. David Tracy, for example, has argued that postmodernity's "attack upon the self-confidence of the modern *logos*" has allowed the truthful power of ancient Christian texts and doctrines to make a "strange return" in our own day.[11] Perhaps his observation can extend to the contemporary retrieval of a premodern style of theological interpretation. Given the remarkable and healthy pluralism in the genres of modern and postmodern theology, I believe that there is room for a speculative style of interpretation that can serve a contemporary eschatology. The proof of such a claim, of course, finally lies in performance, and I will venture such a performance for the reader to judge in the pages to come.

I shall proceed by enlisting the work of Karl Rahner to illustrate in more detail the modern restraint on the eschatological imagination, and conclude this first chapter by proposing a traditional justification for a more speculative approach to eschatology, one that appreciates how a richer use of the eschatological imagination might be theologically warranted and religiously edifying.

ON GETTING IT HALF RIGHT:
RAHNER ON ESCHATOLOGICAL ASSERTIONS

A good example of the modern restraint on the eschatological imagination can be found in the writings of Karl Rahner, especially in his programmatic essay "The Hermeneutics of Eschatological Assertions."[12] Here Rahner insists on the need for a special hermeneutics for understanding eschatological beliefs, a need that seems to be prompted by typically Kantian assumptions regarding the limitations of knowledge. "The idea that such [a special] hermeneutics has been sufficiently catered for by hermeneutics in general," Rahner observes, "rests on the false and primitive conception, that the eschata form a world like any other, so that knowledge of them—in spite of its being determined, like other knowledge, by the object itself—presents no particular problems apart from those of the knowledge of theological realities in general."[13] Eschatology requires a special hermeneutics precisely because the objects of its knowledge are unavailable, and unavailable in a way that encourages error in their proper interpretation. Rahner reminds his reader that eschatology is about the real future that is God's, a future that lies beyond the control of human knowledge or action. God knows the future omnisciently, but God's future is also finitely knowable in principle by human persons since human destiny is a crucial dimension of that future. Yet, acknowledging that God's future may be humanly knowable does not mean that God's future can be known in fine detail by human beings now, within the scope of history. Even though God could reveal everything of the end time to humanity, God has not. Moreover, it would be erroneous to think that scriptural accounts of the end are "pre-views of future events."[14] Such a view reduces the engaged believer to the status of a disinterested voyeur who makes God's future "only what is yet to come from a distance, and no longer that which is at hand in its futurity."[15]

A meaningful eschatology, Rahner argues, is one in which knowledge of the future emerges from the existential circumstances of the believer's life now. The future "is an inner moment of man and of his actual being as it is present to him now. And so knowledge of the future, in so far as it is still to come, is an inner moment in the self-understanding of man in his present hour of existence—and *grows* out of it."[16] Eschatology must recognize the appropriate limitations on knowledge. Vain presumption beckons the interpreter beyond those limits to conjure apocalyptic in the false forms of "phantasy or gnosticism."[17] Eschatology, then, has cause for modesty in its account of God's future which in and of itself cannot be completely known, at least under the epistemic conditions of history. Eschatology must speak strictly out of the present moment as the knowable way in which God's future is encountered in the life of faith. "By and in being oriented toward the future," Rahner claims, "[the human person] must know about his future. But in such a way, that this knowledge of the future can be a moment in his knowledge of the present. And only thus."[18]

This last phrase—"And only thus"—voices Rahner's caution against extending eschatological assertions beyond their properly existential scope of meaning. The concerns of modern epistemology stir this caution, but so too does a particular understanding of God. Throughout his writings, Rahner delights in portraying God as holy mystery, as a wellspring of loving grace whose eternal depths defy comprehension even as they evoke the desire for meaning in human life. As the "Whither of transcendental experience," God remains "the nameless, the indefinable, the unattainable,"[19] the infinite mystery within which human persons discover and actualize the horizon of their own finite mystery. The eschata are the fulfillment of the human quest for God. As divine knowledge they lie hidden in God's being. But more, as divinely willed and gracefully achieved human destiny, the eschata are a dimension of the mystery of God's own being and, as such, share in the infinite mystery within which human persons encounter the "more" of finite transcendence. For Rahner, the eschatological events are mysterious both for epistemological reasons and for ontological reasons. Human knowledge cannot help but fall short of divine being because human knowledge is limited, and divine being is not. Since the eschata share in the divine mystery, they defy speculative description on these two related counts.

An interesting application of this position to a specific eschatological event can be found in Rahner's writing "The Life of the Dead." Here Rahner argues that the persistent courage of human transcendence in the face of life's seemingly insurmountable obstacles illustrates the presence of eternity in time. Eternal life grows out of the present moment as human freedom responds to death productively, raising death from empty destruction to a radical limit before which persons become fully themselves in choosing God. Death is only meaningful as deep loss, Rahner insists, when human life has become something to lose. And only a human life that has already entered eternity here and now by knowingly or unknowingly embracing God's future is worthy of death's meaningful loss. "It is only because we have become immortal in our life," Rahner states, "that death with its menacing and impenetrable mask of destructivity is for us so deadly."[20] Eternal life can only be spoken of meaningfully as the life of the living since we are separated from the dead by the rupture of death.

Even though eternity can be encountered within our personal histories, the eternal life of the dead, Rahner claims, eludes our conceptual and imaginative grasp. While the living "are still creatures *in time*," the dead dwell in the mystery of "absolute nearness to God."[21] Living within the life of God, the dead transcend the scope of our actual experience, and of *their* encounter with eternity, Rahner frankly admits, "there is not much we can say." Faith enables us to say at least that the mystery into which the dead have gone is one of "unspeakable *bliss*." Yet, "the sheer silence of [this] bliss cannot be heard by our ears."[22] This respectful retreat to the ineffable certainly reflects Rahner's Kantian sensibilities. Moreover, these Kantian sensibilities complement his Ignatian mysticism and, so mingled, emerge in a theology of God as inexhaustible mystery, a mystery into which Rahner enfolds the life of the dead. It should be no surprise, then, that Rahner extends the same apophatic regard for the divine mystery to the blessed dead dwelling in the divine life. Just as imagination and expression are utterly humbled before the task of representing God, so too are these temporally bound powers humbled before the prospect of representing the blessed dead, inaccessible as they are in the mysterious life of God. This dual apophasis, Rahner concludes, directs us to seek what we may experience of eternity only existentially in the present moment, where silence, and not speech, is the appropriate response:

We meet the living dead, even when they are those who are loved by us, in faith, hope and love, that is, when we open our hearts to the silent calm of God himself, in which they live; not by calling them back to where we are, but by descending into the silent eternity of our own hearts, and through faith in the risen Lord, creating in time the eternity which they have brought forth forever.[23]

Rahner's eschatological modesty is not an unusual stance in the trajectory of modern theology. Both Protestant and Catholic kinds of liberal theology are governed by Kantian assumptions on the limitations of knowledge, which require that one speaks of the last things immanently, if one speaks of them at all.[24] The same might be said for Reformed theology in a Barthian style, which is happy to employ Kantian epistemology to warrant a classical Reformation understanding of divine otherness and the distance of the dead.[25] But even if Rahner's position is generally illustrative of the modern deferral to Kantian sensibilities, it is especially interesting in the way it advances those sensibilities through a theological understanding of God as mystery. As the heading to this section announces, I am unconvinced by Rahner's argument in toto, though I am willing to concede the validity of one of his two principal points. Explaining this criticism will serve as an introduction to the concluding methodological sections of this chapter.

Rahner is certainly correct in his view that experience and talk of the eschata grow out of the present moment and "only thus" may the eschata be represented theologically. Although this stance possesses a Kantian resonance in the modern period, it is difficult to deny that it is something of a truism throughout the entire Christian tradition, if not in theory then at least in practice. Thomas Aquinas and Kant hold remarkably different assumptions about reality. And yet both would maintain that the workings of imagination and understanding require sensibility, as does the speech that brings them to expression. Both agree that sensibility provides realistic content to our mental operations, even though they explain the formal contributions of subjectivity to the construction of knowledge in different ways. Indeed, one of Rahner's signal contributions to modern theology is his retrieval of this Thomistic teaching on the need of sensibility for representation in light of the Kantian critique of traditional metaphysics.[26] Rahner's retrieval demonstrates the real consistency throughout the premodern and modern periods on the issue of theological representation, namely, that ideation and expression require the contributions of sensibility as the representable. It is no wonder, then, that Rahner discusses eschatology only out of the experience of the present moment, which includes, of course, the existentially present past and the existentially present future. Hermeneutical modesty about the eschata itself would require such a stance, were it not for the even stronger warrant that an alternative position could not be palpably imagined.

Although Rahner rightly regards the present moment as a proper base for thought and speech about the eschata, there is no reason in principle that this safeguard against fantastic speculation need result in the theological conclusions he reaches about the life of the dead. Rahner complements his position on the need for an existential eschatology by enfolding the dead into the divine mystery. This constructive stance in turn justifies his hermeneutics of eschatological statements. If the dead dwell within the divine mystery, then, like the divine mystery, they transcend the concrete particulars of thought and expression. Faith affirms the sheer bliss enjoyed by the blessed dead within the divine life, but the character of that state of blessedness is as indescribable as the divine mystery that both causes and occludes this bliss. Hermeneutical modesty before the eschata is appropriate, Rahner thus claims, for two mutually supportive reasons. First, responsible theological construction must respect the limitations on knowledge set by the sensible conditions of representation. Although Rahner invokes this epistemological principle theologically, its Kantian resonance applies more generally to any form of speculation ventured by reason or imagination. Second, the nature of the blessed dead, engulfed as they are in God, demands that these epistemological strictures be respected for an explicitly theological reason that bolsters the cause of herme - neutical modesty. Rahner extends the proper apophatic regard of faith for the divine mystery to the blessed dead as well, making silence the most apt theological response to the state of blessedness. The dead are distant from the present moment. And even though the present moment might be eschatologically constructed in meaningful ways, the afterlife is not capable of meaningful description. The kind of eternal life enjoyed by the dead, lost as they are in God's own mysterious being, constrains the eschatological imagination to the point of mystical silence.

It is this second half of Rahner's double-sided position that I do not think is correct. For Rahner, the critical judgment that eschatology should respect the legitimate boundaries of knowledge issues in a theological position on the life of the dead that follows the Kantian rule on hermeneutical modesty.[27] While there is good reason for a modern theology like Rahner's to respect the Kantian rule, there is no reason that the epistemological principles informing the rule need shape the representation of eschatological events in the way they do in his theology. Indeed, I shall argue that the relationships between and among several basic Catholic doctrines encourage the theologian to say much more about eschatological events than Rahner is willing, while yet speaking about the eschata in and through the present historical moment, as Rahner insists is proper. Even though Rahner finds both epistemological consistency and theological profundity in what I would call his "thin" eschatology, I shall argue that hermeneutical modesty does not require this approach, and that a "thick" eschatology— one that exercises the eschatological imagination more vigorously— can be much more effective in portraying "the assurance of things hoped for, the conviction of things not seen" (Heb 11:1).

IDOLATRY AND SACRAMENTALITY

Modern theology has been reluctant to engage the eschatological imagination for several reasons. The Kantian critique of metaphysics is one. Another reason, quite frankly, is the fear that any detailed account of eschatological events would simply be vulgar. This fear is not exclusively a modern concern. The Gospel writers were reluctant to describe eschatological events in any detail, even when they recounted what they received as Jesus' own words. The parables of Jesus consistently eschew a literal description of heavenly life, offering instead evocative images of the kingdom of God that stir the human hope for fulfillment. Even though Paul claimed to have had an ecstatic vision of paradise, he refused to describe it (2 Cor 12:2–4), justifying his silence by the sacredness of what he saw and, in an earlier letter, offering the believing community the same evocation of hope that the Gospel writers would: "no eye has seen, nor ear heard, nor the human heart conceived, what God has prepared for those who love him" (1 Cor 2:9). The book of Revelation may seem to be an exception to this biblical reticence. A close scrutiny of the text, however, finds interesting restraint even here. The apocalyptic events it details occur in *this* life and not in the next. That these historical occurrences are portrayed through highly symbolic language seems to convey John's judgment that any literal description of the end time would be common and unworthy of the religious imagination.

The New Testament silence on eschatological events tacitly condemns any sensibility that diminishes the scope of fulfillment to the familiar, and, as a consequence, undermines the hope that faith evinces.[28] But there is another, much more pernicious, kind of vulgarity that seems to be at work in both the ancient and modern constraints on the eschatological imagination, namely, the idolatry that traditionally has been understood as the root of moral evil. Christian salvation is so bound up with the mystery of God's divine life that any imaginative account of the eschata would seem to entail a literal description of God, as though images of the eschata would force the reduction of God to an image of human making. Since idolatry is traditionally understood as the preeminent sin (Gen 3:5; Ex 20:4–6), any thick variety of eschatological description could be counted the work of invidious arrogance much more than the folly of epistemological excess. The age-old practice of negative theology, iconoclastic sensibilities, and the Kantian strictures on speculative theology all in their own ways bespeak the same concern for idolatry in too lavish an exercise of the eschatological imagination.

Sinful corruption, however, presupposes corruptible goodness, and here, in what Christian belief regards as the sacramental character of creaturely reality, one finds theological license for the eschatological imagination. The opening scene in the book of Genesis affirms the goodness of creation, and sees creaturely goodness as a reflection of the Creator's own unbounded goodness. Medieval theology offers a more detailed description of this creaturely virtue by speaking of the transcendental qualities of being, which, like God, is not only good but also one, true, and beautiful. The doctrine of the incarnation consummates the doctrine of creation in the belief that creaturely reality is so good and redeemable that the divine nature could embrace it in the humanity of the Savior, and in the saving participation of that humanity in the resurrection of Jesus. Christian belief in the sacraments as means of grace confirms the capacity of finite existence to mediate the infinitely divine, a belief powerfully professed in the Catholic doctrine of the Real Presence of Christ in the Eucharist. Idolatry is an ever-present concern in theological representation, to say nothing of Christian life, because it moves in the same trajectory as authentic sacramentality, appealing to the same finitude of being as a communication of the divine but now in a way that limits the divine to the given and circumscribable. Idolatry is reductive sacramentality, a constriction that ironically becomes a transgression of the proper terms of relationship between the divine and the creaturely.[29] But prior to this reduction, in the created conditions of reality, lies a resource for eschatology that, though fallen, is both good and redeemed, and which might be put to good theological use.

Having made the point that a fuller exercise of the eschatological imagination need not be idolatrous in principle, I hasten to make another. If eschatological representation *is* guilty of idolatry, it may be so in one of two ways. Eschatology always concerns the reality of God and the divine actions that bring about the eschata. An eschatology could be idolatrous by diminishing God and God's actions to the level of the creaturely. Idolatry of this sort is risked in all theological inquiry, as humanly limited concepts and language try as they may to grasp the infinite. But this kind of idolatry is perniciously accomplished in chiliasm—the literal reduction of God's actions to the events of history. Chiliasm is not a pressing theological problem in our time, although, as a warrant for ideological violence, it has increasingly become a political problem. As was noted earlier, modern theologians have only been willing to engage the eschatological imagination metaphorically, and so have not been seduced by this sort of idolatry.

A second kind of eschatological idolatry would move in the opposite direction, by elevating creaturely persons, things, and events to divine proportions. In one version of this excess, human persons would be elevated to an unqualified mystical union with God as God. Now, it is questionable whether there are actual examples of this kind of idola - try in the theological tradition, which, contrary to the concrete chiliasm of the first kind of eschatological idolatry, would take the form of a spiritualized gnosticism. Meister Eckhart has been accused of this kind of theological failure, a charge encouraged by Eckhart's willingness to include the living as well as the dead in the state of mystical union with God. Leaving aside the legitimacy of this indictment, we need only note that Eckhart's style of mysticism is extraordinarily rare in the tradition, particularly when it is advanced as normative Christian faith and not as the heterodox criticism of it.[30] The Eastern Christian tradition of representing redeemed life as a state of divinization is another example of mystical sensibilities pressed far. But this ancient Greek conception of salvation has proved its orthodox status over the centuries by refusing to dissolve creatureliness into an unqualified union with God.

Given the paucity of idolatrous representations of the creature as God, we can conclude that the modern reluctance to speculate about the eschata is not virtuous avoidance of a seductive theological temptation. Indeed, the fear of this kind of idolatry seems to be stirred by a category mistake. Concerns about idolatry in eschatological speculation derive from the false conflation of eschatological events with the divine being itself, and so the utterly erroneous assumption that a description of the eschata would entail a reductive description of God. The biblical account of creation and the ancient Christian creeds speak of heaven as a created reality, and thus distinguishable from God and God's eternity even as the divine abode. Christian belief maintains that creatures do not lose their creatureliness in eschatological fulfillment, a caution that is affirmed in the Christian hope for an embodied salvation. The Last Judgment may be God's through Christ, but it remains God's judgment on all that is creaturely. Speaking of eschatological events cannot be equated with speaking about God, as much as God is implicated in any talk of eschatological events. Like any dimension of authentic sacramentality, creaturely persons, things, and events could be idolatrously corrupted by their false identification with God. Examples of this kind of sin, though, seem to be rare in the tradition, if they exist at all.

Another way of making this same point, and in a way that highlights the irony at work in modern theological practice, is that our very efforts to avoid idolatry themselves give rise to idolatry. Our theological avoidance of talk about the eschata intends to honor the distance between the divine and the human. And yet, that very gesture itself succumbs to the idolatrous assumption that God's involvement in the eschata warrants their regard through an apophatic lens properly reserved for God. Our good theological intentions fail by making too much of eschatological events and so, by consequence, too little of God, and all in the name of rigorous theological method or mystical profundity.

When all is said and done, the modern reluctance to represent the events of the afterlife issues as much from Reformation sensibilities about authentic sacramentality as it does from Kantian sensibilities about the limits of knowledge. And here, in confessional disputes between Catholics and Protestants, one of the most neuralgic issues was the accessibility of the blessed dead in heaven. The Reformers vehemently attacked the Catholic belief in and practice of the cult of the saints, since it implicated all the points of contention among sixteenth-century Christians. The Reformers saw idolatry in the Catholic veneration of the saints, judging saintly patronage in the afterlife to usurp the mediating role of Christ as Savior. In the view of the Reformers, the saints in heaven valorized the religious actions of ascetics from whom their ranks were drawn. The saints exercised a sacred agency that compromised the very strong doctrine of grace at the heart of Reformation spirituality. Reformation faith thus embraced the notion of the blessed dead as distant from the living. In the afterlife, they were enfolded into the predestinating will of God by which they were chosen from all eternity. The afterlife of the saints was unimaginable because imagining the blessed dead might require the imagination of their activity in heaven, and, in the Reformation reading of Paul, human activity has no graceful integrity of its own.

This last point may serve as a transition to the next step in our argument. If Reformation and Kantian sensibilities have mutually configured modern assumptions about the eschatological imagination, then Catholic sensibilities need to adjudicate the extent to which these concerns are appropriate to its task. Modern Catholic theology rightly has learned much from Kant about the limits of knowledge and the excesses of traditional metaphysical speculation. But Catholic theology should be wary of granting final epistemic authority to philosophical strictures that would have disallowed the great artistic, poetic, and theological exercises of the religious imagination throughout the Catholic tradition. The unity of that tradition suggests that the scandal of an excluded past would make for an equally scandalous present or future. And even though Kantian epistemology nicely supports Protestant sensibilities on the unavailability of otherworldly events, there is no reason at all for Catholic theology to relinquish its peculiar style of Christian sensibility to embrace a style not its own, however rooted that style may now be in the assumptions of more recent theological interpretation. The challenging task for a Catholic theology is not just to imagine the eschata, but more importantly to imagine them in ways that are faithful to the mainstays of Catholic belief and in ways that may serve as icons of hope for believers. Let us continue by suggesting guidelines for accomplishing such a theological project.

THE DOCTRINE OF BODILY RESURRECTION AS AN INTERPRETIVE RULE OF FAITH

If our eschatology will venture a speculative approach to theological interpretation, then I propose that the doctrine of bodily resurrection can serve as a hermeneutical guideline for our efforts. The doctrine of bodily resurrection stands at the heart of the faith since it expresses the first Christian experience of faith itself. Bodily resurrection is a christological belief that affirms Jesus' dignity as the Savior, as the one whom God has "declared to be Son of God with power according to the spirit of holiness by resurrection from the dead" (Rom 1:4). And yet, bodily resurrection is also an anthropological belief that conveys the Christian hope for personal participation in the resurrection of Jesus and the eternal life that it brings. Thoroughly implicated in the doctrine of bodily resurrection is the entire sacramental worldview of Christianity which, in its affirmation of the goodness of creation, warrants eschatological reflection from this world to the next. The doctrine of the resurrection inscribes the entire network of belief, so that its use as an interpretive rule of faith conveys the authentic values of the tradition.

Throughout the ages Christians have believed that life after death finally occurs in an embodied state in which all that makes a person him- or herself, both inner life and outer physical life, continues to exist, fulfilled in the presence of God. This belief explicitly denies any conception of the afterlife in which only an immortal soul finally continues to exist, at the expense of the body. Our earliest written testimony to this Christian belief occurs in the apostle Paul's first letter to the Christian community at Corinth, written in the 50s of the first century. Late in this lengthy letter, Paul addresses a difficult matter that had been brought to his attention by a member of that Corinthian community. It was reported to him that some of the recent Corinthian converts, who initially had embraced Paul's teaching, now had left behind their belief in bodily resurrection in favor of a belief in the immortality of the soul alone.

Paul was scandalized by this lapse in faith on the part of his friends, but it seems to me that the Corinthian reversal in belief is actually very unsurprising. If one were inclined to believe in life after death, then believing in the immortality of the soul alone seems an easier commitment than one to bodily resurrection. The corruptibility of the body can be witnessed with the advance of years, and can be witnessed even more dramatically after death. A belief in life after death that made claims only for the endurance of some invisible and essential dimension of the person impervious to fleshly corruption would seem more defensible before the witness of common sense. This was especially true for some members of the Corinthian Church who were Greek in cultural background and who, in line with some philosophi -cal traditions, may have been accustomed to thinking about the body as an earthly and tragic prison for a naturally immortal soul that was truly and exclusively their self. Earlier in his letter Paul chides members of the Corinthian community for disparaging the body and for forgetting that the "body is a temple of the Holy Spirit within you, which you have from God," and urges them to "glorify God in your body" (1 Cor 6:19–20).

We should not forget that Christianity took nearly all of its basic beliefs from Judaism and that it was Paul the committed Pharisee who claimed to have a vision of the resurrected Christ. Ancient Israelites did not believe in life after death, but did believe in an embodied salvation here and now on God's promised land. Some Jews at the turn of the Common Era had begun to believe in bodily resurrection, but typically as a this-worldly event ushered in by the appearance of the Messiah in Israel.[31] Jews believed in a bodily salvation because they affirmed the goodness of God's creation and especially the goodness of the only creature created in God's image and likeness. The majority Jewish tradition did not view the human being dualistically, as the mind-set of the Greek philosophical tradition did—inner life good and really the self, the body the seat of deathliness and not the self at all. Christians embraced this Jewish belief in the created goodness of the body and conveyed its values to their new belief in life after death. Paul was the first Christian writer to express this belief in the resurrection of the body, if only because his writings are the earliest Christian documents we possess. But the belief in an embodied afterlife may very well have sprung from Paul's rich religious imagination. Chiding the fears of the lapsed Corinthians about bodily mortality in the afterlife, Paul describes the miraculous transformation that he believes God will work, bringing the body in death into the body in eternal life: "So it is with the resurrection of the dead. What is sown is perishable, what is raised is imperishable. It is sown in dishonor, it is raised in glory. It is sown in weakness, it is raised in power. It is sown a physical body, it is raised a spiritual body" (1 Cor 15:42–44).

Now, describing the self in resurrected life as a "spiritual body" is not exactly a detailed portrait of heavenly life. Paul's rhetoric plays on opposites to highlight the miraculous difference between the self in sin and death, on the one hand, and the self raised to eternal life by the grace of Christ, on the other. The self in sin and death is perishable, dishonored, weak, and a physical body. The self raised to eternal life beyond the corruption of sin and death is imperishable, glorious, powerful, and a spiritual body. Paul undoubtedly chose the provocative oxymoron "spiritual body" in order to confound the dualistic expectations of the lapsed Corinthians. By portraying the resurrected self as an inseparable unity of spirit and body, a "spiritual body," Paul insisted that all that makes a person who he or she is—inner life and outer life—is worthy of salvation and the vision of God in heaven.

This holistic understanding of the saved person was affirmed in various ways throughout the later Christian tradition. What Christians profess about Jesus' resurrection is another way of expressing their hopes about their own, and these hopes are powerfully expressed in the four canonical gospels. Mark, Matthew, Luke, and John all close with stories of the first Easter morning, and proclaim the resurrection of Jesus with the consistently striking image of an empty tomb. The body of Jesus, and so Jesus himself, they say, is not to be found among the dead but has been raised by God into new life beyond death. The later gospels of Luke and John share scenes in which the resurrected Christ proves his identity to his incredulous disciples by displaying the physical wounds of his crucifixion (Lk 24:39–42; Jn 20:27–29). In resurrection, he is beyond the suffering and death of the cross. And yet, because the cross shaped who he is, Jesus' resurrected body still shows its terrible effects.

This central Christian belief can serve as a hermeneutical principle for representing the last things. Our approach in this work will depart from the apophatic regard for the eschata so typical of modern theology to follow a speculative path through which the eschata are given thicker description. The doctrine of bodily resurrection offers both warrant and guidance for this endeavor.

The continuity that the doctrine of bodily resurrection affirms between the human person in history and the human person in heavenly life warrants theological speculation about eschatological events. Whether this continuity issues from the personal identity of the believer that Paul described as miraculously transformed into a spiritual body, or whether this continuity issues from the metaphysical identity of creation that Paul described as miraculously transformed into the "new creation" (2 Cor 5:17), both through the power of Christ's resurrection from the dead, it is this same continuity that the eschatological imagination is able to traverse in order to speak credibly about the eschata. The Christian belief in this ontological continuity thus provides a context within which claims for a reflective continuity between "now" and "then" can be made. In making such claims, the theologian speculatively draws on the evidence of this life, the life that will be eschatologically transfigured, in order to imagine the future consequences of God's grace and love.

Representations of that continuity, however, must always respect the "more" of eschatological fulfillment. Speculation, properly accomplished, is not motivated by the reductive desire of fundamentalist literalism. Nor is it an exercise in theological idolatry, with which Luther famously, though unfairly, charged the medieval Scholastic tradition.[32] Speculation must remain an exercise in reflective modesty, fully aware that its results are utterly tentative, even when an ecclesial audience judges them favorably. Speculation authentically offers its findings with respect for Paul's testimony that the events of the eschata finally elude capture by the eye, the ear, or the heart. But in no case should the eschatological "more" be judged beyond the imagination's capacity for finite representation. Indeed, from the perspective of theological anthropology, the imagination might be understood as the created faculty especially graced in its service to the virtue of hope, just as reason might be understood as the created faculty especially graced in its service to the virtue of faith.

The discussion of eschatological issues in New Testament exegesis and theology during the past century has reached a consensus that the most appropriate Christian understanding of salvation takes the form of an "inaugurated eschatology." In this view, the eternity of resurrected life and its sharing in the kingdom of God does not simply lie in an eschatological future beyond death and judgment. Nor has it been utterly realized in history, as a consequence of Jesus' own resurrection from the dead. Rather, eternal life has been "inaugurated" through God's raising of Jesus, an event that begins the graceful gift of salvation already in history.[33] That gift, however, continues to be unwrapped and appreciated anew in all the moments of history as the power of resurrected life wins its victory in time over the powers of sin and death. Although the gift is given and its benefits accrue in time, its contents are revealed more fully in God's future, in the reality of eternal life beyond death and in the completely shared eternity of bodily resurrection that Christians believe will be enjoyed after the Last Judgment.

Such an inaugurated eschatology faithfully represents the orthodox doctrine of bodily resurrection. Just as this doctrine professes the belief that the body we "already" have will, but has "not yet," come to the fulfillment of resurrected life, so too does an inaugurated eschatology insist on continuity between the redeemed but still redeeming present and the redemptive "more" of resurrected life in God's eschatological future. This consistency between the doctrine of bodily resurrection and an inaugurated eschatology's redemptive coupling of present and future provides further warrant for our appeal to bodily resurrection as a hermeneutical rule for eschatological speculation. But it also sheds light on the interpretive benefits of this approach.

The goal of eschatological speculation is not to achieve gnostic knowledge about the end of the world, the Last Judgment, or the life to come. The goal is to engage the eschata seriously through the imaginative construction of theological icons that profess the hope that comes with faith and, through this exercise, to inspire hope in the midst of the struggles that faith ever faces in life. To the degree that an inaugurated eschatology appreciates the way in which God's future is already re-creating the present moment, any speculative account of the eschatological future will offer important resources for imagining the existential configurations of God's grace. Modern theology has become quite used to thinking that its reflection only has existential value within the Kantian strictures on knowledge, as though talk of the eschata themselves would only be a vain projection of this life as the life to come. I submit that the meaningful speculative construction of the last things in a manner consistent with the entire network of Catholic belief and practice, in turn, may be able to illumine the same beliefs and practices with an eschatological light that cannot be contained by the Kantian strictures. In this regard, talk about historical events can have its meaningful point of departure in talk about eschatological events just as much as talk about the last things necessarily issues from an existential standpoint.[34]

With these hermeneutical guidelines in mind, let us begin the task of imagining the eschata with the hope that our results might enrich the pluralism of postmodern theology and the living faith of the Church.

CHAPTER 2

Imagining the Life of
the Blessed Dead

If meaningful speculation about the last things is a legitimate option for contemporary theologians, then what exactly should they take as their subject matter? And how should their imaginations go about the task of representing the claims of Christian hope? There is no circumscribed answer to the first question. Theologians, and all Christians for that matter, should be willing to speak about any and all matters of faith and hope whenever they have something edifying to say. And there is little doubt that the last things capture the very heart of what Christians find edifying, since they are faith statements about the ultimate meaning of the believer's life in relation to God. The classical listing of the last things is fourfold: death, judgment, heaven, and hell. Thus, the last things are concerned with the eternal consequences of the divine judgment that God passes upon our earthly histories at their definitive end. This constellation of concerns in turn includes a host of others suggested by the fourfold list, among them the Catholic beliefs in purgatory and the communion of the saints, the eschatological fulfillment of the Church, the redemption of history in its entirety, and the role of forgiveness in defeating the heritage of sin.

All of these eschatological topics might be the subject matter of meaningful theological speculation and, in the following chapters, we will have occasion to treat them all in more or less detail.

The second question posed in the opening lines above requires a more nuanced answer. Christians are eager to speak about their existential encounters with God, Christ, and the Spirit in uncountable ways: as testimony to God's providence in their lives; as expressions of gratitude for the Savior's life, death, and resurrection; and as accounts of the Spirit's inspiring presence in the temporal currents of society and history. Yet this kind of speaking proceeds from the actual evidence of the present moment, from what Christians experience in their minds and hearts. This emotional starting point in the life of faith is always tied to concrete circumstances in the world and in our shared lives with others. These existential contours to our experience guide the imagination in speaking about the "conviction of things not seen" (Heb 11:1). They provide moorings for theological discourse that are anchored in the particularities of life in which faith both flourishes and struggles. Talk about the last things is somewhat different, as we have seen in the previous chapter. The last things are events and ways of being that Christians believe they will fully experience eschatologically. This otherworldly setting for the last things has led many theologians wrongly to think that an apophatic silence is the proper response to the eschata or that talk about the eschata must be reduced to the experience of the present moment, as though the eschata were only meaningful as religious metaphors for this-worldly life.

I have argued that the doctrine of the resurrection of the body can be enlisted as a methodological rule for the theological representation of the last things. As much as the doctrine of bodily resurrection affirms the "more" of resurrected life, it yet insists that there is a real continuity between the self in this life and the self as it shares in the resurrection of Christ in the life to come. This claim for personal continuity justifies speculation about the eschata to the degree that such speculation reflects the inaugurated eschatology that has been a mainstay of the tradition since the time of Paul. The Christian belief that the power of Christ's resurrection from the dead causes the resurrection of believers does not maintain that the effects of this cause only begin on the other side of death. Rather, the tradition's inaugurated eschatology insists that the graceful power of resurrected life has already spilled into the lives of believers with Christ's resurrection from the dead. The New Testament witness, as well as the consistent sense of the faithful throughout the ages, expects that resurrected life will be consummated after death, as a consequence of God's judgment, and that the state of resurrected life will be raised to an eschatological "more" that exceeds the grasp of worldly imagination. And yet, the continuity of the saved self, a continuity assured by the continuity of resurrected life before and after death, enables believers to speculate meaningfully about the "more" of resurrected life out of their experience of resurrected life now.

I would like to linger on that last point just one more moment in order to clarify the means and the end of the theological endeavor I am commending. I did not say that the goal of eschatological speculation was somehow to surpass the limits of worldly imagination by an extraordinary intuition of the eschata, as though the goal of eschatology were the immediate experience and representation of a "new creation" that has yet to appear. This theological goal would be impossible to achieve. Nor did I say that the goal of eschatological speculation was to project the historical experience of resurrected life here and now, in the midst of the vagaries of fallenness, into the future dimensions of the eschata, as though the eschata fully revealed would be no more than faith's present experience of them. This theological goal would be achievable, though any result would be the worst kind of reductionism that failed to respect the transcendence of God's kingdom yet fully to come. Rather, the hermeneutical rule for eschatological speculation that I will follow finds empirical resources for imagining the eschata in our existential experiences of redemption, which is to say, in our present experience of already standing in a resurrected life gracefully secured by the life, death, and resurrection of Jesus Christ. Since resurrected life is as continuous as the selves who enjoy it, the theological imagination can legitimately draw on the evidence of resurrected life now in order to reflect meaningfully on the eschata that have yet to be revealed. The hiddenness of the eschata to believers on this side of the eschaton requires that such reflection remain speculative. But in order to express the depth of Christian hope, eschatological speculation must capture not only the eschatological resonance of the present moment but also the "more" of the eschatological future. Even though the eschatological more in and of itself exceeds the limits of theological imagination, it may be speculatively accessible, in limited ways, through the more familiar paths of existential hope.

The success of any particular eschatological proposal is, of course, a matter of performance. It can only be judged appreciatively if it is faithful to the existential hope of the Church and, in its speculative dimensions, imaginatively suggestive enough to offer a credible rendition of the future eschata, and by doing so to inspire the present hope of the Church even more. In this chapter, I will attempt this kind of theological speculation by engaging the central Christian eschatological belief in life after death and, specifically, by attempting to imagine a particular feature of the life of the blessed dead. There is nothing especially original about imagining the life of the blessed dead. Throughout the centuries, theologians, graphic artists, poets, and, most recently, filmmakers have crafted portraits of heavenly life in order to elucidate the content of faith and hope, to say nothing of the fullness of divine and human love that any expression of heavenly life will seek to convey. Before offering my own eschatological portrait, I would like to introduce the theological task I have described formally to this point by considering two previous attempts at the same project. We will begin with Thomas Aquinas's account of the wholeness of resurrected bodies in heaven in his work *Summa Contra Gentiles*, and proceed to Jona than Edwards's attempt to describe heavenly life in his two sermons, "Heaven Is a World of Love" and "Serving God in Heaven."

AQUINAS ON THE HEAVENLY STATE
OF RESURRECTED PERSONS

Thomas Aquinas's (1224–1274) lengthy work *Summa Contra Gentiles* was written between 1259 and 1264. A reasoned defense of the faith before an imagined audience of unbelievers, it was completed two years before he began his theological masterpiece, the *Summa Theologiae*. Thomas did not complete the *Summa Theologiae*. In December 1273 he suffered a breakdown after which he did not write, and he died three months later in March 1274. When Thomas put down his pen, he was at work on the third and final part of his theological *Summa*, which undoubtedly would have ended with a discussion of eschatology. Given the consistency of Thomas's thought, it would be reasonable to assume that the contours of his presentation would have followed his closing treatment of eschatology in the *Summa Contra Gentiles*. There Thomas addresses a host of eschatological topics such as the resurrection of Christ, the resurrection of believers, heaven, hell, purgatory, and the Last Judgment. Most of his treatment of the theme, though, is devoted to speculation about the heavenly state of resurrected persons. After affirming the traditional belief that the resurrection of Christ causes the resurrection of believers, Thomas constructs a lengthy explanation of how human bodies that suffer corruption in death can come to wholeness in heavenly life. This concern in turn leads him to imagine what saved persons are, do, and, more importantly, do not do in the afterlife.

Thomas's discussion wrestles with the seemingly insuperable problem that deathly corruption poses for the Christian belief in the unity and integrity of the human person in eternal life. Following the medieval method of anticipating the objections of opponents, Thomas catalogues the best counterpositions before advancing his own theological solutions. Of the seven objections he considers, two will serve to illustrate the reasonable challenge to a belief in bodily resurrection, and their solutions will illustrate Thomas's insistence that resurrected persons in heaven do not lack the wholeness of their created nature. First, Aquinas rehearses the objection that natural changes of all sorts on the part of bodies in this life would make the restoration of wholeness in the resurrection "extremely unseemly." Hair, fingernails, and toenails are constantly clipped from the body and disposed. Moreover, "other parts of the body . . . are covertly resolved by the action of the natural heat," a reference to the bodily function of defecation in which, like the previous examples, what was once a dimension of the body is sloughed off and ceases to participate in corporeal unity. But, the objection continues, if bodily unity is complete in the resurrection, and "these all are restored to the man rising again, an unseemly enormity will rise with him."[1] The restoration of complete unity in resurrection would seem to lead to a bizarre, and indeed, monstrous self.

Second, Thomas lays out an objection that is an amazing thought-experiment in physical identity. It occasionally happens, he states, "that some men feed on human flesh, and they are nourished on this nutriment only, and those so nourished generate sons." In such a circumstance, the flesh of the eaten becomes a part of the eater's body, and, through the eater's procreative activity, part of the bodies of the eater's offspring too. "Therefore," Thomas observes, "the same flesh is found in many men."[2] This fact seems to present crucial difficulties for the integrity of the resurrection, since the cannibal's food seems to prevent the wholeness of the person who was his meal and the restoration of the person eaten seems to deprive the cannibal and his offspring of their entire physical selves.

Thomas solves these problems in ways that affirm his belief in the complete physical integrity of resurrected selves. He addresses the first objection considered above by noting that the unity of corporal parts lies primarily in the soul to which the body is joined. But even the flux of bodily change on this side of death subverts neither one's sense of personal identity nor the judgment of others that the same physical person, though one ever changing, stands before them. Like a fire that is always the same fire even though the wood of its fuel is burned to ash and constantly replenished, the human body remains one in this life in spite of its undeniable change. "Man," Thomas claims, "is not . . . numerically different according to his different ages, although not everything which is in him materially in one state is also there in another."[3] And if physical change poses no difficulty for physical identity in this life, in principle it can pose no difficulty for physical identity in resurrected life. The cannibal conundrum could also follow the lines of such naturalistic explanation, especially if one imagines a modest meal on the cannibal's part and so minimal bodily loss to the person eaten. "For it is not necessary," as his answer to the previous objection made clear, "that whatever has been in man materially arise in him." But what if the imagination presses to the point of a very hungry cannibal or one, as

Thomas envisaged, who ate only human flesh? In either case, bodily loss, and so personal integrity, would be far too great to explain by the ordinary course of bodily flux. In this case, Thomas proposes, the resurrection of the body is a miracle that may require a bit more of the miraculous in such extraordinary circumstances. Quite simply, "if something is lacking, it can be supplied by the power of God."[4]

Having affirmed the holistic integrity of the self in resurrected life, Thomas presses further by imagining the state of resurrected persons in heaven. His Aristotelian metaphysics of the human person nicely supported the classical Christian belief in the resurrection of the body. Aristotle's hylemorphism explained the human person as a union of a formal principle of actuality, the soul, and a material principle of potentiality, the body. By Thomas's day, Christians had long believed that the body and soul, separated at death, would be reunited at the Last Judgment and together begin the eternal destiny that only the soul had begun at death. But just as a disembodied soul is no more a person than a soulless corpse, Thomas insists that it is "contrary to the nature of the soul to be without the body" and that "nothing which is contrary to nature can be perpetual."[5] Thus, Thomas found philosophical justification for the claims of the ancient creed, and reasonable support for his efforts to imagine heavenly life after the Last Judgment had been passed on all and the unity of the self had been achieved by the miracle of resurrection.

Many of Thomas's speculative results are gathered through a *via negativa* that says what heavenly persons are by saying what they are not. Those raised from the dead, Thomas avers, will not die again. Although he musters several arguments to prove his point, Thomas here expresses the heart of Christian hope that Christ's resurrection from the dead will have saving benefits for believers in their own resurrection. The afterlife will not be a continuation of earthly life, which always remains fast in the grip of sin and death. The bodies of those raised to heavenly life will possess a "different disposition,"[6] even if resurrected persons will continue to possess the same nature assured by the unity of soul and body. Yet the difference in disposition between the earthly body and the raised body will lie in the incorruptibility of the latter into which the former will be transformed.

This *via negativa* of no death and no corruptibility continues in Thomas's judgment that resurrected persons will not eat food and not engage in sexual love. Thomas understands eating, drinking, and engaging in sex as dimensions of the body's earthly corruption, and so it is hardly surprising that he would imagine heavenly life without them. Even though food, drink, and sex promote life prior to death, Thomas thinks of them as deathly activities in the afterlife that would subvert the notion of heavenly glory that fills his imagination. Yet, intent on demonstrating the compatibility between faith and reason in this philosophical *Summa*, Thomas takes pains to show the logic of his denials. If food were consumed in the afterlife, it would be converted into the body through digestion. But since a glorified body would not be capable of defecation, everything consumed in heaven would contribute to the growth of the body to the point that the person "will achieve a size beyond moderation."[7] When one considers that the eating of food and the resulting growth will take place forever, the thought-experiment leads to the unhappy conclusion that heavenly dining "will cause an increase in some dimension and we will have to say that the body of the man who rises will be increased to infinity"[8]—a prospect that would lead to an unidentical self in resurrection, to say nothing of a rather crowded heaven.

The denial of sex in heaven occupies more argumentative space than the denial of food. Medieval biology understood the male contribution to the generative act as the formal principle of life, and the male's semen to be the product of superfluous nutrition. Since Thomas had already proved that resurrected life would preclude eating, the sexual act, imagined as intercourse between a man and a woman, would likewise prove to be impossible. But even if the biological energy for sex in heaven were possible, then other deeper problems would arise. Sexual union, Thomas states, "is ordered to generation." Unless sexual union after the resurrection was to be in vain, "there will be human generation then just as there is now." Such a prospect presents a host of problems. Those born in heaven would not participate in the Last Judgment, the great social event on the calendar of salvation in which "all who have the same nature receive life at the same time."[9] But perhaps the Last Judgment would not be required for those born after it for an even more problematic reason. If those born in heaven are the issue of incorruptible bodies, then one might think they would be born without original sin, beyond the power of death, which is the cost of sin, and so without need of the Savior's redemption. Thomas suggests between the lines that such beings would not be human beings since they would not be children of the first parents and, as such, shareholders in their sin. If, on the other hand, those born after the resurrection were born corruptible, then their death will occur in heaven, a state in Christian belief beyond all death, to say nothing of the corruption that their corruptible heavenly origin would presuppose. Were these consequences not enough to subvert the thought-experiment, the heavenly birth of children in corruption would require their death and resurrection, which, in turn, would compromise the universality of the Last Judgment.[10]

Thomas presents many more arguments that follow along the same lines, and all portray the same heavenly imaginary. Heaven is a state in which the saved finally are restored to the wholeness of their earthly selves, body and soul, and in their wholeness transformed beyond death into the glory of perfect beatitude in the presence of God. In this state, Thomas assumes, the saints do not engage in activity, since the Beatific Vision is the fulfillment of all desire, and in desire's gracious loss there is no motivation for action and nothing to do except passively to enjoy the consummate bliss of the divine life.[11]

Thomas could have spent his time discussing a great number of activities in which resurrected bodies will not engage in heaven. His preoccupation with the activities of eating and having sex probably reflects his commitment to ascetical values. Thus interpreted, his denial of food and sex in the afterlife expresses the ascetic's commitment to diminished physical satisfaction in eating and drinking, as well as to the vow of celibacy. This reading finds support in Thomas's insistence that the bodily pleasures instigated by food and sex, and, he infers, bodily pleasures of any sort, would be unseemly in heaven. "In the present life," he argues, "it is a disordered and vicious thing to use food and sexual union for mere pleasure and not for the necessity of sustaining life and begetting offspring."[12] Pleasure, he claims, drives the body to serve those higher ends, but pleasure is not an end in itself.

The perfect order of the desireless life of the risen will not require the earthly promptings of pleasure, for pleasure, Thomas judges, is not virtuously directed to the good of others but merely toward its selfish satisfaction.[13] Since ecclesiastical values privilege the ascetical life as the closest imitation of Christ and so the surest path to heavenly reward, Thomas fashions his image of the resurrected person along the lines of the idealized ascetical body. Even though all are not ascetics in this life, all will have ascetical bodies throughout eternity.

If the life of ascetical renunciation governs Thomas's *via negativa* in eschatological description, then this "asceticizing" of heaven continues in another important renunciation that determines how Thomas imagines what transpires in heaven. Having established that the blessed dead will not engage in the acts of eating, drinking, or sexual union, Thomas proceeds to a more sweeping judgment: "From this one can see, finally, that all the business of the active life—it seems ordered to the use of food, to sexual activity, to the other necessities of the corruptible life—will come to a halt. Therefore, only the occupation of the contemplative life will persist in the resurrection."[14] In the *Summa Theologiae*, Thomas would take pains to argue that the contemplative life is superior to the active life in every way. The contemplative life, he claims, is nobler and more meritorious than the active life.[15] Indeed, the contemplative life is prior to the active life in its very nature "since it deals with things that are prior and more excellent; and hence it moves and directs the active life."[16] These judgments reflect any number of values, chief among which is Thomas's belief that the ascetical life, shaped by its devotion to contemplation, is morally superior to the lay life, which is ever preoccupied with the business of day-to-day concerns. A second value, however, is that Thomas conceives of eternity as a state in which persons judged worthy of heavenly life will find their ultimate happiness solely in the contemplation of God.[17] As we have already noted, these two values are mutually related. Catholic beliefs about the salvational priority of the ascetical life inform Thomas's understanding of resurrected life—not only in the renunciation of bodily pleasure but also in the renunciation of lay preoccupations. In turn, Thomas's conception of eternal happiness as the contemplation of God justifies the authority of ascetical vows and their practice. These values intertwine to energize a remarkably sophisticated argument for a heavenly life in which the saints are utterly at rest, enthralled before the glory of the Beatific Vision.

JONATHAN EDWARDS ON WHAT
THE SAINTS DO IN HEAVEN

Whereas Thomas imagines the blessed dead dwelling eternally in a state of consummate quiescence, Jonathan Edwards (1703–1758) imagines the occupants of heaven very differently disposed. In a 1738 sermon entitled "Heaven Is a World of Love," Edwards describes both the geography of heaven and the ties of community that there bind the saints together. Heaven, he claims, "is the palace, or presence-chamber, of the Supreme Being who is both the cause and source of all holy love."[18] The presence of God fills heaven, as does the very reality of love that God is by nature. Heaven is a place in which there are "none but lovely objects." There are no odious persons in heaven, for "all the persons who belong to that blessed society are lovely."[19] Moreover, heavenly things—and there are, Edwards insists, heavenly things—are lovely and "perfectly lovely." Whatever beauty earthly things possess is always diminished by the "contrary" and the "sinful." But in heaven all limitations will dissolve away in the fullness of existence. There, God's love will be illuminated by the brilliant glory of the Son of God and be poured out in the "perfect sweetness" of the Holy Spirit.[20] Wherever the inhabitants of the heavenly city cast their eyes, "they shall see nothing but beauty and glory." Moreover, in heaven the saints will find all the things "which appeared lovely to them while they dwelt on earth far beyond all they could see here, the things which captivated their souls, and drew them away from the most dear and pleasant of earthly objects."[21]

Edwards simply takes for granted that God is the focus of the loving activity of the saints in heaven, an assumption that is hardly surprising since it is the love of God's own being that animates heavenly life. "As the saints will love God with an inconceivable ardor of heart, and to the utmost of their capacity; so they will know that he has loved them from eternity, and that he still loves them, and will love them to eternity."[22] But since heaven is a world of love, the divine emotion forms relational bonds between and among all of the saints as well. "All that whole society" of the saints in heaven "rejoice in each other's happiness; for the love of benevolence is perfect in them."[23] The saints all delight in the prosperity of each other, even though their stations are not equal. Heaven, for Edwards, is set in a hierarchy. Some of the saints are higher in glory because they are higher in holiness. And yet, those who are lower will find no cause for jealousy or envy in these differences. Since the love of the saints toward one another "will always be mutual and answerable,"[24] the heavenly community ever will be motivated to share its love perfectly and without the impediment of sinful resistance:

> Heavenly lovers will have no doubt of the love of each other. They shall have no fear that their professions and testimonies of love are hypocritical; they shall be perfectly satisfied of the sincerity and strength of each other's love, as much as if there were a window in all their breasts, that they could see each other's hearts. There shall be no such thing as flattery or dissimulation in heaven, but there perfect sincerity shall reign through all. Everyone will be perfectly sincere, having really all that which they profess. All their expressions of love shall come from the bottom of their hearts. The saints shall know that God loves them, and they shall not doubt of the greatness of his love; and they shall have no doubt of the love of all their fellow heavenly inhabitants.[25]

Edwards is convinced that these bonds of love and fidelity will be strengthened all the more by the knowledge that the heavenly society will continue forever, with each of the saints knowing that "all their beloved fellow saints shall live forever in glory with the same love in their hearts."[26]

Although Edwards insists that all the heavenly inhabitants, freed from the tumults of sinful strife, will enjoy "ineffable quietness," "tranquility," and "quiet rest,"[27] his account of the heavenly life clearly envisions those dispositions of the blessed dead quite differently from

Aquinas. For Edwards, the beatific or, as he calls it, the beatifical vision produces a serenity and peacefulness in heavenly life that dwells within social activity. The blessed dead enact the bonds of loving relationship that tie them together in a community of the saints.[28] They continue to experience the love of God and saintly friendship anew, and to give sincere voice to the beauty and the joy that flourish in a world without enmity, sin, and betrayal. Aquinas's contemplative understanding of the Beatific Vision leads him to the imaginative assumption that the saints are so intellectually enthralled before God that all their activity ceases. For Thomas, words and deeds by their very nature are teleological, goal-oriented whenever authentic, and in God all goals are so consummately fulfilled that words and deeds become superfluous. Indeed, to Thomas's mind, their presence in heaven would only be proof that their agent was shy of heaven and thus lacking the vision of God. Edwards imagines a different heaven in which quiet, rest, and tranquility do not preclude activity, and even busyness.

In a sermon preached on March 14, 1731, and entitled "Serving God in Heaven," Edwards describes in further detail the activity of the saints in heaven. The reasonable creature, he avers, finds happiness in the perfection of its nature, and "'tis more excellent in the creature to be in action than in a state of inactivity."[29] The human person's powers of action are the endowment of God, and by "his giving of him such noble and excellent powers of action as he hath done, it is evident that he made him for action."[30] It is tempting to interpret this theological anthropology as an expression of Edwards's Puritanism, particularly as an extension of the Puritan doctrine of regeneration to heavenly proportions. Certainly there is much to support this reading, though it is hardly exhaustive. One should not overlook the degree to which the inductive style of Edwards's theology shapes his anthropology. As a theologian of pragmatic sensibilities, Edwards is inclined to define human nature functionally rather than metaphysically. Edwards believes, no doubt, that God's grace is proved by action. But he believes just as surely that actions shape the character of the human person, and so much so that any account of personal integrity, in this life or the next, must catalogue the results of the God-given power of action.

While believers are obliged to act in service to God in this world, the saints in heaven exercise their powers of action readily and freely, without the slightest burden of responsibility. In this world even faithful believers must always contend with their own sinfulness, which causes them to struggle in acting to please God. But in heaven, Edwards claims, saintly acts in service to God flow copiously from the will:

> The thing which God requires of his creatures is to be holy, to do holy actions, to be holy as he is holy; but the saints in heaven will have such an high esteem and admiration of God that they will greatly delight in conforming to him. It will be a great pleasure to 'em to be conformed to him whose beauty they constantly behold with exaltation and ecstasy of soul, and whose glory they cease not day nor night to extol.[31]

For Edwards, this saintly behavior radiates God's love, as all things in heaven do. "True love," he assures his congregation, "is an active principle; it desires to show itself not only in words, but in deeds, by doing something for the beloved."[32]

In Edwards's later sermon "Heaven Is a World of Love," we needed to read between the lines in order to reconcile his descriptions of saintly action in heaven with his insistence that heaven is a place of quiet and rest. "Serving God in Heaven," however, intentionally delights in the paradox. "'Tis true," Edwards confirms, "the heavenly state is a state of rest: they that enter into heaven, they enter into Christ's rest. . . . But this don't hinder but that their state will be a state of action and employment. We need not suppose that they spend their time in doing nothing: no, the saints never are so active as in heaven." This is not to say, however, that their activity will be laborious or cause them to tire. Animated by a love for God and flourishing within the love of the saintly society, the blessed dead "will have no need of ceasing, to take their rest; it will be all rest."[33] Saintly activity is itself heavenly refreshment, an engaged form of heavenly peace in which enacted virtue brings tranquility to holy character. And just as heaven is never ending, so too is the virtuous activity of the saints, whose moral powers "shall be used forevermore." This unlimited horizon for saintly activity enables their powers to be "perfected in heaven" so that the holiness of the saints increases as they continue to serve God. The saints, Edwards insists, "shall perpetually behold God's glory and perpetually enjoy his love. But they shall not remain in a state of inactivity, merely receiving from God; but they return to him and shall enjoy him in a way of serving and glorifying him."[34]

ANOTHER PROPOSAL: FORGIVENESS IN HEAVEN

Aquinas and Edwards share a theological commitment to engage in speculation about the life of the blessed dead. To many contemporary theologians, their willingness to venture this kind of inquiry is typical of their premodern understanding of the theological task—quaint perhaps, but hermeneutically unsophisticated and far too willing to attend to the object of hope rather than hope's existential struggle and its capacity to enliven the moral life. Yet it seems to me that Aquinas and Edwards should be applauded for their eschatological seriousness rather than chided for their theological naiveté. Both make extraordinary efforts to imagine the fulfillment of God's biblical promise to "wipe away the tears from all faces" and to "swallow up death forever" (Is 25:8). Both parse the living encounter with grace in order to represent the final consequences of grace, when "everything old has passed away" and "everything has become new" (1 Cor 5:17). Both offer inspiring accounts of heavenly life that encourage believers to consider an eschatological "more" in faith, hope, and love derived from the contexts of their respective Christian traditions.

As much as Aquinas and Edwards are committed to the same eschatological project, they accomplish it in very different ways. Aquinas imagines an afterlife in which the personal identity of the resurrected self is of paramount importance, and, as we have seen, he imagines that the identity of all in the afterlife has been transformed by the ascetical ideals that the Catholicism of his day valued so highly. The active life ceases in favor of a never-ending contemplation of God in

the Beatific Vision which, he assumes, enthralls the saintly contempla-
tor into a state of passive wonder. Edwards imagines the afterlife in
New England Puritan fashion as a never-ending life of virtue, which
perfectly yet increasingly continues the moral improvement that those
regenerated by grace began in earthly life. He delights in imagining
an aesthetic heaven, filled with beautiful things and beautiful persons,
whose heavenly service is energized by God's love, which permeates
every corner of heaven.[35]

In their study *Heaven: A History*, Colleen McDannell and Bernhard Lang argue that two genres of heavenly description have persisted throughout the Christian centuries: a theocentric view and an
anthropocentric view.[36] In the former, attention to heaven as God's
realm accentuates the differences between heaven and earth, and results in a conception of the saints as quiescent. In the latter, God fades
into the background as heaven is imagined in finer detail, with a premium placed on the actions of the saints. Like any typology, this
one is painted in broad strokes and were the types applied respectively
to Aquinas and Edwards, they would require nuanced qualification.
Aquinas, for example, speaks of the heavenly life as contemplative, but
insists on the continuity of persons from earthly to resurrected life.
Edwards certainly stresses the activity of the saints in heaven, but not
at all to the diminishment of God's heavenly presence. Yet there is no
denying that these general types fit the heavenly speculation offered
by Aquinas and Edwards. Since our project here is to recover the premodern willingness to speculate about the afterlife in a contemporary
eschatology, our proposal will fall into one of these two broad types.
And since our project is not to imagine God or heaven itself but the
life of the blessed dead, then the pages that follow will offer a sketch
of heavenly life that is illustrative of what McDannell and Lang call
the anthropocentric view. Unlike Aquinas, and much more like Edwards, I will portray resurrected life by attending to the character of
the blessed dead, and, even more, to the formation of their heavenly
character. I will do so by envisaging forgiveness as an ongoing moral
endeavor of the blessed dead, an endeavor that completes the salvation of the saints in heaven into eternity.

What Does Jesus Do in the Afterlife?

Caroline Walker Bynum has observed that to "twentieth-century non-Christians and Christians alike, no tenet of Christianity has seemed more improbable—indeed, incredible—than the doctrine of the resurrection of the body."[37] Anyone who knows the rich ways that bodily resurrection animated the faith of premodern believers cannot help but be struck by its absence in contemporary Christian belief. When contemporary Christians imagine the afterlife, they tend to do so dualistically, as the continuance of a disembodied soul. Thinking in the manner of ancient Platonists, they assume that the fullness of the self resides in its invisible dimensions, beyond the fluctuations of the body that eventually are rife with old age, disease, and death. The creed, however, professes belief in the resurrection of the body and so insists on an afterlife in which the entire person is saved. Ancient Christians not only believed in bodily resurrection but also went to great lengths to imagine how it would occur and how it would perdure, as their art and theological speculation testify.[38] The resurrected Jesus was a paradigm for their religious imaginings, and we would do well to follow their time-honored example by making the resurrected Jesus a paradigm for imagining the life of the blessed dead in the pages to follow.

Paul's discussion of the afterlife in 1 Corinthians 15 is the earliest Christian testimony to Jesus' resurrection as a model for the resurrection of believers. For Paul, the denial of the resurrection of the dead on the part of the new Corinthian converts amounted to a denial of Jesus' resurrection, since, Paul infers, the resurrection of Jesus is the graceful source and cause of resurrection itself (1 Cor 15:12–19). Yet Jesus' resurrection remains in the background of Paul's concerns as he tries to sketch a holistic account of the believer's resurrected life. The narrative commitments of the later evangelists put the resurrected Jesus in full view of the believer as a paradigm for imagining the afterlife. In its original form, the Gospel of Mark portrays the resurrection of Jesus only in the powerful image of the empty tomb. The resurrected Jesus makes no appearance (Mk 16:1–8), as he does

in the longer ending and in the later gospels. Matthew includes two appearance scenes—to the women leaving the tomb and to the disciples
in the closing passage—that offer little detail of Jesus' new resurrected
life (Mt 28:9–10, 16–20). Luke and John make much of post-Easter
appearances, writing elaborately of Jesus' resurrected life. As different
as their accounts of the post-Easter Jesus are, these gospel writers yet
treat the appearances in consistent ways that can inform our project.

It is something of a commonplace in the interpretation of the
later resurrection appearances to highlight the issue of Jesus' identity,
and to do so by noting the ways the gospel writers stress the reality of
Jesus' resurrected body. Both Luke and John acknowledge that Jesus'
resurrected body is different from his body before Easter. His resurrected body is not easily recognized, as demonstrated in Luke's story
of the disciples on the road to Emmaus (Lk 24:13–32) and John's
story of Mary Magdalene mistaking the resurrected Jesus for the
gardener (Jn 20:11–16). His body appears or disappears miraculously,
and so is not subject to the ordinary conditions of worldly existence
(Lk 24:31, 36, 51; Jn 20:19, 26). The evangelists make the very same
point about the resurrected Jesus that Paul had made about resurrected life decades earlier: that the body in resurrection transcends
the limitations of the body in death (1 Cor 15:42–44). And yet, while
acknowledging the saved and saving difference in the person of the
resurrected Lord, both Luke and John are especially intent on show-
ing that this Jesus is the same person who was born and lived and died
on the cross. Both do so by having the resurrected Jesus make his
wounded body the proof of his identity. The Lucan account has Jesus
say to his startled disciples before whom he has appeared: "'Look at
my hands and my feet; see that it is I myself. Touch me and see; for
a ghost does not have flesh and bones as you see that I have'" (Lk
24:39). In one of the most compelling scenes in all the gospels, John
has the disciple Thomas make the crucifixion wounds the proof of
Jesus' resurrected identity, and Jesus is happy to oblige when he appears to him (Jn 20:24–29).

Interpretive attention to Jesus' embodied identity in the resurrection is an important corrective to the dualistic understandings
of afterlife that prevail in contemporary Christian communities. If

Jesus' afterlife is normative for the afterlife of believers, then the New Testament narratives insist on the indispensability of embodiment for identity, and so for the saved identity of the blessed dead. And yet this close relationship between identity and embodiment can occlude other aspects of Jesus' resurrected identity that are just as crucial for the eschatological imagination. Embodiment, after all, can be conceived statically, as a state of being conveyed by the mere fact of physicality. There is a sense in which Jesus' demonstrative use of his body as a marker of continuous identity in Luke and John encourages such a view. Considered in this way, embodiment is a quality of identity as inert as a metaphysical essence. I propose that we broaden the scope of Jesus' resurrected identity by attending to his embodied actions in the appearance scenes. These actions, Jesus' "doing" in his resurrected life, can enliven our imagination about the life of the blessed dead.

What does Jesus do in his resurrected life? According to both the Apostles' Creed and the Nicene Creed, Jesus is "seated at the right hand of the Father" and he "will come again" to judge the living and the dead.[39] A literal reading of the ancient professions of faith seems to suggest that the resurrected Jesus is now inactive, waiting until the end of time to continue his saving work as the Son of God. Luke and John imagine things differently. Even though these gospels together offer precious few pages on the resurrected life of the Risen Lord, they do consistently present the identity of Jesus through his actions. The richness of Scripture, its own fecund sacramentality, offers many possible descriptions of such actions.[40] I would like to focus on the following: the way that Jesus keeps his promises; the way that Jesus bears the pain of his life without reproach; the way that Jesus reconciles failure; and the way that Jesus shows himself to be who he is.

Fulfillment is the most obvious theme that runs through the resurrection accounts. The gospel writers narrate the resurrection of Jesus as they do to proclaim the truth that all lives, all of creation, and all of history have been fulfilled in the Easter event. All four gospels express this fulfillment through the image of the empty tomb, and the Synoptic Gospels bring this image to clear articulation in the announcement of the resurrection by heavenly messengers. We should note, though, that this fulfillment is something that Jesus does, not only in the eventfulness of the resurrection itself but also in the way that this event is his keeping of a promise. Mark's gospel makes this point most clearly. Mark presents the resurrection of Jesus as a dramatic surprise after the seemingly hopeless tragedy of Jesus' tortuous death. Yet Mark expects that surprise will be transformed into purpose as readers recall the crucial scene at the center of the gospel in which Jesus' identity is under discussion. In response to Jesus' question " 'But who do you say that I am?' " (Mk 8:29), Peter declares that Jesus is the Messiah. This response prompts Jesus to explain what being the Messiah means: "Then he began to teach them that the Son of Man must undergo great suffering, and be rejected by the elders, the chief priests, and the scribes, and be killed, and after three days rise again" (Mk 8:31). Even though this passage characterizes Jesus' explanation as instruction, the Easter event seems to raise it to the heights of promise, and, in light of the Easter event, to the summit of a promise fulfilled.

Promises are the most important words that persons speak since they extend personal relationship into an unseen future in which faithfulness may be broken. A promise bespeaks constancy of character. It verbalizes the speaker's most serious intention to be a committed self beyond the present moment. A promise kept is the fulfillment of personal character as it stands in relation to others, and that fulfillment is achieved in the struggles that keeping a meaningful promise entails. If we consider Jesus in resurrection as someone who has kept his promise to be the Risen Lord, then this is a promise that he has made to be most fully himself by facing the trial of torture and death so that, through his resurrection from the dead, God could destroy death for all.[41]

The role of the crucifixion in the fulfillment of Jesus' promise to save the world brings us to another of his activities in the afterlife. The resurrected Jesus bears the pain of his life without reproach. This forbearance is not simply resurrection behavior but extends from Good Friday to Easter and beyond. Jesus remains an innocent victim throughout his false indictment, his torture, and his terrible execution. And though innocent, he refuses to reproach the many agents of imperial power who enact its violence. In resurrection, Jesus continues to act in this way. He calls attention to his wounds in order to stir the resurrection faith of his disciples. But he does not lay blame for their infliction, either historically by mention of Roman violence or the betrayal of a friend, or theologically by mention of sinful humankind.

Jesus' disposition in this regard offers an interesting contrast to Job's in the face of his innocent suffering. In order to make the innocence of Job's suffering utterly clear, the author of the ancient book leaves no doubt in the opening scene that it is God, and not Job, who bears responsibility for all the evil that suddenly befalls the just man (Jb 1–2). Job voices his innocence with like clarity. His eloquent speeches lament the terrible injustice that has been done to him. He reproaches God for what he rightly believes is God's guilt, and he reproaches his friends for their pious defenses of God and their easy willingness to blame the victim. In noting this difference between Jesus and Job, I do not mean to suggest that Job's response is inappropriate. Job's lament is courageously prophetic. Railing against the injustice of his suffering, he speaks righteously on behalf of any faithful believer beset by undeserved suffering. His words attempt to end the violence that has entered his life by naming its cause. Jesus, of course, is no stranger to prophetic speech of this sort. In scene after gospel scene he speaks against the power of evil at work in the world, and especially against its effects in the lives of the marginalized. Jesus, though, does not raise his voice to protest or to blame with regard to his own suffering, either before or after the resurrection. In the afterlife, Jesus' wounds identify who he is, but they are not his evidence for the injustice done to him or for the guilt of the perpetrators. Jesus' unwillingness to reproach his offenders defines a higher standard of moral response that achieves an eschatological clarity in his resurrected life, when the irreversible evil done to him cannot be checked by lament, and reproach would only perpetuate the reciprocity of blame that makes new victims. Job himself may approach this higher standard in his final silence before God (Jb 42:1–6).

Another activity of the resurrected Jesus is his reconciliation of failure. The Gospels consistently agree that Jesus died alone. Jesus and his message may have inspired discipleship in the later years of his life, but the spectre of the cross led his disciples to flee in the face of danger and worldly judgment. Scripture scholars often point out that the disciples' abandonment of Jesus is such a scandal for the early Church that its acknowledgment in all four gospels is strong evidence of its historicity. Certainly this most bitter of injustices, at the hands of friends and not strangers, must be counted first among those that Jesus does not reproach. In spite of this terrible offense, the resurrected Jesus both forgives failure and carries his forgiveness to the point of reconciliation. The best example of this relentless forgiveness appears in Jesus' reconciliation of Peter in John's gospel. In the gospel's closing scene, Jesus asks Simon Peter three times if he loves him, and three times Peter affirms his love. With each affirmation, Jesus presses Peter into the commitment that he lacked the night before Jesus died, when Peter, fearing his own arrest, three times denied his association with Jesus. The resurrected Jesus does the work of reconciliation not only by the symmetry of his forgiveness but also by entrusting Peter with responsibility for the nascent Church. With every confession of Peter's love, Jesus urges his care toward the faithful with the words "Feed my lambs," "Tend my sheep," "Feed my sheep" (Jn 21:15–17). It is Jesus who allows Peter to mend their broken relationship and it is Jesus who strengthens their renewed friendship by a remarkable act of faith in their future together. Having denied Jesus and, by so doing, having participated in the breaking of his body, Peter now is charged with the task of nurturing the body of Christ in the world.[42]

The final activity of the resurrected Jesus that I would like to consider is the way he shows himself to be who he is. In his important book *The Identity of Jesus Christ*, Hans Frei makes the interesting observation that Jesus is most himself in his resurrection.[43] This claim seems rather strange to a time in which the question of Jesus' identity is typically answered by yet another scholarly reconstruction of the historical Jesus. Frei approaches the identity of Jesus in quite a different way by attending to Jesus' character, his integrity as a person. Jesus' character cannot be described on the basis of historical evidence, for such evidence is lacking and, even more, holds little interest for faith. A believer's regard for the person of Jesus has all the evidence it needs in the biblical narrative where Jesus' character takes shape in the events of his life, death, and resurrection.

In describing Jesus' character, Frei resists the modern inclination to think of identity as a function of subjectivity. Personal identity, he argues, does not well up in inner feelings but takes shape as one's intentions are consistently brought to action in the course of life. This rather un-Romantic and empirical approach to identity might seem more compatible with the historian's rational regard for Jesus up to the point of his death. To the contrary, Frei maintains that the gospels portray Jesus not simply as a person who said and did things from birth to death, but as a person whose words and deeds are consummated in his resurrection from the dead. As Frei puts it, "To know *who* he is in connection with what took place is to know *that* he is. This is the climax of the story and its claim. What the accounts are saying, in effect, is that the being and identity of Jesus in the resurrection are such that his nonresurrection becomes inconceivable."[44] The resurrection is not an event that functions as a kind of "add-on" to Jesus' life, even one in which he becomes extrinsically "more" than he was prior to his resurrection. For Frei, the resurrection is the event that provides unity to all that Jesus said and did such that Jesus becomes most fully who he is precisely in his resurrection from the dead. By the same token, we can say that all that Jesus says and does in his afterlife stands in continuity with his preceding character-forming words and deeds.

Frei makes a wonderful observation here that describes exactly how believers encounter Jesus' graceful presence, itself a function of who he is believed to be, namely, the Risen Lord. This last activity of the resurrected Jesus—that he shows himself to be who he is—is actually a more general account of the other activities that we have already considered, all of which manifest Jesus' identity by demonstrating his character in action. It would be interesting to consider whether and how Frei's observation about the resurrected Jesus applies to believers in ways that can allow us to speculate meaningfully about their own resurrected life.

Jesus' Resurrected Life and Ours

Jesus' resurrected life is interesting in its own right, as everything about him is. Our interest in his eschatological deeds, though, has been prompted by what they might mean for the resurrected life of believers. The Christian belief that our common humanity shares in Jesus' resurrected life justifies this comparison, as does the way that Jesus' actions set the standard for Christian discipleship. And yet, whatever homologies between Jesus and believers justify our comparison, there are important differences to consider. First and foremost, Jesus is the Savior, the divine Son of God, and so is exceptional in every respect, including his resurrection. Jesus' resurrection is not the received gift of eternal life, as is ours, but the gift itself, the event that redeems the world. Moreover, Jesus' bodily resurrection occurs three days after his death. In Christian belief, the bodily resurrection of believers does not occur until the Last Judgment.[45] Until that event, the disembodied souls of the blessed dead experience the fulfillment of heavenly life. This difference between Jesus' resurrection and our own means that we cannot speak literally of the embodied actions of believers in resurrected life until the miracle of bodily resurrection has taken place.

It is important to note, however, that the tradition has affirmed a real consistency in the life of the blessed dead before and after the eschatological union of body and soul. This is expressed most clearly in the fourteenth-century teaching of Benedict XII. Condemning the theological views of his predecessor John XXII, Benedict taught that the disembodied soul in heavenly bliss enjoys the fullness of the Beatific Vision, and that the resurrected union of soul and body after the Last Judgment adds nothing to this experience. John held the view that bodily resurrection was required for the Beatific Vision to occur at all, since the metaphysical integrity of the person dwells in the union of body and soul. John thus imagined a heavenly wait for the soul in a diminished afterlife before the resurrection, deprived of the Beatific Vision. The purport of Benedict's authoritative teaching was that saved persons do not experience varying degrees of heavenly bliss throughout their lives in blessedness. The resurrection adds nothing to the redeemed encounter with God in the Beatific Vision.[46] It is interesting to notice that the same religious concerns motivated both sides in this disagreement. The integrity of the saved person mattered to both John and Benedict, the former finding it in the unity of the soul and body and the latter in the unity of undiminished, heavenly joy. In this controversy, as in everyday life, the immediate satisfaction of longing trumped metaphysical consistency.

Benedict's teaching affirms that, before God, the self remains wholly itself, even when the effects of deathly fragmentation linger into the afterlife in the separation of soul and body. His position is not that the body does not matter, for Christian sensibilities demand that it does. Rather, he maintains that the unity of the self-same person—in soul and body—is never lost in the presence of God. This unity of the saved self before and after bodily resurrection in Benedict's teaching provides a traditional warrant for speaking of the activity of the blessed dead as embodied even before the resurrection, if not exactly then at least in anticipation of eschatological destiny. This proleptic warrant enables us to transcend the difference between Jesus' afterlife and the afterlife of believers prior to resurrection, and in such a way that Jesus' afterlife can be paradigmatic for thinking about the blessed dead on this side of the Last Judgment.[47] Let us consider, then, the embodied actions of the resurrected Jesus as a heuristic for thinking about resurrected life.

What might it mean for the blessed dead to imitate the way that Jesus keeps his promises in resurrected life? The promise that served as our earlier example was nothing less than Jesus' divine promise to save the world. For merely human persons, of course, this promise is inimitable since there is no respect in which they can make or keep it. In the case of the blessed dead, we must consider the eschatological fulfillment of promises that are morally much more ordinary.

One way of considering the realm of human sinfulness is as a tragic collection of broken promises. This conceptualization has its roots in the Jewish covenant, which is a set of promissory relationships between God and the people of Israel, between God and individual human persons, and among human persons. To live by keeping these promissory relationships is to live in faithfulness to God and one's neighbor. To live by breaking these promissory relationships is to sin. The brokenness of sinful lives is nothing other than the broken-ness of promises to be faithful in relationship. This is not to say that every promise we make must be kept in order to be faithful to God, our neighbor, and ourselves. As Margaret Farley has demonstrated, some of our promises are conditional, and changes in time and circumstance may require their redefinition or even their responsible dissolution.[48] As a moral rule, though, the inability to keep a promise represents sin-ful failure, whether the promise is explicit or tacitly defined by the ex-pectations of personal relationship. For all but the extraordinary saints, death marks the loss of worldly opportunity to keep unkept promises or to mend relationships severed by sinful betrayal.

If we imagine the task of discipleship extending into the afterlife, then perhaps we can think of the blessed dead as engaged in the moral task of promise keeping. This engagement can be like Jesus' embod-ied action to the extent that the blessed dead continue to be faithful to promises they have kept in their earthly lives. Promise keeping be-comes transformative imitation of Jesus when the promises broken in the course of earthly life are renewed and faithfully kept eschatologi-cally. To imagine the blessed dead as active in this way is to imagine them engaged in overcoming sin, particularly sin of their own mak-ing. Or, to express the same idea from another angle, to imagine the blessed dead active in this way is to imagine them at work in securing the ties of moral relationship. Since moral relationship takes shape in a communal setting, there is no reason for us to conceive this activity in a dyadic fashion, as though love, friendship, or commitment flour-ish only between two personal partners, or to conceive relationship as transpiring only among the blessed dead. The Catholic notion of the communion of the saints assumes that the living and the dead are bound together in a network of relationships as the one body of Christ, even if we are too accustomed to think of the moral life of the Church triumphant as quiescent. And if Martin Buber's existentialist analysis of personal relationship can be instructive for thinking about the communion of the saints, then no personal relationship in this world or the next transpires without itself sharing in, and being grace-fully nourished by, personal relationship with God.[49]

The advantage to this focus on promise keeping is that it enables us to imagine the communion of the saints as an activity in which the blessed dead participate by imitating Jesus' resurrected life. We can observe this as well in the second kind of embodied action on the part of the resurrected Jesus. We noticed that Jesus bears the pain of his life without reproach. He refuses to indict those whose sin has brought him to suffering and death. Even though prophetic speech indicts the injustice of sin and can be extraordinarily virtuous, there is something especially inspiring about Jesus' unwillingness to blame or even to speak at all of the causes of his suffering. A high Christology might explain Jesus' silence as his self-assured confidence in a saving plan scripted from all eternity. Since the events of cross and resurrection have destroyed the power of suffering, there is no reason for the resurrected Jesus to credit the causes of suffering at all by speaking of their power in his life. His silence bespeaks his victory. A better explanation would attend to Jesus' character as demonstrated by his consistent actions. In this perspective, Jesus' achievement as a person lies in his willingness to forgive those who have done him harm. Jesus is very explicit in offering words of forgiveness in the Gospel of Luke as he hangs dying on the cross (Lk 23:34). Attending Jesus' articulate act of forgiveness is the striking silence of his unwillingness to reproach those who have done him harm. Jesus' refusal to blame should be understood as a behavioral precondition for his forgiveness of both strangers and friends, and thus as an indispensable dimension of this astounding act of forgiveness itself.

It is interesting to notice how closely the ancient creeds join the eschatological events of "forgiveness of sins" and "resurrection of the body." As tempting as it may be to understand the forgiveness of sins exclusively as an act of God that saves the forgiven, a fuller appreciation would include the responsibility of believers to forgive those who have done them harm, as expected in the only prayer that Jesus taught his disciples (Mt 6:12). This activity may take place in earthly life, and yet, in sinful failure, often does not. In light of this common failure, perhaps we could imagine the life of the blessed dead in the activity of offering forgiveness eschatologically. The forgiving actions of the blessed dead imitate Jesus' unwillingness to reproach those who have done him harm as the beginning of real forgiveness and also the third embodied activity of the resurrected Jesus that we noted earlier, namely, his reconciliation of failure. The way in which Jesus forgives Peter makes it very clear that forgiveness is a task that blossoms in the conscious work of reconciliation. Jesus' efforts at reconciliation are powerful manifestations of grace, and through these actions Jesus allows Peter to renew their relationship and to profess his love. The same may be said for the life of the blessed dead. To be a disciple of Jesus means that, even in the afterlife, the bonds of reconciliation that unite the communion of the saints must be forged in the work of forgiveness, made and remade in acts of love that grace those who forgive as much as those who are forgiven.

Becoming Most Oneself in Resurrected Life

Hans Frei's compelling interpretation of Jesus' resurrection helped us to understand what Jesus does in the afterlife, and in a way that embraces all of his other eschatological actions. Jesus, he noted, becomes most himself in his resurrection. His very person, his character as demonstrated in his actions, is completed in the events of his resurrected life. We can conclude this chapter by considering how this last, and most comprehensive, description of Jesus' deeds in the afterlife can serve as a paradigm for the life of the blessed dead.

Applying Frei's description of Jesus' resurrected life to the blessed dead immediately poses problems. Jesus, after all, led a sinless life, and so his resurrection is easily and consistently imaginable as his personal fulfillment. Indeed, Frei's very point is that careful readers of the gospel find a remarkable continuity between who Jesus was in his earthly life and who Jesus is in his afterlife. Any talk of the resurrected fulfillment of believers as an imitation of Jesus would need to acknowledge that this imitation, like any act of Christian discipleship, is always limited by the transcendence of Jesus' divine nature and the transcendence of his sinless humanity. If the blessed dead can be described as becoming who they most are in heavenly afterlife, then this becoming must be understood as a transformation brought about by God's grace. Resurrected life is nothing less than a miracle through which, faith holds, believers will become much more than who they were in life, and yet in a way that fulfills who they always were. In Paul's language, this transformation is a "new creation" in which the power of sin, "everything old," has passed away (2 Cor 5:17). The personal continuity of the blessed dead thankfully is not beholden to the standard set by Jesus. Their salvation, becoming who they most are, to some degree entails becoming who they were not: persons broken by their sin and the sin of others. This miraculous continuity, one that yet abides in spite of the personal burdens of sin, is largely the work of God's grace.

The Catholic argument of this chapter, though, has proposed that who we become in resurrected life continues to transpire by grace and works, and has suggested that the resurrected actions of Jesus provide a model for discipleship even in the afterlife. For the blessed dead to continue to be who they are, they must act in character. But acting in character for the blessed dead, being who they truly are even as they are transformed by grace, requires their imitation of Jesus. This imitation remains a task, and even a challenge, precisely because the effects of sin linger in resurrected life. Like the wounds on Jesus' resurrected body, the effects of sin—both responsibility for it and its victimizing consequences—continue to inform personal identity in resurrected life. This is not to say that sin is still a possibility for the blessed dead. The possibility of sin would be a meaningless notion apart from its actuality, and to allow for the actuality of sin in the life of the blessed dead would be to concede that redemption could be undone. Rather, the transformation that makes the blessed dead who they most are is only real and meaningful to the extent that its gracefulness neither annuls the effects of sin nor reduces the redeemed to a less-than-personal existence. The effects of sin mark the identity of the person who perpetrated and suffered them, just as much as do the salutary effects of virtue. And to be a person shaped in identity by both good and evil presupposes rational and willful agency, not only in this life but also in the life to come. For the blessed dead to be themselves they must continue to act, and act in ways that communicate their character as the saints. To be most fully themselves, they must exercise saintly character toward the heritage of sin as well as toward the heritage of grace.

We can imagine this moral activity continuing to take place long after the final judgment has been passed on all and the number of the saints in heaven is complete. To do so would assume that the saints are most themselves not only in blissful repose before the glory of the Beatific Vision but also in the virtuous work of forgiveness that is as never ending as the effects of sin in resurrected life. Our appreciation of the communion of the saints increases if we imagine the blessed dead presently engaged in the same graceful activity of reconciliation, both among themselves and toward those in earthly life where the actuality of sin ever threatens the solidarity of the saintly community. Our appreciation of the communion of the saints increases even more if we envision this saintly activity not only as the ardent moral behavior of the blessed dead but also as the task of those in earthly life who aspire to become most themselves in resurrected life. Just as we imagined that the reconciling activity of the blessed dead extends throughout heaven and earth, so too should we imagine the same scope of Christian discipleship for those in earthly life. While there are differences in the communion of the saints, there finally is no difference among all the saints, living and dead, in their responsibility to imitate Jesus in all their natural and supernatural relationships.

It may seem as though the description of the blessed dead offered in these pages is more an account of life in purgatory than of heavenly life. Perhaps this is so because we are unused to imagining the effects of sin lasting in heavenly life, and inclined to think that the blessed dead so share in the eternal life of God that, like the divine nature, they are impervious to the sort of change that the exercise of character demands. For the blessed dead to be themselves, though, they must continue to be persons shaped by the history of sin. For the blessed dead to be most fully themselves, they must continue to act in the afterlife in imitation of Jesus' own resurrected life in ways that defeat the burden of sin that they both made and suffered. The negotiation of sin is certainly the business of the dead in purgatory. But it is important to imagine heavenly life continuing that task in its own way, for less a conception risks the loss of our selves in all their integrity.[50]

The images of resurrected life presented here do not aspire to literalism, and they certainly do not claim to be exhaustive. They remain interpretable acts of the imagination and stand in the company of many others that might be warranted by Scripture and tradition. Theology should not shrink from the task of thickly describing the eschata, a practice that has been valued highly in the Christian tradition. In spite of the modern dismissal of such activity as pious caprice, imagining eschatologically can be a serious exercise in faith and hope. However modest our results must be, they can be an effective rejoinder to the mystical silence that now so often measures a meaningful theology of the afterlife. Our modest results have proposed that one answer to the interrogative title of our first chapter—for what may we hope?—is that we may hope to be busy in heavenly life at the work of redemption, whose gift we have received.

CHAPTER 3

Time, Judgment, and Competitive Spirituality

A Reading of the Development of the Doctrine of Purgatory

Speculation about the life of the blessed dead brought us to the tentative conclusion that all of the saints, extraordinary and ordinary, are busy in the afterlife at the ongoing work of forgiveness, and that this eschatological activity is a realized norm for Christian virtue in all the dimensions of the communion of the saints. As the previous chapter closed, I observed that imagining the blessed dead in this way might seem odd to a tradition inclined to think of the Beatific Vision as a state of ecstasy that is utterly, and so ironically, static. Busyness in the afterlife cuts against the grain of a traditional metaphysics of eternity and pious expectations of heavenly life as a sheer state of repose. Even more, my proposal for a thicker description of a heavenly life in which the blessed dead are preoccupied with the business of reconciliation seems nearer to traditional images of life in purgatory. Conflating heaven and purgatory risks the unseemly positions that heaven is stained by sin or that purgatory shares too much in the glories of heaven. Perhaps the most troublesome aspect of a purgatorial dimension to heaven is that the association itself takes purgatory too seriously for a time that has regarded it with theological indifference.

For many Catholics in the postconciliar Church, purgatory has fallen off the eschatological map. One reasonable explanation for why this has occurred might run along the following lines. The theological and pastoral reception of the Second Vatican Council highlighted the power of God's grace in bringing believers to salvation, and that emphasis undermined the detailed accounting of personal virtue and sin in the Tridentine merit system. This accent on the graciousness of divine love brought about a seismic shift in Catholic belief and practice. Conservatives in the Church would continue the explanation by concluding that the postconciliar theology of God's infinite mercy and compassion tragically eclipsed the preconciliar sense of the power of personal sin. This diminishment of the sense of sin has had repercussions for a host of other mutually related beliefs and practices that explains the contemporary indifference toward purgatory. The diminishment of a sense of personal sin has been attended by a transformed understanding of the saintly life as an epiphany of virtue, though not virtue achieved through difficult struggle with sin. The diminishment of the sense of personal sin has led to the virtual disappearance of the sacrament of penance in popular Catholic practice, a change in religious behavior that reflects the loss of a belief in the rigor of divine judgment. And since purgatory is about judgment, it is hardly surprising that the doctrine of purgatory has largely disappeared from Catholic belief and practice.

This chapter, though, offers a somewhat different explanation for the disappearance of purgatory in contemporary Catholic belief and practice, and one that does not reduce its disappearance to the tragic. That explanation will depend on an argument that I offer in the body of the chapter for the development of the doctrine of purgatory. My purpose is to reflect on the development of the doctrine of purgatory in order to appreciate the workings of judgment in the Catholic tradition. I will not attempt a theological retrieval of the doctrine of purgatory, nor am I interested in trying to describe the life of the dead in purgatory in the manner of my account of the blessed dead in heaven. I am entirely open to the possibility that there is value in such a retrieval, but that is not my project here. Nor does my analysis intend to suggest that the doctrine of purgatory is an inauthentic development in the teachings of the Church. Instead, the doctrine of purgatory will serve as a resource for elucidating the anxieties and hopes that attend the Catholic belief in divine judgment. I readily concede at the outset that my argument will not please professional historians. It is sweeping in its historical scope, speculative in its judgments, and leads, in the end, to constructive conclusions. The story I tell will have historical contours and its main characters will be Catholic Christians who have lived their lives in the tradition's two, broad vocations: ascetics and laypersons. I begin the story by considering the recent revival of scholarly interest in purgatory that has been prompted by the work of Jacques Le Goff.

EXPLAINING PURGATORY

No study has had a greater influence on our understanding of the development of purgatory as a Catholic belief than Jacques Le Goff's *The Birth of Purgatory* (1981).[1] Le Goff argues that purgatory came into full bloom as a Catholic belief and doctrine rather late, in the twelfth century. Established at that time as a "third place" in the afterlife along with heaven and hell, purgatory became "an intermediary other world in which some of the dead were subjected to a trial that could be shortened by the prayers, by the spiritual aid of the living."[2] Hints of such beliefs abound in the earlier tradition, whether in affirmations of otherworldly purgation or in ancient accounts of near-death experiences in which the believer is conducted on a journey through hell so that, chastened by the terrible sight, he or she can regard earthly life as an opportunity for repentance.[3] But, for Le Goff, nothing in the earlier tradition compares with the elaboration of purgatory in the religious imagination of twelfth-century Europe.[4] Purgatory not only achieved specificity as a third place but also took shape in a detailed theology of retribution, sacrifice, penalties, pardons, and spiritual exchange among the dead and the living. Purgatory has continued to capture the Catholic imagination until very recently, achieving doctrinal definition in the late medieval period and enjoying "a more ample existence . . . in the leading Catholic styles of the fifteenth to the nineteenth centuries." Since Le Goff concedes that "Purgatory is rooted in the theology of the post-Tridentine catechism,"[5] he might have carried this period of flourishing to the eve of Vatican II, in the aftermath of which belief in purgatory has all but disappeared.

Central to Le Goff's thesis is his attribution of the twelfth-century birth of purgatory to social-historical causes. Cities began to rise in Europe at this time, creating a third, social group of merchants alongside the traditional two of empowered nobles and clergy, on the one hand, and the powerless peasantry, on the other. The binary eschatological destinies of heaven and hell were now imaginatively supplemented by a third, temporary destination that projected the new intermediate social group into the afterlife, along with all the social ambiguity of future success and failure that typified the life of the new merchant group. In Le Goff's words: "Between the great (lay and ecclesiastic) and the small (rural and urban workers) an intermediate category had been born, namely, the 'bourgeois,' who formed a group so diverse that I prefer not to speak of it as a class."[6] Le Goff does not reduce the birth of purgatory to the single cause of social stratification in the urban development of the High Middle Ages. He insists that it would be absurd to argue that "the bourgeoisie created Purgatory, or that Purgatory in one way or another derived from the bourgeoisie, assuming a bourgeoisie even existed at the time."[7] Rather he makes the more modest or, as he calls it, "hypothetical" interpretation that medieval men and women could only think and imagine in terms of their social and economic structures, and that dramatic changes in these structures could not help but be reflected in their thinking about life after death. It is difficult to disagree with Le Goff on this point, at least as a partial explanation of the development of this doctrine.

As an *Annales* historian, Le Goff is strongly committed to social historiography. And yet, in spite of this commitment, he troubles over the adequacy of this explanatory approach in the book's concluding pages. He admits that his argument has made purgatory the "key component" in explaining the medieval system of ideas. Purgatory holds this central place in his argument since, in his judgment, it captures something new in the developing structure of late medieval society. Early medieval thinking moved in a binary framework that reflected the feudal social division of rich and poor, empowered and disempowered. The twelfth century witnessed a shift to a trinary mode of thinking that mirrored the appearance of the new merchant class, and that valorized purgatory in an otherworldly landscape that previously had highlighted the eternal binaries of heaven and hell. The newness of an elaborate theology of purgatory in the later Middle Ages represented the newness of the nascent urban culture and accounts for the centrality of purgatory in Le Goff's social-historical explanation. But, Le Goff wonders, "Isn't it possible that the real energizing and organizing force of the system lay not in Purgatory but in Heaven?" Even though the sources portray purgatory as a place of suffering, perhaps "Purgatory's center of gravity may have shifted so far toward Paradise as to make the desire for Heaven the energizing force of Christian doctrine."[8] Wondering next about the adequacy of his account from the opposite direction, Le Goff questions whether belief in purgatory developed as it did in order for "the Church to preserve the belief in Hell everlasting" by "introducing a temporary Purgatory mainly to throw the inextinguishable fires of Hell into sharp relief."[9]

These are challenging questions to raise at the end of a rather ardent argument, and they show Le Goff's admirable capacity for self-criticism. Le Goff does not answer these questions, nor does he pose them only to dismiss them and reclaim the explanatory power of his argument. His book ends with the questions left standing, testimonies to what he describes as his nagging anxiety about the adequacy of his argument.[10] And this is a productive anxiety indeed. Had Le Goff pursued these questions and argued in heavenly or hellish directions, one expects that he would have constructed theses that resembled the one advanced in the book he did write, his scholarly mind-set and method unswervingly committed to social historiography. But his questions also delimit the boundaries of social-historical explanation by highlighting the importance of religious emotions in a system of doctrine, and so in any attempt at historical explanation. Perhaps, Le Goff considers, the *yearning* for heaven or the *fear* of hell are more central to Christian concern about the otherworld than purgatory itself, and perhaps purgatory is but a derivative way of speaking about the yearning for heaven or the fear of hell, or possibly even both!

Religious emotions like yearning and fear, of course, always unfold in determinate social-historical circumstances that mold them in complex ways, and so a more complete study of these emotions would need to explain the particular cultural setting that produced them. And yet, this same observation applies, mutatis mutandis, to a predominantly social-historical explanation. Even though religious beliefs and practices can be explained as a function of social-historical causes, they, in turn, can produce powerful religious emotions whose consistent meaning contributes to the integrity of an identifiable religious tradition. As much as these meaningful emotions are particularized by time, place, and circumstance, they may shape the determinate historical conditions within which they appear and to an extent that obliges the interpreter to consider the causal consequences of their consistent meaning over time.

I now consider this point with respect to purgatory. "Purgatory-like" beliefs have flourished throughout Christian history, especially in Latin Christianity, in what eventually came to be identified as the Roman Catholic tradition, and even in the popular culture where these beliefs have had currency. Origen's third-century belief in earthly life as successive reincarnations in which the soul is gradually educated to conformity with the divine will; Augustine's fifth-century mention of a supernatural, purifying fire in *City of God*; Gregory the Great's seventh-century stories of near-death experiences in which believers return to life after experiencing a vision of hell so that their sins could be purged by renewed moral effort in this life; Catherine of Genoa's classical sixteenth-century account of the late medieval theology of purgatory as an otherworldly third place; Le Goff's observation that this classical theme saw variations in a "Counter Reformation purgatory, . . . a baroque Purgatory, a romantic Purgatory, and a Sulpician Purgatory";[11] and the widespread practice of purgatorial intercession in Tridentine Catholicism in general to the eve of Vatican II—all testify to the consistent appearance of purgatory-like beliefs in the tradition. If one assumes that this consistent appearance expresses at least the possibility of consistent and meaningful religious emotions, then the interpreter cannot ignore that possibility in proposing historical explanations. Any effort to explain why these purgatorial beliefs have persisted throughout the tradition is susceptible to the same kind of reductionism about which Le Goff worried in his approach. Moreover, social-historical criticism rightly has made us wary of essentialist tendencies in homologous explanation. Nevertheless, the abiding expression of the same kinds of religious hopes and fears begs for explanation at the level of the historically similar, just as much as beliefs marked by time and place beg for explanation at the level of the historically different.

In the pages that follow, I explore how the consistent appearance of the religious emotion of anxiety, fueled by competition for heaven between and among martyrs, ascetics, and laypersons, does much to account for the development of the doctrine of purgatory in the Catholic tradition. I do not consider this perspective on the development of the doctrine of purgatory to be exhaustive. I offer the argument presented here only as another layer of explanation that, if credible, may complement the many recent scholarly accounts of the doctrine of purgatory.

ESCHATOLOGICAL ANXIETY

Purgatory is not explicitly mentioned among the four last things: death, judgment, heaven, and hell. But purgatory is entirely about the judgment that believers expect to face in the afterlife as a consequence of their lives here and now. The first shades of belief in what later developed into the medieval doctrine of purgatory appear as early as Augustine's fifth-century speculations about judgment in *City of God*. In book 21, the North African bishop opines that "not all men who endure temporal pains after death come into those eternal punishments, which are to come after that judgment. Some, in fact, will receive forgiveness in the world to come for what is not forgiven in this . . . so that they may not be punished with the eternal chastisement of the world to come."[12] This early conception links purgation to the judgment that God has made on those who suffer otherworldly pain. But judgment in Christian belief is not confined to supernatural purgation. Judgment has been a matter of concern from the tradition's earliest days, no doubt because it assesses the believer's consummate relationship to God, and so the believer's eternal destiny.

The early Christian conception of judgment was bound up with the zealous belief in Jesus' imminent return to the world as eschatological judge. Christian hope in this saving event drew on the religious energies of the Jewish apocalyptic tradition, which may have inspired the preaching of Jesus himself. One possible textual candidate for this influence is the Jewish book of Daniel, whose vision of the Son of Man "coming with the clouds of heaven" (Dan 7:13) captured first-century Christian imagination on the manner of Jesus' return. Daniel sees the end time as God's judgment on his people that will "bring some to everlasting life, and some to everlasting contempt" (Dan 12:2), a judgment of division that would later appear prominently in the Gospel of Matthew. The theology of the Q material, written or orally transmitted sayings of Jesus on the responsibility of discipleship, highlights the judgment that early Christians expected to accompany the coming of God's kingdom. Jesus' exhortations to virtue of the highest order in the Q sayings make impending judgment a horizon before which Christian commitment finally will be proved. Even though Matthew and Luke (75–85 CE) wove the Q material into larger gospel frameworks that tempered its apocalyptic fervor, they yet followed Q in making the judging expectations of Jesus the criterion of virtuous action for their Christian communities. These late first-century churches could aspire to ethical heights that required even the love of one's enemies (Mt 5:44; Lk 6:27), believing as they did that such virtue was an obligation for those who lived in an already immanent kingdom of God.

The early Church defined the criterion of judgment not only by the teaching of Jesus but also by the martyr's extraordinary example of Christic imitation. The book of Revelation, written around 100 CE, provides early testimony of the martyrs' privileged place in the apocalyptic drama. As the events of the end time unfold, John sees the "souls of those beheaded for their testimony to Jesus and for the Word of

God" standing before those enthroned and "given authority to judge."
The martyrs are vindicated for their sacrifice by sharing in the "first
resurrection," by which they "came to life and reigned with Christ a
thousand years" (Rev 20:4, 5). Their immediate judgment and salvation distinguishes them from other believers. As "blessed and holy"
and as "priests of God and of Christ," the martyrs provided a measure
in the late first-century Church of the most authentic discipleship to
which believers might aspire in their own appearance before the judge
who would soon vanquish the powers of the world.

It is interesting to speculate about what sort of emotions were
stirred in the earliest Christians by this expectation of judgment upon
the return of Christ. Paul, writing in the middle years of the first century, chastises members of the Christian community in Rome for
judging each other when it is only God's place to judge. "For we will
all stand before the judgment seat of God," he writes, where "each of
us will be accountable to God" (Rom 14:10, 12). And yet Paul's strong
doctrine of grace seems to expect the parousia as an irresistible wave
of grace that will bring those baptized in Christ to heavenly bliss in
spite of their sinfulness. For Paul, human sinfulness is as inescapable
as the death that he believes sin causes (Rom 5:12). All are judged un-
favorably by the Jewish Law since no deed that issues from human
nature can bring a person to righteousness before God. "I can will
what is right," Paul concedes, "but I cannot do it. For I do not do the
good I want, but the evil I do not want is what I do" (Rom 7:18–19).
This Pauline style of faith, then, takes for granted that God's judgment on every human life, and, even more, on every human deed leads
to the verdict of condemnation (Rom 5:16). All human beings deserve
a death that is final and from which there is no rescue. In Paul's view,
God's love and mercy are not beholden to this just verdict but instead
break it to pieces. Out of the rubble of sin, death, and condemnation,
God brings forth the surprising and undeserved gift of eternal life in
the resurrection of Christ from the dead, which, Paul believes, brings
in turn the gift of resurrected life to believers (1 Cor 15:12–19). Since
Paul's audience comprises newly baptized Christians who have expe-
rienced this gift of eternal life, his letters testify consistently to the

victory of grace, even to the point that they make no mention of final condemnation or hell. The Pauline style of faith understands the resurrection of Christ to have annulled God's righteous verdict of condemnation on human sin, and so the emotion that characterizes its belief before the coming judgment is gratitude.[13]

The style of faith that we find in the Synoptic Gospels of Mark, Matthew, and Luke is quite different, as is the range of emotions it likely evoked in believers. Here, the grace of God that breaks into the world in the life, death, and resurrection of Jesus expects the proof of discipleship in deeds that imitate the Savior's life and by which the believer will be judged. Judgment in this style of faith does not move in the trajectory of Pauline thought. God's judgment presupposes human responsibility not only for sin but also for virtue. Moreover, judgment in this style of faith highlights the believer's active decision before the alternatives of moral achievement or moral failure, and ultimately before the eschatological destinies of heavenly glory or infernal condemnation. Even though we find these beliefs about judgment in all three of the Synoptic Gospels, they are so pointedly expressed in Matthew that we will name this style of faith "Matthean." In words that echo the eschatological sensibilities of Q, Matthew conveys this sense of judgment sharply in the reproach Jesus brings on the cities that fail to repent before his "deeds of power":

> Woe to you, Chorazin! Woe to you, Bethsaida! For if the deeds of power done in you had been done in Tyre and Sidon, they would have repented long ago in sackcloth and ashes. But I tell you, on the day of judgment it will be more tolerable for Tyre and Sidon than for you. And you, Capernaum, will you be exalted to heaven? No, you will be brought down to Hades. (Mt 11:21–23)

For Matthew, this judgment of division—in Jesus' words—cannot be separated from the return of the Son of Man. "'For as the lightening comes from the east and flashes as far as the west, so will be the coming of the Son of Man. . . . Then two will be in the field; one will be taken and one will be left. Two women will be grinding meal together;

one will be taken and one will be left. Keep awake therefore, for you do not know on what day your Lord is coming'" (Mt 24: 27, 40–42).

Matthew completes this vision of eschatological division in a passage that exerted a profound influence on Christian belief in the Last Judgment. Continuing to explain the end times to his disciples, Matthew's Jesus says: "'When the Son of Man comes in his glory, and all the angels with him, then he will sit on the throne of his glory. All the nations will be gathered before him, and he will separate people one from another as a shepherd separates the sheep from the goats, and he will put the sheep at his right hand and the goats at the left" (Mt 25:31–33). This judgment is rendered on the fruits of discipleship. Those who have earned the crown of heaven fed the hungry, gave drink to the thirsty, welcomed the stranger, clothed the naked, cared for the sick, and visited the imprisoned (Mt 25:35–36). Jesus condemns those who did not accomplish these deeds to "the eternal fire prepared for the devil and his angels" (Mt 25:41). This same logic of division appears in Mark and Luke to the extent that Jesus calls believers to a discipleship of deeds measured by the sacrifice of the cross, a standard that Jesus had defined in his own saving death and that each martyr profoundly imitated in the act of becoming a saint.

The Matthean style of faith, no doubt, was satisfying to believers since it became the majority belief of the Christian tradition. But the satisfaction it brought also occasioned a certain kind of concern that I call "eschatological anxiety." By this term, I mean emotional consternation about one's eternal destiny, which, in a Christian context, amounts to worry about the final integrity of one's life, about its ultimate meaningfulness or meaninglessness, about its consummate happiness or desolation. This anxiety emerges in the prospect of a judgment before God in which one's deeds and misdeeds truly matter. As already noted, the Pauline style of faith assumes that all human deeds are wanting. Sin seeps so deeply into every natural act that there is no natural virtue. But the Matthean style of faith presupposes the believer's active responsibility before real alternatives in eternal destiny. Believers in this style of faith understand their acts of discipleship to be energized by the grace of Christ. Perseverance on the gospel's difficult road cannot be credited to human powers alone. And yet, human initiative makes a distinct contribution to the journey of salvation and without it there is no righteousness before the divine judge. That such action is measured by the high standards provided by the ethical commands of Jesus in Scripture, his passion and death, and the martyr's heroic example of imitation—and all before the prospect of Christ's imminent return as judge—certainly stirred anxiety among early believers whose ethical performance fell short of their martyred peers, an anxious group of nearly all.[14]

Christian faith in the Late Antique world developed along the lines of this Matthean style of faith, proliferating as a religious perspective that Peter Brown has called the "peccatization" of the world.[15] As the apocalyptic expectations of the first century receded, and, even more, as the age of persecution ended and Christianity entered the ordinary time of late Roman Antiquity, judgment took shape in the believer's sense of sin and in the need of forgiveness before God's righteousness. By the fifth century, Brown argues, Christians came to be especially concerned about the *"peccata levia*, the day-to-day sins"[16] of those who were not blatantly saints and not blatantly the damned, that is, the Christian masses who were increasingly visible in the emerging feudal world. All the baptized, whether monastic or lay, imagined the Christian life as an extended purification of the soul in preparation for its eschatological encounter with God. Even though grace was assumed to be at work in the believer's salvation, "the center of gravity of the imaginative structure associated with the notion of purification rested heavily on the individual and on his or her ability to take on full responsibility for his or her own healing."[17] The late Roman legal system provided a cultural context in which the Matthean style of faith could more exactly take account of every sin and measure the virtuous recompense owed God, a calculation that mirrored the secu - lar amnesty that violators of imperial law sought from the emperor. Brown points out that this understanding of the Christian life as an accounting for sin valorized personal death as the moment of eschatological encounter with God. "Neither in late antiquity nor in the early middle ages," he avers, "should we underestimate the silent pressure exercised on all Christians by the inscrutable anomaly of death. . . .

In the Christian imagination, the moment of death was an exact re-flection, in miniature, of the terror of the Last Judgment."[18]

It is not surprising that personal death would gain prominence as the moment of eschatological encounter with God. This shift re-flected the cultural assimilation of Christianity into Mediterranean society, its embrace of the day-to-day life of the civic realm where, as Brown points out, the believer struggled constantly to make amends for his or her day-to-day sins. Christian life became quotidian for a host of reasons: the end of persecution, the rise of the institutional church, and the alliance of political and ecclesiastical authorities. But we should not overlook the fact that Christian life also became quo-tidian because the imminent apocalypse expected by the earliest Chris-tians did not occur. In response, Christians retheologized their reli-gious worldview, particularly with respect to the time of judgment. The return of Christ was relegated to a more distant future and in-vested with the same communal proportions of judgment that first-century Christians had expected soon. This Last Judgment was distin-guished from the particular judgment that each believer would face at the time of death as a disembodied soul, a judgment in which the body would share when it was miraculously resurrected and united with the soul on the last day.[19] Personal death replaced the first-century expec-tation of the apocalypse as the catalyst of eschatological anxiety. Most importantly, the belief in a particular judgment immediately after death quotidianized judgment by enveloping it in the ordinariness of death. As much as the hour of one's own death became religiously extraordi-nary, "fearful, or simply awe-inspiring"[20] as the moment of appearance before the divine judge, the ordinariness of death as a human event, witnessed often in the deaths of others, wove judgment into the daily circumstances of life. To the degree that the moment of death was in-vested with the believer's portfolio of discipleship, judgment made its way back in time into the believer's every sinful and virtuous deed.

Time thus became saturated with judgment as the concern for eternal destiny was extended not only forward so to speak, from a par-ticular to a reiterated Last Judgment, but also backward into every mo-ment in the believer's life. Unfolding ordinarily in a de-apocalypticized temporality, judgment became an ongoing event in a protracted period of time in which every word and deed entered into the balance of divine justice. As I will show, this new Christian sensibility on time and judgment provided a setting for the development of the doctrine of purgatory in the late Middle Ages.

COPING WITH THE MARTYRS

The cult of the saints in the Late Antique world is usually explained as a religious practice shaped by the culture of patronage that flourished in Mediterranean society.[21] The veneration that believers accorded the saints mirrored the bonds of the patron–client relationship, its ties of power and need and its exchange of favors now transferred into the currency of the supernatural and the believer's desire for resurrected life. As a coda to this customary explanation one might also consider how the rise of the cult of the saints contributed to the domestication of judgment and constituted an interesting site for the negotiation of eschatological anxiety in the early Church.

The martyrs continued to provide the standard for Christian virtue throughout the age of persecution, their faithful deaths defining the earliest Christian understanding of the saint. The delay of the parousia, however, led Christians to redefine their conception of judgment and the normativity of saintly imitation. As noted above, the fact that Christ had not returned required the delay of the last day into a more distant future. The Church relinquished the book of Revelation's idea of a "first resurrection" of the saints into a chiliastic reign of Christ for one thousand years, a loss that strengthened the belief in heavenly life after death that appeared in the tradition as early as Paul's letters. A changed notion of the "first resurrection" of the martyrs, though, continued to resonate in the practice of burial *ad sanctos*. Judging the martyr's physical remains to be sacred, Christians of the early centuries began the practice of regarding their burial places as holy ground, sanctified by the martyr's charismatic presence. The shrine became the destination of pilgrimage, a place to petition the saint for favors that kept deathliness at bay, and also a burial ground for the community's beloved dead. Since the martyr had already passed through

judgment and gained divine favor, believers buried their dead in proximity to the saint in the hope that the ordinary faithful would share in
the martyr's "first resurrection,"[22] now conceived as the privilege the
martyr would enjoy in being raised to physical wholeness first of all
on the last day.[23] The practice of making the shrines into cemeteries
assured the physical closeness of the dead to the saint on the day of
judgment, an intimacy that, through the power of grace and ample
hope, would allow the ordinary believer to participate in the martyr's
most favorable judgment.

We might think of this practice, centered in the authority of the
martyr's judgment, as a further domestication of eschatology. The
practice of burial *ad sanctos* conceded the delay that Christians had
come to expect in the approach of the end time, nearness to the relics serving as a substitute for what first-century Christians believed to
be the nearness of a parousia brought by Christ himself. Christians
continued this domestication of eschatology by depositing the relics
of the saints into the newly built churches of the fourth and fifth centuries. The relative permanence of the new structures, which reflected
an ecclesiology of accommodation to the new era, testified to the distance of the end time and to the routinization of the sacred in ordinary
time. And as the life of the Church was extended into a future that
led all the way to the distant end of the world, a premium began to be
placed on the Christian life as a more limited horizon of years within
which believers struggled to act virtuously in order to make recompense for the failure of sin. Within this more compact and personal-
ized eschatology, the believer's death now became the focal point of
judgment, a death packed with all the moments of life that fell under
the divine scrutiny and for which the believer was held accountable.

Christian life thus became a duration for the exercise of virtue
and the avoidance of sin, a limited time charged with eternal consequences. The cult of the saints was an acknowledgment on the part of
the faithful that a few Christians—indeed very few—had used their
time extraordinarily well. Believers who came in need to the saints
knew that they, the ordinary, were among the many whose sins out-
weighed their virtuous deeds. The difference between the saint, as
one of the few, and the sinner, as one of the many, animated the cult.

The martyr's virtuous difference as an extraordinary imitator of the Savior availed the power of eternal life to believers. The difference of the martyr's favorable judgment, accessible to the believer through the martyr's intercession, was a remarkable comfort to the needy faithful who could share in the saint's exceptional difference. But the martyr's difference also stood as a threatening measure of what a believer's life could be. The martyr's death was the consummate act of discipleship since it mirrored Jesus' death on the cross, a standard of virtue that few Christians could, or were willing to, match during the persecution. After the persecution ended in 313 CE, the martyr's achievement was placed beyond the possible circumstances of discipleship, securing the authority of the martyr's judgment throughout the tradition. This made the martyr as much a source of eschatological anxiety as a source of eschatological comfort. The martyr's favorable judgment by God was one in which believers could participate through the martyr's cult. But it was also a judgment on the lives of believers that stirred fears about their own judgment.

It would be interesting to consider the rise of Christian asceticism from the turn of the fourth century as a way of negotiating the eschatological anxiety incited by the martyr's judgment. At one level, the notion of the ascetic as holy person was a response to the acculturation of Christianity. The martyr's sacrifice exhausted the early notion of the saint. As the age of persecution ended and the Roman authorities stopped making martyrs, Christians sought an alternative understanding of saintly imitation and found it in the nascent ascetical movement. Ascetical men and women imitated Jesus by willing the sufferings of his passion into their bodies and, by doing so, believed that they shared in his saving atonement in an extraordinary way. Unlike the martyrs, though, the ascetics carried their imitation to a point far short of death. Since the society in which they lived was not hostile to their religious endeavors, martyrdom was not an option. Indeed, as Christian belief provided a matrix of meaning for medieval society, ascetics were celebrated as holy persons from whom the ranks of the new saints were drawn, the most accomplished ascetics earning the crown of exceptional holiness. But as much as ascetics were revered for the vows they took and strove daily to keep, their religious achievements flourished under the shadow of the earlier ideal of sainthood. Even the most devoted consecrated lives that ordinary believers acclaimed still struggled to justify themselves before the martyr's most favorable judgment. Two well-known examples from the hagiographical tradition make this point.

In Athanasius's *Life of Antony*, we see an early expression of this eschatological anxiety. Written shortly after Antony's death in 356, the text records the ascetical achievements of one of the first and certainly one of the most revered Egyptian monks. Athanasius portrays Antony's lifelong denunciation of fleshly desire as a context for his devoted contemplation of God. At every turn in this difficult journey, Antony faced temptations of the mind and the body, and even physical beatings at the hands of the devil, who was intent on bringing the monk to ruin. Antony's steadfast commitment to the ascetical life led his fellow Christians to regard him as a living saint. Some expressed their admiration by following his example directly, retreating to the desert to live the hermit's life. Others simply wanted to be near him, as though sharing his physical presence placed them in the ambit of sacred power. In the narrative, this pious attention from the faithful proved a distraction to Antony, who fled from all this enthusiastic notice by making an abandoned fortress his monastic cell and living in it alone for twenty years. The faithful were undeterred by Antony's desire for solitude and kept watch outside the fortress, initially content just to be near the holy man. But eventually his admirers grew impatient and "tore down and forcefully removed the fortress door." Antony, Athanasius writes, "came forth as though from some shrine, having been led into divine mysteries and inspired by God." He continues:

> And when they beheld them, they were amazed to see that his body had maintained its former condition, neither fat from lack of exercise, nor emaciated from fasting and combat with demons, but was just as they had known him prior to his withdrawal. The state of his soul was one of purity. . . . He maintained utter equilibrium, like one guided by reason and steadfast in that which accords with nature.[24]

And "through him," Athanasius testifies, "the Lord healed many of those present who suffered from bodily ailments; others he purged of demons. . . . He consoled many who mourned, and others hostile to each other he reconciled in friendship."[25]

Athanasius clearly draws connections here between Jesus' resurrection and Antony's appearance to the crowd. Antony's ascetical regimen seems already to have produced a resurrected body in this life, one that has banished the traits of deathliness and that, by presence alone, is a conveyer of graceful, healing power. Antony is Christ-like by virtue of an extraordinary discipleship forged in ascetical sacrifice. But even though this scene offers imaginative allusions to Jesus' resurrection, Athanasius does not describe the fortress simply as a tomb but as a shrine. The more direct comparison that the text offers is one that measures the new ascetical saint against the high standard of the martyr, pressing the case for Antony's worthiness as holy man. Amazingly, Athanasius portrays Antony as though he were a living relic, and so an animated version of the martyr's charismatic corpse. "Buried" in the shrine, he is yet salvationally present to the faithful who seek him, as were the relics of the martyrs to earlier generations. Like the martyr, he brings physical and spiritual healing to those who approach him in need. Athanasius undoubtedly believes that Antony's remarkable discipleship has already garnered God's favorable judgment. He possesses the spiritual stature of the martyr even though he did not suffer a martyr's death. And yet, Athanasius's justification is riddled with eschatological anxiety, the fear that even Antony falls short when measured against the martyr's established authority.

Athanasius expresses this anxiety even more directly in his narrative. During the persecution of Egyptian Christians under Maximin in the early fourth century, Antony placed himself in danger by ministering to those who were arrested and sentenced to imprisonment or forced labor. Athanasius describes Antony's bravery in standing by the victims as a source of wonder to the prefect who enforced the writ of persecution. Athanasius, though, does recognize that Antony's witness fell short of the ultimate sacrifice and feels the need to explain: "For, as I said before, he also prayed for martyrdom. He seemed, therefore, like one who grieved because he had not been martyred, but the Lord was protecting him to benefit us and others, so that he might be a teacher to many in the discipline that he had learned from the Scriptures."[26] Athanasius confronts the problem of the martyr's threatening judgment by offering a more direct comparison between martyr and ascetic and an apology for Antony's way of life: "When finally the persecution ended, and Peter the blessed bishop had made his witness, Antony departed and withdrew once again to the cell, and was there daily being martyred by his conscience, and doing battle in the contests of faith. He subjected himself to an even greater and more strenuous asceticism, for he was always fasting."[27] Athanasius invokes martyrdom here as a metaphor for the ascetic's struggle with sin, which, given the facts of Antony's life, is the only kind of martyrdom he can achieve. The use of the metaphor testifies to the martyr's authority and to Athanasius's judgment that, to be a holy man, Antony must wear the martyr's mantle in some way.

This same eschatological anxiety is also evident in a much later hagiography, Bonaventure's *Life of Francis*. Written in 1260, the longer version of Francis's life hails the saint as a person of "extraordinary sanctity" and as "an example for those who would be perfect followers of Christ."[28] Seven centuries after Francis's death, Pope Pius XI would officially grant him the title *alter Christus*, "another Christ," but Bonaventure already assumes this to be so and his account of the life did much to earn Francis the formal papal honor. Bonaventure describes the saint as a remarkable imitator of Jesus, even to the point that Francis performed many of the miracles that Jesus worked in the Gospels, including the changing of water into wine.[29] Identification with Christ, Bonaventure tells the reader, was Francis's ascetical goal. He "longed to be totally transformed into him by the power of ecstatic love," and worked ardently at this task by reliving Jesus' forty-day fast in the desert—"secluded in a lonely place, shut up in a cell, with as little food and drink as possible, fasting, praying, and praising God without interruption."[30] But as much as Christ remains the paradigm for Francis's spiritual striving in the text, it is interesting to see how Bonaventure regards the martyrs as a measure of Francis's saintly quest, and a threatening measure at that.

Francis's approach to the religious life can only be described as competitive, an observation that Bonaventure specifically offers. He notes that "whenever he saw anyone more poorly dressed than he, Francis immediately censured himself and roused himself to imitate him, as if he were competing in a rivalry over poverty and feared to be beaten by another."[31] Always venturing more in this competition, Francis set out for Syria in his sixth year of ascetical practice. His goal, Bonaventure states, was "to preach penance and the Christian faith to the Saracens and the infidels."[32] His motivation for making this journey was to meet the high standard set by the tradition's earliest saints, for Francis took up this quest "burning with a desire of martyrdom,"[33] presumably a possible consequence of preaching the gospel in the Muslim world. Bonaventure describes this same desire as a constant companion to Francis on his evangelical mission: "But the fruit of martyrdom had so attracted his heart that he desired a precious death for the sake of Christ more intensely than all the merits from the virtues."[34] We see the same motivation ascribed to Francis in a return to the Middle East seven years later in the midst of the dangers of the Fifth Crusade. Undeterred by threats to the lives of Christians, Francis is portrayed by Bonaventure as an "intrepid knight of Christ . . . not terrified by the fear of death, but rather drawn by desire for it."[35]

The climax of Francis's hagiography occurs in his reception of the stigmata in the last years of his life. Yet, it is interesting to see how this profound event, in which Francis miraculously develops the wounds of Christ's crucifixion on his body, unfolds under the specter of the martyr's extraordinary sacrifice. Bonaventure depicts Francis's holiness as a context for this remarkable act of divine favor, and judges his holiness by the achievements of his ascetical life. The "man filled with God," Bonaventure testifies, "understood that just as he had imitated Christ in the actions of his life, so he should be conformed to him in the affliction and sorrow of his passion."[36] Even though Francis's lifelong asceticism has brought him the recognition of his religious culture, in his (and Bonaventure's) mind a yet higher standard of Christic imitation set by the martyrs judges even the most excellent performance of virtue. "And although [Francis's] body was already weakened by the great austerity of his past life and his continual carrying of the Lord's cross, he was in no way terrified but was inspired even more vigorously to endure martyrdom."[37] Bonaventure feels compelled to justify Francis before the martyr's complete sacrifice even as he describes the exact moment that Francis received the stigmata and shared intimately in the wounds of the cross: "Eventually he understood by a revelation from the Lord that divine providence had shown him this vision so that, as Christ's lover, he might learn in advance that he was to be totally transformed into the likeness of Christ crucified, not by the martyrdom of his flesh, but by the fire of his love consuming his soul."[38]

It is strange to find that the martyrs proved to be such a threat to the tradition's later ascetical saints, even to extraordinary figures like Antony and Francis. But so seems the evidence, at least as it is conveyed in the judgments of Athanasius and Bonaventure, which are separated in time by nearly a millennium. That Athanasius and Bonaventure place their ascetical heroes in competition with the martyrs is testimony to the martyr's remarkable achievement and an expression of the eschatological anxiety that this achievement stirs in them as they work ardently to fashion their own. Our understanding of the late medieval development of the doctrine of purgatory, however, requires us to attend to the temporal dimension of this competition, particularly to the different ways in which saintly acts unfold in time.

The martyr's defining saintly act transpired in a moment, or, to be exact, in however short a time that it took for the sufferings of martyrdom to culminate in death. The martyr's saintly act was threatening not only because it imitated the Savior's death so closely but also because the clarity of such imitation could shine forth in a single moment in which the ambiguities of spiritual struggle and sinful weakness were eternally banished. Even if their lives were remembered as extraordinarily virtuous, the martyrs distinguished themselves as saints instantly in the act of faithful dying. The definitiveness of this temporal moment, and not only the action that filled it, stood as a challenge to the ascetical model of saintly practice that flourished in the tradition after the age of persecution. Those aspiring to ascetical sainthood found themselves in a spiritual competition with the martyrs, a competition that in principle they could not win in the course of their lives because of two insuperable obstacles. First, the martyr's consummate sacrifice transcended imitation since ascetical aspirants soon flourished in a Christian culture that celebrated rather than threatened their lives. Second, the singularity of the martyr's saintly act was compressed into a brief temporal moment that then became timeless. Spiritual achievement so impressive that it could be accomplished at once earned an equally instant judgment accompanied by the certainty of saintly status. By comparison, the ascetical path to sainthood was lifelong and fraught with the uncertainties of self-doubt and moral failure, to say nothing of constant and wanting measure against the standard of martyrdom. Even in the hagiographies of living saints like Antony and Francis, whose spiritual achievement was widely acknowledged and celebrated by their contemporaries, temporal duration became a field of eschatological anxiety in which the most worthy ascetics continued to compete, always venturing more in order to secure the favorable divine judgment they sought.

COPING WITH THE ASCETICS

In the Catholic imagination, purgatory is a multivalent place. Its sufferings are portrayed as extreme and mild, physical and psychological, as laden with guilt and as occasions of joy. This multivalence extends to the scholarly interpretation of purgatory. Philippe Ariès, for example, calls attention to how purgatory mitigates the power of hell.[39] Barbara Newman highlights gender issues in the interpretation of purgatory by raising interesting questions about the religious aspirations of medieval women.[40] Reminded of Dante's poetic celebration of the desire for heaven on the part of purgatorial sufferers, Jacques Le Goff ponders whether another tenable alternative to his argument might very well be that purgatory was "more a pre-eternity than a post-existence."[41] Without any claim for interpretive exclusivity, I follow a lead offered by Pierre Chaunu in his intriguing study of early modern attitudes toward death in the city of Paris. Here Chaunu argues that purgatory negotiates the problem of duration, not only in its metaphysical state as a temporal realm but also, and more importantly, in the character of its temporality as an extended time defined only by the indeterminate events of the Second Coming and the Last Judgment.[42] Thus, I include this notion of duration in my discussion of eschatological anxiety in Catholic discipleship.

As much as historians disagree about when exactly to date the appearance of the doctrine of purgatory, a scholarly consensus has emerged that an explicit and widespread belief in purgatory did not develop until the late Middle Ages. That belief was accompanied by the first theological reflections on the place of purgatory in the life of faith and even the first speculations on what life in purgatory was like for the souls who suffered there. The doctrine received formal ecclesiastical approval, with varying degrees of explicitness, at the Second Council of Lyons (1274), the Council of Florence (1438), and the Council of Trent (1563). Even though there is mention of otherworldly purgation in Augustine's *City of God* and a host of purgatory-like ideas in the writings of the ancient church fathers and in early medieval texts, the evidence strongly suggests that the doctrine of purgatory developed relatively late in extensive Catholic belief and practice.

It is interesting to consider why this was so. Why did a belief like purgatory, which enjoyed popularity for centuries after its appearance, emerge rather late in the tradition? This question is different from Le Goff's, which asks what new and particular social circumstances gave rise to the new belief and all the practices that attended it. Posing the question of origin with appeal to the tradition considers the appearance of new or, at the very least, more explicit religious beliefs and practices within a larger network of meaning that they serve and promote through the behaviors of those who believe and enact them. This religious tradition, of course, is utterly woven into all the other strands of culture, and so much so that only the most artificial abstraction could configure it idealistically, or as something sui generis. And yet, as a dimension of culture with an enduring coherence of its own, a religious tradition offers a framework of explanation that is an important perspective to consider in accounting for any historical etiology, especially those that concern thematically religious instances of origin, like the burgeoning late medieval belief in and practice of purgatory. If purgatory was a widespread and meaningful belief for Catholic Christians from the twelfth through the twentieth centuries, the question of why its development came so late in the tradition is at least as meaningful as the question of why purgatory seems to have largely disappeared from Catholic belief and practice in our own day. I now consider how the traditional trajectory of what Peter Brown calls the "peccatization" of the world and what I have called the "quotidianizing" of judgment made its way into medieval Catholicism in a way that negotiated the eschatological anxiety of the laity.

I have noted that the martyr's instantaneous virtue and judgment set a standard of discipleship that challenged hagiographers as different as Athanasius and Bonaventure. As much as these biographers were convinced of the saintly stature of their exemplary ascetics, they still worried that their spiritual heroes fell short of the martyr's measure and did all that they could to justify their saint in the way they told his story. This tension in the hagiographies may or may not have represented the actual feelings of Antony and Francis themselves. The writings only allow us to make judgments about the views of their authors. Later Christians counted both Athanasius and Bonaventure in the company of the saints. But in their own day, the hagiographers were ascetics struggling with the eschatological anxiety instigated by the martyrs' consummate holiness and which they expressed so clearly in their literary defenses of their ascetical masters. Martyrs and ascetics were spiritual rivals, though only, of course, in the ascetic's retrospective judgment. As the consecrated life became the shape of extraordinary discipleship after the age of persecution, the martyr's example stood before the ascetic's vows as a practically unreachable goal. Every moment in the ascetic's life offered an occasion for reminder that the ascetic was not a martyr, and so less holy than the martyr. Time so considered defined the ascetic's life as a negative field of judgment. And yet, the ascetical lifetime also offered a means of negotiating this eschatological anxiety. Every moment in the ascetic's life offered an occasion for the imitation of Christ. None of these acts could compete with the martyr's single act, offered to God in the moment of complete sacrifice. But all these acts together, filling the longer temporal duration of an ascetical lifetime, could and did justify the holiness of the monastic life and, in extraordinary cases, monastic saintliness. Time so considered defined the ascetic's life as a positive field of judgment.

The development of the doctrine of purgatory can be considered with regard to this background, though now as a stage for the relationship between the ascetic and the layperson. In his study of relations between the living and the dead in the Middle Ages, Patrick Geary offers a succinct description of the role of ascetics in their wider social world:

> Monastic communities performed two religious functions vital to medieval society at large. First, clerics prayed for the salvation and well-being of the local population, particularly their benefactors and supporters. Inclusion in the prayers of the religious during one's lifetime and after one's death was a vital concern to a population obsessed with the insecurity of this life and the uncertainty of the next. Second, through the divine office, the Mass, and the cult of the saints whose relics were honored in the community's church, the regular clergy fulfilled the ritual actions necessary to keep the spiritual powers benevolently disposed toward human society.[43]

Monks provided spiritual goods for the laity. But, as Geary notes, laypersons provided for the clerics as well, by contributing directly or indirectly to the financial support of their communities. This exchange, however, was far from equal. The clerics mediated the power of eternal life to an eschatologically anxious culture. Clerics possessed this power by virtue of their commitment to a consecrated life that, at least in principle, filled time with extraordinary acts of discipleship. This difference in vocation, and all that attended it, stirred a different sort of eschatological anxiety in the wider reaches of the Christian population. The layperson's eschatological anxiety was not measured by the martyr but by the ascetic, who now stood in medieval culture as a living standard of Christian devotion, of a life that was worthy of heavenly reward.

If the martyr arose in the ascetic's judgment as a daunting spiritual competitor, then a certain kind of competitiveness also characterized the layperson's relationship with the ascetic. Unlike those who vowed a consecrated life, laypersons did not choose to enter the fray of extraordinary discipleship. Rather, they found themselves in a system of relationships that I call a "hierarchy of discipleship" defined by the valued distinction between the clerical life and their own. Within this stratified spirituality, a forced competition entered the religious imagination of the layperson that was simply a product of vocational difference. Time proved to be an important dimension of the competitive relationship between the ascetic and the layperson, just as it did in the relationship between the ascetic and the martyr. The ascetic's entire consecrated life provided a temporal trajectory within which a saving judgment could be earned. This extended time for virtue negotiated the martyr's instantaneous judgment. The ascetical lifetime validated its spiritual worthiness through a duration filled with virtuous quantity that competed as best it could with the martyr's singular act of imitative quality. This same duration, though, validated the ascetic's spiritual worthiness with regard to the lower end of the hierarchy of discipleship. If, as Peter Brown claimed, the peccatization of the world in early Catholic Christianity compressed the spiritual portfolio of judgment into all the deeds of a lifetime completely embraced in the believer's hour of death, then the consecrated life, believers assumed, was especially well positioned to meet the demands of divine judgment. This is not to say, of course, that believers did not encounter abominably sinful ascetics and remarkably saintly laypersons in their day-to-day experience, and take account of these anomalies in their eschatological expectations. Yet, the vocational difference between ascetics and laypersons defined a competitive field on which, it was assumed, the ascetic had an overwhelming eschatological advantage. This advantage worked to soothe the ascetic's anxiety before the martyr, just as much as it provoked the anxiety of the laity before religious lives judged in principle to be more.

The relations in the hierarchy of discipleship described here first appeared as the age of persecution ended in the early fourth century and the ascetic took the place of the martyr as the paradigmatic holy person in the living experience of the Church. The development of the monastic movement in the early Middle Ages and the proliferation of religious orders throughout medieval times instantiated the hierarchy of discipleship in the Christian worldview, an outlook that embraced not only this world but also, I would suggest, the world to come. Perhaps the doctrine of purgatory developed slowly and came to popular acceptance rather late in the tradition, partially at least, because its development was a function of the institutionalization of monasticism, the working of the hierarchy of discipleship into the Christian order of things, and with that hierarchy, the various kinds of eschatological anxiety that it stirred in the lives of ascetics and laity. Considered from this perspective, the birth of purgatory negotiated the eschatological anxiety of the laity by finding a solution to the problem of competitive judgment in temporal duration. In a manner similar to the ascetic's lifelong lengthening of the temporal field of competition with the martyr, belief in purgatory lengthened the layperson's temporal field of competition with the ascetic.[44] Purgatory allowed the laity to cope with the eschatological anxiety engendered by the consecrated life by extending the time for a satisfactory judgment on one's life into a temporal realm beyond death, one limited in duration only by the end of time and the Last Judgment—a time that could be described, quite literally, as "all the time in the world."

This vast purgatorial horizon of time allowed for the forced competition between ascetics and the laity to be conducted on a more level playing field, one that stretched the believer's lifetime of judgment into the otherworld so that time could serve the believer in a way that it may not have in the course of earthly life. In some respects, the effect of this temporal lengthening allowed the layperson's life to be more like the ascetic's, in much the same way that the ascetical paradigm of the saintly life allowed the ascetic to be more like the martyr. We see this otherworldly "asceticizing" of the layperson's purgatorial life in several ways.

First, and minimally, purgatory conflated the layperson and the ascetic in their shared need for purgation after death. Accounts of purgatory abound in their descriptions of the need for purgatorial suffering on the part of monks and nuns. The late twelfth-century French version of *St. Patrick's Purgatory* by Marie de France charts the otherworldly journey of the Irish knight Owen, who, though still alive, enters purgatory to witness its terrible sufferings. After the tortures of purgatory are detailed in scene after scene, a narrator's voice enters the text to deliver a homily on the penitential sufferings that compares them to the sufferings of the monastic life:

> Not even cloistered monks
> (Who think they lead a harsh life
> On account of their confinement)
> Know what sort of pains and torments
> Are in the places we have described
> And set before you.[45]

The chiding tone directed toward the monk assures the layperson that even the most rigorous forms of ascetical self-denial pale before the sufferings of purgatory that nearly all, in the end, will share. In a letter written sometime between 1173 and 1179, Hildegard of Bingen relates the extraordinary sufferings of a soul in purgatory. Burning in a house consumed by a "fierce fire," the punished soul "glowed like red-hot iron," its sufferings greatly multiplied by stinging scorpions and devouring boars. Hildegard ends her account of the vision by observing that this soul would not be lost to hell in spite of its great sins, because "while living in the body, it had been disciplined by its superiors in accordance with the Rule, and, by God, through physical infirmity."[46] The soul enduring such punishments is that of a sinful ascetic.

This same minimal conflation also occurs in Dante's purgatorial sojourn. In canto 18, Dante discovers the remarkable penance allotted for the sin of sloth: the guilty must run in purgatory without pause. Among the moving throng is a soul who apologizes to Dante for his apparent rudeness in conversing on the run and who acknowledges both his guilt in deserving such punishment and his identity as the abbot of San Zeno at Verona.[47] Canto 19 relates even more prominent ascetical penance in the realm of avarice where Dante encounters Pope Adrian V, who lies prostrate on the ground, bound hand and foot, his eyes forced to contemplate the material object of his sinful desire. When Dante kneels beside him out of respect for his ecclesiastical station, Adrian demurs "'Straighten your legs, rise up, brother, . . . do not err: I am fellow-servant with you and with the others unto one Power.' "[48]

As much as these texts conflate the ascetic and layperson by stressing the sinfulness of ascetics, few depictions of purgatory undermine the hierarchy of discipleship more than the fifteenth-century *A Revelation of Purgatory* by an unknown woman visionary. The author imagines the ecclesiastical hierarchy in purgatory, with all groups distinguished and suffering in particular ways. Married men and women are pierced with flaming goads by devils who then force-feed them pitch and round out the punishment by drawing them apart, "bone from bone."[49] Single men and women are roasted on spits and consumed by "adders, snakes, and toads," and then dragged through the fire on sharp hooks by devils who complete the torture by dismembering their hearts and genitals.[50] This account of the suffering of laypeople, though, comes later in the text. The author begins by observing that in the fire of purgatory is "every kind of pain" imaginable and "every sort of Christian man and woman living here in this world, no matter what rank they were."[51] Of all these ranks, clerics are placed first in the catalogue of suffering, not only in their order of appearance in the text but also in the degree of their penitential pain. "But among all the pains that I saw of all men and women," the visionary claims, ". . . it seemed men and women in the ministry of the Church had the greatest pain in that sight."[52]

Having set the scene of clerical suffering, the visionary immediately recounts the appearance of a soul named Margaret, "a sister living in a religious house" who pleads for intercessory prayers and masses to end her purgatorial suffering. The suffering soul is described as "marked with severe wounds, as though she had been rent with combs," and as "wounded and torn." Her heart is rent with "a grievous and horrible wound; from it there came sparks, and from her mouth a flame."[53] The visionary details Margaret's terrible suffering at the hands of devils who align their vile torments with particular sins she committed in life. Turning her attention to the suffering endured by all in purgatory for particular sins, the visionary warns that lechery "was the [sin] most severely chastised, and especially that of men and women of Holy Church, whether they were religious or secular."[54] Devils wield razors to mangle the "heads and prelates of Holy Church," whose suffering reaches a crescendo as they are eviscerated for betraying their priestly vows.[55] And yet, even among the suffering clerics there are further distinctions to be made:

> It seemed that religious men and women had a hundred times more pain than secular priests and secular women had, for they were cast onto cruel wheels and turned about with intense fire, and adders, snakes, and devils were always around them. And the devils turned the wheels so fast that I could not see them, but very horribly they cried, as if all the world had cried at once. And this pain, father, had religious men and women and prelates of Holy Church—more pain than secular priests or secular women.[56]

The more rigorous the ascetical vows, the more intense the purgatorial punishment, an imaginative depiction of the "third place" that utterly inverts the earthly hierarchy of discipleship and narrows the judgmental distance between ascetics and laypersons.[57]

Purgatory allowed the conflation of ascetics and laypersons in another, more important way that drew on the Christian belief in the productive power of suffering. In this regard, the textual evidence suggests that the layperson becomes like the ascetic, and, even more, can become an ascetic through purgatorial suffering.

Striking examples of this ascetical transformation occur in Marie de France's *St. Patrick's Purgatory*. The local bishop counsels the knight Owen to prepare for his journey to the underworld by placing himself "among the good men of a monastery, [o]r among the canons of a convent; [t]hen he [Owen] would be more certain to accomplish his purpose."[58] A prior who keeps the purgatorial gates, which are an inner door of an Irish church, insists that Owen ready himself by remaining in the church "for fifteen days, [f]asting and praying, keeping vigils, [a]nd performing acts of mortification."[59] The layperson must act like a monk in order to face the test of expiation. As Owen enters purgatory and wanders "far underground" through ever-increasing darkness, he breaks into a "winter light at dusk" that reveals a

palace [that] had all around it
One continuous wall,
Constructed of columns, arches,
Vaults and *wandiches.*
It resembled a cloister,
Suited for men of religion.[60]

The palace seems to be an ante-room to heaven, a place of transition between purgatory and eternal glory, though it is clearly still in purgatory since a man whom Owen meets inside warns him to "conduct yourself bravely, [o]r you will perish here" amid the sufferings that the reader is about to encounter outside the palace walls. The speaker is described as "the master and prior" of fourteen other men who together greet him as he enters. The fifteen receptionists are portrayed as "[r]ecently shaved and tonsured [a]nd dressed in white vestments . . . , [a]ppearing to be men of religion."[61] That the monks are "recently" tonsured is especially interesting. They may be so for the unlikely reason that they all died recently as novices and have quickly found their way to glory, for it is clear in the text that they are in a state of beatitude beyond the sufferings of purgatory. Another, more likely, explanation is that their recent tonsuring is the mark of their expiation through purgatorial suffering, which, in turn, would suggest that the successful negotiation of purgatory can bring the layperson to the ascetical vocation.

The text does not suggest that expiation always has this effect. In fact, later in the account, after Owen has witnessed scene after scene of purgatorial torture, he enters the earthly paradise that Adam and Eve inhabited before the Fall. There he sees all who have met the measure of purgatory and who, in the glory and happiness of completed penance, await ascent to the celestial paradise above. The layperson is mentioned, which suggests that purgatory does not end for all with the profession of monastic vows. Yet, even there, the layperson moves in the overwhelming company of ascetics:

He also observed religious folk
Walking in procession.

It seemed to him that no one had ever seen
Such a splendid procession
Anywhere or at any time,
Nor one so nobly arranged.
He saw forms of men and images
Of every age, and likewise
Of every order.
Great was that company of folk.
All were differently attired,
According to their orders.
Some were dressed like archbishops,
Others like bishops,
One like an abbot, another like a monk,
A priest, a deacon, a canon,
Subdeacon, acolyte,
Or layperson, chosen by God.[62]

Clearly, this vision of purgatory's effects makes the ascetical path the standard of the saved state. The "layperson" is engulfed in the larger procession otherwise elongated by "religious folk." By walking with them, the layperson becomes like them, sharing in the decided majority of their redeemed glory and in a way that vocationally elevates the layperson to the status of one especially "chosen by God" (laie gent, a Deu eslite).[63]

A different version of this asceticizing of the layperson through suffering appears in what eventually became the developed theology of purgatory in the late Middle Ages. A clear and interesting illustration is Catherine of Genoa's *Trattato* on "Purgation and Purgatory," a transcription of her visions that appeared in 1522, twelve years after her death. Whereas Marie de France's *St. Patrick's Purgatory* presents a realm of infernal tortures and a hell itself for those whose sins are too great to make expiation and win release, Catherine imagines a very distinct "third place" whose sufferings are joyous because they bring a soul to the glory that God's favorable judgment has already secured for it. Catherine's description of these joyous sufferings could quite easily be read as an idealized portrayal of the monastic life, as an

account of the same aspirations and goals that motivate ascetical renunciation. The souls in purgatory, she avers, are beyond the envy of
comparison with their peers. "Such is their joy in God's will, in His
pleasure, that they have no concern for themselves but dwell only on
their joy in God's ordinance."[64] The souls exhibit the virtue of humility
in community, all the while undergoing sufferings that are productive in bringing the soul to salvation. "This joy [in the desire for para-
dise]," Catherine states, "increases day by day because of the way in
which the love of God corresponds to that of the soul, since the impediment to that love is worn away daily."[65]

Another testimony to the joyful sufferings of purgatory appears
in the *Probation* of the late sixteenth-century Florentine visionary
Maria Maddalena de' Pazzi. In one of her vivid and "lived" visions,
transcribed by her Carmelite sisters, she wandered the convent garden as though it were purgatory, searching for her recently deceased
brother. De' Pazzi's purgatory is a place of horrible tortures, and yet,
when she finds her brother, she is pleased to find that his sufferings
are delightful:

> That night she was looking for her brother's soul. We understood
> that because, when she stopped, she said: "Oh, where is my little
> soul? Isn't he here among these ones?" And, when she found him,
> she was very happy and, showing a great joy, she spoke to him in
> a compassionate way: "Poor one, you suffer so much and are still
> very happy? You burn and are so cheerful?"[66]

Like Catherine of Genoa, Maria Maddalena de' Pazzi portrays purgatorial sufferings as fulfilling. Much in the manner of ascetical denial,
they pave a path to spiritual perfection that brings the soul to God.
Catherine presses this identification even further in her treatise. Just
as the saintliness of the martyrs was defined by terrible suffering and
just as the suffering of accomplished ascetics like Antony and Francis
increased with their degree of holiness, so too does Catherine expect
the soul in purgatory to know greater suffering as it advances in spiri -
tual perfection. "Yet this joy [in God's overwhelming love]," Catherine insists, does not do away with one bit of pain in the suffering of

the souls in purgatory. As the soul grows in its perfection, so does it suffer more because of what impedes the final consummation, the end for which God made it; so that in purgatory great joy and great suffering do not exclude one another.[67]

The record of Catherine's final vision makes the same connections between the ascetic and the soul in purgatory but does so more directly. Her concluding discourse describes the inner disposition of the soul in purgatory. And yet, from her words, it is difficult to distinguish between the comportment of the disembodied soul and the expected comportment of the monk or nun. Casting herself in the role of participant-observer, Catherine describes the purgatorial experience as her own, even though, as a visionary still alive, she has not passed though the death and divine judgment that would bring her into the state of purgation. "I see my soul alienated from all spiritual things," she claims, "that could give it solace and joy." In this desired state of spiritual acedia, the soul "has no taste for the things of the intellect, will, or memory, and in no manner tends more to one thing than to another."[68] This detachment fosters and finally culminates in an abandonment of all "things," "places," and "persons" that detract from the spiritual path:

> So vehement is the soul's instinct to rid itself of all that impedes its own perfection that it would endure hell itself to reach that end. For that reason the soul tenaciously sets about casting aside all those things that could give the inner self specious comfort. It casts out the least imperfection. Cutting itself off from all except those who seem to walk the way of perfection, the soul concentrates itself, preferring not to frequent places where those persons find their pleasure.[69]

Now, there are no "things" or "places" in Catherine's purgatory, as there are in other late medieval depictions of purgatory. And even though there are other "persons" in purgatory, Catherine began her treatise with the observation that the suffering souls in purgatory are unaware of each other as possible distractions from the consuming fire of God's purifying love.[70] It would seem that Catherine has projected the goals and temptations of her own ascetical life into purgatory and has done so to the degree that ascetical renunciation has become the descriptive template for otherworldly purgation. That an ascetic would speak of the otherworld out of her own experience is hardly surprising. Yet, we cannot overlook the fact that Catherine understands herself to be describing the purgation of all the souls that are, or ever have been, or ever will be in purgatory. And since the vast majority of these suffering souls were laypersons in their earthly life, the vision of purgatory that she presents extends the field of ascetical aspiration and accomplishment to laypersons, thus allowing them to achieve in purgatory's extended time what they did not in the course of their earthly lives.

All these ways in which the layperson is asceticized in purgatory diminished the competition between the layperson and the ascetic in the hierarchy of discipleship. The development of the doctrine of purgatory enabled the layperson to cope with the ascetical ideal of saintliness by extending the time in which divine judgment could be worked out for the layperson. The texts I have considered provided the layperson with the opportunity to affirm the integrity of the lay state by insisting that laypersons were no worse than, and sometimes even better than, ascetics as they suffered the purgatorial consequences of divine judgment. Even more, what became and remained the developed theology of purgatory from the time of Catherine of Genoa to the instructional manuals on purgatory from the early twentieth century[71] enabled laypersons to participate in the ascetical life eschatologically by undergoing sufferings that were joyful and sanctifying. It is not surprising that laypersons like Dante and, probably, Marie de France would diminish the purgatorial difference between ascetics and believers like themselves, since that difference reflected their religious disadvantage before the divine judgment. More surprising, perhaps, is the fact that depictions of purgatory are largely the work of ascetics who seemingly acted against their religious self-interest by asceticizing purgatorial suffering in the ways I have considered. What might account for the willingness of ascetics like Hildegaard, Catherine, and so many others from the late Middle Ages to the mid-twentieth century to diminish their difference from the laity in their accounts of purgatory? Or, to pose the question from another angle, what advantage *did* ascetics find in their own contributions to the development of the doctrine of purgatory? Several answers together might contribute to an understanding.

First, one should not overlook compassion as a motivation for the willingness of ascetics to embrace all the dead into their state of hierarchical difference. As much as the hierarchy of discipleship encouraged ascetics to value their difference from the laity, the preeminent Christian virtue insisted on the love of neighbor which, in eschatological perspective, hoped for the salvation of all. Considered from a more particular emotional perspective, the conflation of laypersons and ascetics in purgatorial suffering allowed ascetics to imagine the assured salvation of their family members, from whom they had been distanced by their consecrated life. The purgatorial conflation of the lay and ascetical saints derived to some degree from a heartfelt commitment to the communion of the saints.

But ascetical self-interest also played a role in the development of the doctrine of purgatory. As much as ascetical compassion affirmed the latitude of the communion of the saints, that compassion was only one ingredient in a rich mixture of motivations that included the very strong desire to highlight the distinctiveness of the monastic vocation. The ascetical life provided a template for purgatorial suffering, since late medieval Christians simply assumed that the hierarchy of discipleship was true and that its redemptive standards had to be negotiated in one way or another. Once the late medieval theology of purgatory described its sufferings as joyful and spiritually productive, the "third place" became an otherworldly monastery that valorized the ascetical life as the surest path to glory. Purgatory's ascetical template allowed all its suffering souls to participate in the monastic life, even though all believers would have assumed that nearly all were the souls of laypersons. At the same time, this metaphorical widening of the monastic vocation in the afterlife strongly affirmed the authority of the ascetical life and its status in the competitive style of religion that itself led to the development of the doctrine of purgatory.[72] In addition to this self-interest in the realm of religious *mentalité*, one should not overlook, even if it merits only a mention here, the financial benefits that accrued to clerics through almsgiving associated with the release of purgatory's suffering souls.[73]

Finally, and most importantly for the argument offered here, purgatory allowed ascetics to cope with ascetics. We have seen that all ascetics were challenged by the high standard set for the religious life by the martyr's extraordinary example and that even the most influential hagiographies—the stories of Antony and Francis—made every effort to justify the lives of the greatest ascetics before the ancient measure of martyrdom. Catholic culture, though, in any time and any place is far more familiar with the lives of ordinary ascetics, those who have lived a life devoted to the Church that, like most lives, is a mixture of virtuous and sinful deeds. Ascetics were subject to the same kind of eschatological anxiety that coursed through the merit system, an anxiety that for most was triggered much more by the tradition's saintly ascetics like Antony, Francis, and the founders of orders than it was by the martyrs. Purgatory offered ascetics the same advantage that it offered to laypersons: a wider field of time in which judgment could be adjudicated by productive suffering that drew the soul closer to the accomplishments of the greatest saints.[74] For most ascetics, the differences in the hierarchy of discipleship were as threatening as they were to laypersons and so required the balm of purgatorial time in which differences between believers mattered less, judgment extended beyond death, and, as I will consider in my concluding section, personal virtue that had mattered so much in the competitive religion of earthly time now mattered not at all.

COMPETITIVE RELIGION IN
ESCHATOLOGICAL PERSPECTIVE

Purgatory's multivalence achieved its otherworldly variety through a host of this-worldly interests. Interests defined by social change, class, finance, patronage and exchange, ecclesiastical politics, and the desire for justice all contributed to the origin and development of purgatory. Here I have proposed another layer of explanation that might be added to these and other possible causes, namely, anxious longings prompted by traditional belief in the hierarchy of discipleship. Purgatory temporally stretched judgment in order to negotiate the burden of religious competition in a peccativized Catholic culture, a burden centered in the aspirations of ascetics but borne by all the faithful. In this concluding section, I reflect theologically on the appearance and disappearance of purgatory in the eschatological imagination of Catholic believers. I have already considered the appearance of purgatory in all sorts of ways, though there is still one more important matter to explore. I have more thoughts regarding the disappearance of purgatory in the last forty years.

One of the most interesting aspects of the late medieval theology of purgatory is the belief that the suffering souls are utterly passive with respect to their own state of remediation; they can do nothing to improve their condition, diminish their suffering, or shorten their time of purgation. Although they have been judged favorably by God and have been assured of the Beatific Vision, the suffering souls can do nothing on their own behalf to bring their final state of salvation to completion. Thomas Aquinas explained the formal metaphysics of this passivity as early as the thirteenth century. Souls separated from their bodies at death, he argues, are immutable, since in this state there is no bodily desire to change the soul's enacted disposition toward its ultimate end, whether toward eternal beatitude or toward eternal damnation. Beyond death, the soul dwells "in a state of rest in the end acquired,"[75] an inactivity that characterizes the souls in purgatory as much as it does the saints in heaven and the damned in hell.[76] This position accounts for the finality and unchangeability of God's judgment on every life immediately upon death. After all, if souls could change in their disposition toward their final end, then God's judgment could be undone. And yet, even though God's judgment cannot be undone in any of the three otherworldly places, purgatory is a realm where the soul's "state of rest" is as much a matter of its passivity as of its immutability.

Catherine of Genoa described the inactivity of purgatorial suffering in a manner that became authoritative for the later tradition. The souls in purgatory, she claims, dwell "only on their joy in God's ordinance, in having Him do what He will."[77] "Content in God's will" and having none of their own, the souls only feel "sorrow over their sins"[78] and lack any trace of ego or sense of competition with their fellow souls: "These souls cannot think, 'I am here, and justly so because of my sins,' or 'I wish I had never committed such sins for now I would be in paradise,' or 'That person there is leaving before me,' or 'I will leave before that other one.' . . . Such is their joy in God's will, in His pleasure, that they have no concern for themselves."[79] In Catherine's vision, the soul relinquishes itself to its suffering, which it "willingly accepts as a mercy."[80] God is utterly the agent of the soul's purgation. "In so acting," she testifies, "God so transforms the soul in Him that it knows nothing other than God; and He continues to draw it up into His fiery love . . . [where it] feels itself melting in the fire of that love of its sweet God."[81] Insisting most pointedly on the soul's passivity in all this, Catherine confesses that "if we are to become perfect, the change must be brought about in us and without us; that is, the change must be the work not of man but of God."[82]

Catherine's sensibilities on the passivity of the souls in purgatory prevailed throughout the later tradition, as far as the pastoral treatises of the early and mid-twentieth century. And yet, they did not prevail without contest. In his homiletic manual entitled *The Poor Souls in Purgatory*, Paul Wilhelm von Keppler, bishop of Rottenburg at the turn of the twentieth century, insists that the souls in purgatory are "sentenced to a state of inactivity, which, however, is not a state of rest, but full of restlessness and an eager desire to act."[83] Quite unlike Catherine, who touted the joyfulness of purgatorial passivity, Keppler ever accentuates the anguish of the souls in their inability to act, a motif that highlights the terrible loss of free choice in a religion that prizes meritorious action as the path to God. "In this state of passivity," Keppler declares, "the Poor Souls must feel doubly that painful want of the sacramental graces which were at their disposal during life. On earth, they were able to draw graces to themselves . . . which would have . . . secured their immediate salvation."[84] And now, in purgatorial time, such opportunities have vanished. Martin Jugie, a French theologian who flourished in the mid-twentieth century, agrees with Catherine that "there can be no question of merit after death" and that "after death, the soul does not change."[85] Jugie, though, was deeply suspicious of any explanation that would make purgatorial sufferings "a purification only,"[86] a view that to his mind would overlook the charitable actions of which the suffering souls are capable. Unlike Catherine, who maintains that the suffering souls are unaware of each other in the purifying power of divine love, Jugie sees purgatory as a region of "perfect fraternal charity." The "doing" of the souls, however, is limited to their praying for each other and for the living,[87] an activity that Jugie carefully laces with the passivity traditionally expected of the suffering souls. The prayers of the souls for others, he insists, lack "satisfactory value" or the possibility of merit and possess only "impetratory force, the proper efficacy of prayer considered in itself." For Jugie, the act of intercessory prayer in purgatory seems to be meager to the point of inaction. "It could be compared," he says, "to the gesture of a poor man who holds out his hand to a rich,"[88] an analogy bent on asserting the passivity of the penitent dead even in the midst of an argument for a residue of their activity.

In spite of their nuanced differences, these views on the passivity of the dead in purgatory consistently represent the same concerns. First and foremost, passivity in purgatory reflects the metaphysics of judgment that Aquinas articulated so clearly and that extends throughout all three dimensions of the otherworld. The eternal judgment of God constrains what the saved and the damned may do to the same degree that it constrains what they may be. In this traditional worldview, both eternal joy and eternal suffering are passive reactions to objective, supernatural conditions, respectively, the Beatific Vision and the torments of hell. Purgatorial passivity is an odd mixture of both joy and suffering, though both emotions here too are passive reactions to an immutable divine judgment still in a temporal process of being fulfilled. Second, the passivity of the souls in purgatory was vital to the practice of intercession on the part of the church militant, the faithful in life who enacted the values of ascetical culture on behalf of those in purgatory, including the suffering souls they assumed they themselves would one day be. This passivity is important even to a theorist like Jugie, who is reluctant to relinquish all doing on the part of the suffering souls so that his purgatory retain some semblance of ascetical virtue while yet insisting with the tradition that purgatorial acts bring no merit to their agents.

In line with the argument presented here, I would suggest another dimension of purgatorial passivity that might aid in explaining both the origins of the doctrine and its recent disappearance. I have observed that a contributing factor to the development of the doctrine of purgatory may have been an effort on behalf of all the faithful to negotiate the competitive style of religion that gravitated around the ascetic's vocation. Purgatory, I have suggested, tempered the eschatological anxiety that permeated the Catholic culture of works by allowing the laity to be the ascetical sufferers that they were not and ascetics to be better ascetical sufferers than they were, all within a protracted time of judgment that lowered the bar—and the anxiety—of competitive religion. It would be interesting to consider the passivity of the suffering souls as a further negotiation of this anxiety. As much as believers imagined purgatory as a supernatural monastery, they insisted, paradoxically, that it be portrayed as a place where the suffering souls were passive, unable to engage in the very behavior so competitively valued in the ascetical culture of Catholic Christianity. The passivity of purgatory affirmed the finality of divine judgment and fostered the ascetical values of the merit system by placing the suffering souls in need of intercession. But perhaps another layer of explanation is that the passivity of the suffering souls expressed the heartfelt desires of all believers for the end of competition and the quelling of the eschatological anxiety that issued from life in a peccativized world. Viewed from one angle, the passivity of purgatory anticipated the eschatological goal of heavenly rest. Considered, though, from the perspective of the development of doctrine, the passivity of purgatory expressed deep religious yearnings for inaction before a divine judgment already rendered and certain, even if not quite completed. Purgatory, so understood, was a place of struggle where the prevailing values of the entire system of belief were at once encoded and deconstructed, figuratively canonized and subverted, and, in the complexity of Catholic faith, both accepted and rejected.

Admittedly, this is a speculative interpretation, but one that might be justified if measured against the backdrop of the religious emotions competitively at work in Catholic Christianity. Thus regarded, the passivity of the suffering souls negatively conveys a rebellious desire that contributed to the development of the doctrine of purgatory. One way to test the coherence of this interpretation is to see how the doctrine of purgatory behaves in the absence of competitive religion. My hypothesis in this experiment must be that purgatory disappears where competitive Christianity is not the regnant style of faith. Two historical sites will serve as my testing grounds: the Christian culture of sixteenth-century Lutheran and Reformed Protestantism and one strain of post-Vatican II Catholic faith.

At first glance it seems as though my argument leads to the conclusion that the purgatorial desire for passive quiescence before the divine judgment was a seed of the Reformation that blossomed in the Protestant doctrine of grace alone. Certainly the Catholic belief in the passivity of the suffering souls and the Lutheran and Reformed belief in grace alone share a similar desire for a completed salvation where God's will prevails over all human initiative. Both beliefs acknowledge a state in which human helplessness surrenders before the divine judgment. At most, perhaps, one could understand the Lutheran and Reformed traditions to have expressed this general Christian desire in a host of determinately doctrinal ways. The differences between the Catholic and Protestant beliefs in passivity before God, though, are far more striking. The Lutheran and Reformed traditions moor this passivity in a doctrine of predestination, which places God's saving decision in eternity and makes all human actions worthless sins in the eyes of God. Catholic Christianity consistently has judged a strong doctrine of predestination to be religiously unacceptable. The medieval Catholic tradition rejected it first in the later work of Augustine, even as it accepted so many other features of Augustine's theology and person as utterly authoritative. And since the Council of Trent, modern Catholicism has decisively rejected the Protestant claim for eternal election, finding the doctrine's denial of the efficacy of free choice and natural responsibility for virtue as well as for sin to be inconsistent with its theological understanding of the human person.[89]

The Catholic yearning for passivity before divine judgment is not a desire for the certainty of the eternal decree but rather a desire for tranquility in the face of a particular kind of eschatological anxiety that has achieved its meaning in the context of moral, and even saintly, struggle.

The Reformation doctrine of grace alone provides a relevant point of comparison with the passivity of the suffering souls especially because its acceptance entailed the rejection of the competitive religion of the medieval Catholic tradition and the doctrine of purgatory that developed from it. The doctrine of *sola gratia* subverted the religious value of the ascetical life, which, I have shown, was the center and energy of Catholic competition. The Reformation understanding of grace as sheer divine gift meant that the ascetic's vocation was misdirected and, even more, an exercise in vanity, since grace could not be earned. That same judgment extended to the ordinary discipleship of the laity, who strove for a salvation measured by the ascetical standard. And finally, that same judgment extended to the doctrine of purgatory, which negotiated in complex ways the eschatological anxiety that attended this competitive style of religion.[90] For Luther, "purgatory and all the pomp, services, and business transactions associated with it are to be regarded as nothing else than illusions of the devil, for purgatory, too, is contrary to the fundamental article that Christ alone, and not the work of man, can help souls."[91] In the *Institutes*, Calvin puts his dismissal in the form of a rhetorical question: "But if it is perfectly clear from our preceding discourse that the blood of Christ is the sole satisfaction for the sins of believers, the sole expiation, the sole purgation, what remains but to say that purgatory is simply a dreadful blasphemy against Christ?"[92] If Reformation sensibilities teach the formal lesson that purgatory disappears where strong grace prevails, then perhaps we have some direction for understanding the remarkable loss of belief in purgatory since Vatican II.

As I begin to assess my second historical site for the disappearance of belief in purgatory, it is important to note that the doctrine has not disappeared entirely from contemporary Catholic culture. A tradition is always a constellation of beliefs and practices being made and remade in every passing moment. Its variety and diversity are as characteristic as the unity that believers claim for it. Within this diversity, some Catholics still believe in purgatory ardently enough to participate in all the practices associated with engaged belief in the "third place." And yet, purgatory has largely disappeared from Catholic belief and practice in the past half century, a phenomenon that begs for theological explanation.[93] My introductory remarks noted that one reason for the disappearance of belief in purgatory might lie in the way that the theological and pastoral reception of Vatican II highlighted the power of God's grace, and to a degree that undermined the detailed accounting of personal virtue and sin in the Tridentine merit system. I conclude by reflecting on this observation in light of my lengthy argument.

Even though conservative interpreters of Vatican II stress the unchanged continuity of its teaching with previous tradition, it is difficult to explain the extensive developments in Catholic belief and practice after the council as much to do about the same or, as conservatives are more inclined to hold, a series of misinterpretations of what the council really taught. *Lumen gentium*'s teachings on the universal call to holiness and the common priesthood of all the faithful challenged believers to reimagine the meaning of the traditional notion of the hierarchy of discipleship in a way that accentuated the baptismal vocation of all believers.[94] This ecclesiology, complemented by the same document's teaching on salvation outside the church and the church's embrace of the modern world in *Gaudium et spes*, encouraged believers to envision God's grace as efficacious beyond the means of the institutional church, a view supported by the influence of Rahner's theology on and after the council. The postconciliar emphasis on the availability of God's grace had a host of effects on Catholic belief and practice. It depeccativized the world. It dulled the pointed sense of God's judgment that believers felt upon their lives. It calmed the eschatological anxiety that had filled Catholic lives throughout the earlier tradition. It subverted the advantage that the ascetical vocation had found in the hierarchy of discipleship. And, finally, it caused the virtual disappearance of belief in purgatory as the tradition's late-developing and creative way of negotiating a sinful world, God's judgment, eschatological anxiety, and the burden of the ascetical vocation in the hierarchy of discipleship.[95]

The loss of purgatory, then, was the loss of competitive religion, a loss cheered by some in the Church, lamented by others, and unconsciously lived out by so many more. Where the loss of competitive religion has entailed the believer's oblivion to meaningful guilt and a sense of judgment in the face of personal and systemic sin, there something of value has vanished from the tradition and is in desperate need of recovery. But the loss of competitive religion can also be understood as an authentic development in the tradition, a loss that brings the possible gain of a novel style of Catholic faith that we could describe as "noncompetitive." Although a number of sociological rubrics have been proposed to name the many ways of being Catholic since the council, I have not encountered the rubric "noncompetitive," which I offer not as a sociological but as a theological description that cuts across a number of Catholic behaviors that might be distinguished from the competitive religiosity of earlier Catholic belief and practice. For help in elucidating this Catholic style of faith, I enlist the important work of Kathryn Tanner.

Tanner has argued that a noncompetitive understanding of Christian life is one deeply attuned to the graciousness of God as the giver of the gift that grace is. Since God's gifts are truly gifts and not entries into a system of barter and exchange, they cannot be returned through reciprocal action on the part of the graced that is commensurate with what is given. By their very nature, God's gifts dash any possibility of this kind of conditional reciprocity precisely because the persons who receive them are themselves created gifts:

> God's gifts efface themselves in their giving because God's gift-giving, unlike any gift-giving among creatures with which we are familiar, is total, productive without remainder of its recipients. Because we *are* these gifts, we are not aware of having received them, as we would be in any ordinary case of gifts transferred from someone else's hands to us. Recognition of these gifts is itself, then, a gift from God.[96]

And if even an appreciative faith is a divine gift, then no conditional return to God is expected or even possible. For Tanner, God's unconditional giving communicates the divine life itself, shared as acts of complete self-giving without return among the persons of the Trinity. God's utter graciousness is simply who God is as much as it is what God does.

Understanding God's being and acting in this way means that "God's gift-giving is non-competitive." God's giving to one does not come at another's expense. "What is given," Tanner explains, "remains the possession of the one giving."[97] Grace is not a commodity that can be transferred to and then possessed by the recipient since the graced person, in the act of creation, is a divine gift too, and not some personal site for the exchange of value with God or other competing persons. God's giving does not work in that way. And even though so much giving and receiving in the world does, Tanner insists that a proper theological regard for the human person would recognize the Christian obligation to imitate the manner of God's gift giving, which sets the standard for true relations in all of creation. "If our lives together imitate God's giving to us," Tanner argues, "we should not need to hold what we are or have as our exclusive possessions, or claim with respect to them exclusive rights of use, against others."[98] When owning becomes a function of giving, as it does in the act of creation, possession and rights of use relinquish any sense of propriety and become the common currency of all. And this means that

> our lives as individuals should be constituted and enhanced in their perfections as we share our lives with others in community, identifying ourselves thereby as persons in community with others and not simply persons for ourselves. We perfect one another in community as our operations to perfect our own gifts and talents enter into and supplement the operations of others in a combined venture for goods otherwise impossible.[99]

Such "relations of non-exclusive possession and identification only make sense," Tanner insists, "where giving to others and having oneself are not in competition with one another."[100]

Tanner's reflections clearly lead in the direction of a social ethic, which, while very important, is not my principal concern here.[101] Nevertheless, her thoughts on grace are a suggestive resource for explaining the present Catholic moment. If a noncompetitive style of Catholic faith has appeared in the wake of Vatican II, then Tanner's theology seems to suggest that it derives from a strong emphasis on the power of grace and an appreciation on the part of believers that the efficacy of grace devalues religious competition. Without competition among believers for a favorable divine judgment, all the dynamics of the hierarchy of discipleship dissolve away, and with them some of the typical forms of belief and practice that have flourished throughout Catholic history. For some in the Catholic Church, this change in belief and practice constitutes a fateful loss. Yet, with this noncompetitive style of faith comes a host of possible gains to the tradition. The loss of competitive religion may have resulted in a paucity of vocations to the ascetical life, but the rise of a noncompetitive style of faith has witnessed a new appreciation for the baptismal responsibilities of all believers. The loss of competitive religion may have diminished the practice of auricular confession, but the rise of a noncompetitive style of faith may have increased Catholic devotion to the Eucharist and its reception, perhaps the clearest ritualistic expression of a noncompetitive Catholic sensibility. The loss of competitive religion may have resulted in a loss of devotion to the saints and their heroic spiritual achievements, but the rise of a noncompetitive style of faith may have led to a new awareness of the social dimension of Catholic ethics in an increasingly globalized world. The loss of competitive religion may have resulted in the collapse of a Matthean style of faith, but the rise of a noncompetitive style of faith may have recovered Pauline dimensions of the Catholic tradition that have been too long overlooked.

A possible objection to this account of novel development in recent Catholic tradition is that it makes Tanner's theology of grace a template of explanation, one that requires Catholic anthropology and ecclesiology to fit the Procrustean bed of a classically Protestant theology of grace. But Tanner's stance is not classically Protestant. Its insistence on a noncompetitive understanding of grace and the

Christian life seems to entail the rejection of a doctrine of double predestination, a rejection on which a Catholic theology of grace will always rightly insist. Moreover, Tanner's theology of grace does not undermine the believer's responsibility for his or her words and deeds as
the recipients of divine grace. As important as these words and deeds
are, though, for the faithful Christian life, they do not enter into a system of exchange with God or into competition with others that would
make grace a commodity instead of a gift. "God's giving is not owed
to creatures," Tanner states, "but if those gifts are being given unconditionally by God to all in need, creatures are in fact owed the goods
of God by those ministering such benefits, without being or having
done anything in particular to deserve them. Our good works, in short,
are not owed to God but they are to the world."[102] This understanding
of the relationship between grace and works thoroughly respects the
teaching of the Council of Trent that human initiative comes at the
prompting of grace and yet our works are freely chosen and matter
for our salvation, not as merit but as acts that imitate, however minimally, God's noncompetitive gift giving. This understanding of grace
and works also opens some promising avenues for an interpretation
of the communion of the saints, as we shall see in our final chapter.

If a desire for the end of competitive religion inhabited purgatory
in the passivity of the suffering souls, then perhaps that desire continues to live on even in purgatory's absence, ironically in a postconciliar style of faith that is typically blamed for purgatory's disappearance. Whether a noncompetitive style of Catholic faith can endure
and thrive as the tradition to come depends on whether an authentic
Catholicism is possible without an ascetical center of gravity for the
pressing soteriological issues of time and judgment. It is interesting
to consider that the late medieval blossoming of purgatory coincided
with the rise of Western individualism. Perhaps the competitive élan
of the hierarchy of discipleship was energized even more by that cultural event and translated imaginatively into the extended time of
purgatorial judgment for the individual believer. Catholic believers
will always and rightly be concerned about their individual judgment.
A noncompetitive style of faith, though, may be more inclined to
broaden that concern to include all peoples and all of history. In this

theological perspective, salvation is as much a corporate as it is an individual event and the time of history is as important for negotiating the salvation of the human community as the supernatural time of purgatory has been for negotiating God's judgment on individual believers in light of the ascetical standard. A noncompetitive Catholic faith, then, is rife with eschatological implications for the ancient traditional belief in the Last Judgment and the communal proportions of salvation.

No doubt, a noncompetitive eschatology will be attended by its own brand of anxiety, as will any account of the Christian life that is serious about judgment. But it will be an anxiety shared by believers who trouble about their undeserved reception of God's innumerable gifts. This will not be an anxiety stirred by the competitive envy of the least who aspire to be the most, but rather an anxiety disturbed by the sinful possibility of competition for God's favor in a community of solidarity rightly appreciative of God's graceful subversion of competitive judgment.

Figure 1. Christ in Majesty. *Last Judgment* mosaic (13th–14th c.). Baptistery of
San Giovanni, Florence. Photo © DeA Picture Library/Art Resource, NY.

Figure 2. *Last Judgment*
fresco, Giorgio Vasari
(1511–74) and Federico Zuccari
(ca. 1540/41–1609). Basilica di
Santa Maria del Fiore,
Florence. Photo: Scala/Art
Resource, NY.

Figure 3. Details of the Damned, *Last Judgment* fresco, Giorgio Vasari and Federico Zuccari. Basilica di Santa Maria del Fiore, Florence. Photo: Nicolo Orsi Battaglini/Art Resource, NY.

Figure 4. *Last Judgment* mosaic (11th c.). Cattedrale di Santa Maria Assunta, Torcello, Italy. Photo: Alinari/Art Resource, NY.

Figure 5. *Last Judgment* fresco, Giotto di Bondone (1266–1336). Scrovegni Chapel, Padua, Italy. Photo: Scala/Art Resource, NY.

Figure 6. *Last Judgment* fresco, 1538–41,
Michelangelo Buonarrotti (1475–1564). Sistine
Chapel, Vatican Museums and Galleries, Vatican
City. Photo: Alinari/The Bridgeman Art Library.

Figure 7. Detail of the Damned, *Last Judgment* fresco, Michelangelo Buonarrotti. Sistine Chapel, Vatican City. Photo: Scala/Art Resource, NY.

Figure 8. Detail of Christ and the Virgin Mary, *Last Judgment* fresco, Michelangelo Buonarrotti. Sistine Chapel, Vatican City. Photo: Art Resource, NY.

Vater heilige sie/Ich heilige vnd Opffere mich für sie Mit meinen wunden etc.

Es ist nur ein Mittler.

So wir sündigen/haben wir eine versprechen beim Vater/Darumb last vns getrost zu dem gnadenstul tretten

Ich bin der weg/Niemant etc.

Sihe das ist das lamb Gottes etc.

Trincket alle darauß. Matthe. 26.

INRI

Alle Prophe ten zeugen von diesem/das kein ander name un ter dem himel sey. Act. 4.13.

Figure 9. *On the Difference between the True Religion of Christ and the False, Idolatrous Teaching of the Antichrist*, woodcut, Lucas Cranach the Younger (1515–86). Kupferstichkabinette, Staatliche Museen, Berlin. Photo: bpk, Berlin/Staatliche Museen/Jorg P. Anders/Art Resource, NY.

Figure 10. Untitled Woodcut, Lucas Cranach the Younger (1515–86). Photo: The Warburg Institute, London.

Figure 11. *Adoration of the Trinity*, Albrecht Dürer (1471–1528). Kunst-historisches Museum, Vienna. Photo: Erich Lessing/Art Resource, NY.

CHAPTER 4

Imagining the Last Judgment

Purgatorial time was imagined to extend, and so to equalize to some degree, the duration of spiritual competition for heavenly reward in the otherwise unequal hierarchy of discipleship shared by martyrs, ascetical saints, ascetics, and laypeople. In order to serve this purpose, though, purgatorial time was imagined to be an odd sort of time. Like time in the natural world on this side of death, purgatorial time measured change, specifically the purgative change for the better that prepared the soul for the Beatific Vision. And like natural time, which seems sometimes to pass quickly or slowly, this supernatural time possessed a kind of flexibility in the Catholic imagination, which could just as easily imagine purgatorial time to pass quickly or slowly. What made purgatorial time odd, and so different from natural time, was that its supernatural duration, whether imagined as long or short, was not beholden to natural duration. A personal story can illustrate this point.

I can recall a moment in church as an eleven-year-old in 1963. The Second Vatican Council had just begun, but had not yet influenced Catholic parish life. Mass was celebrated in Latin and the faithful followed along in their missals, books that provided an English translation side-by-side with the Latin text of the liturgy. My missal was a recent gift and so new to me. As I explored its pages I noticed that this edition supplemented the words of the sacred liturgy with pages of prayers suited for all sorts of occasions and circumstances. I noticed that some of these prayers concluded with a notation that a partial indulgence could be earned by their recitation, and by fulfilling other devotional conditions defined by the Church. A partial indulgence is the remission of some of the time of purgation fixed by God's particular judgment at the moment of the believer's death, and fixed in a way proportional to the sinfulness of the believer's life. The indulgence is a pardon, offered by the grace of God and mediated by the offices of the Church, and simply by intention may be earned for oneself as a future purgatorial sufferer or for another who will be or who is now believed to be in purgatory. One prayer especially caught my eye, since it assured the remission of five hundred years of purgatorial suffering. In a self-centered mood that day, I said the prayer with the intention of claiming the indulgence for myself.

The indulgence was especially appealing because the prayer to which it was attached was especially short—no more than six or seven lines. I recall feeling utterly relieved that I could so easily remit so much purgatorial suffering. Indeed, my relief was founded on my quick assumption that five hundred years vastly exceeded whatever purgatorial time I would amass in a lifetime and that this really good indulgence had already gained me the straight road to heaven. But then the future theologian in me, looking closely at the page, made more of the fact that this was a partial, and not a plenary, indulgence. Its fulfillment promised to remit only some, and not all, of the purgatorial suffering owed God. And that distinction immediately propelled my imagination into purgatory's odd temporal parameters. If five hundred years could be remitted so easily, then perhaps one's time in purgatory could last for thousands, or hundreds of thousands, or even millions of years.[1] Needless to say, this was a moment of eschatological anxiety, the likes of which has characterized Catholic culture through nearly all of its history, and for which, I have argued, purgatory was a partial, and not a plenary, solution.

Purgatory's supernatural time is odd because it is not limited by the boundary of personal death, which, for all but the very young and the very unreflective, becomes in life an existential index for marking time. The suffering souls in purgatory have passed beyond death and so its boundary no longer provides temporal orientation, causing the Catholic imagination to drift between images of purgatorial suffering as thankfully short or as distressingly long in duration. And yet, purgatorial time is finite, and not simply because each and every suffering soul eventually will be purged of sin and gain release. Purgatorial time is finite because in Catholic belief purgatory will cease to exist at the Last Judgment. The Last Judgment limits worldly time and purgatorial time, just as it capitulates all judgment. It is to this most unusual and underdeveloped eschatological doctrine that I turn in this chapter.

Modern believers have received the Christian doctrine of the Last Judgment in the most bifurcated of ways. On the one hand, fundamentalist Christians have breathed new life into the age-old doctrine, the most hopeful and literal-minded of their number finding in the vagaries of our time the clearest signs of the imminent end of the world and the appearance of Jesus to judge the living and the dead. On the other hand, the Last Judgment has been one of the most neglected doctrines among nonfundamentalist Christians. Even though many Christians profess belief in the Last Judgment in the words of the Nicene Creed—"he will come again in glory to judge the living and the dead"—few find that the doctrine resonates in their spiritual imagination or holds currency in their daily practice of the faith.

There are many reasons for this modern neglect on the part of nonfundamentalist Christians. The traditional sensibility regarding divine judgment seems to have disappeared for many Catholics in the postconciliar period. The eschatological anxiety that attended the expectation of divine judgment for so many generations of believers seems to have dissipated in the present ecclesial moment through an ardent belief in a divine grace so compelling that it has undermined the tradition's competitive spirituality. Another reason is that the cultural value assigned to personal individuality in the modern period encourages Christians to imagine what judgment they will only in terms of the particular judgment passed by God immediately after death. Belief in the Last Judgment has always assumed that God's particular judgment will be confirmed at the end of time, and so, in light of this contemporary attraction to the particular judgment, the Last Judgment seems rather redundant. The Last Judgment too seems to be a thoroughly mythologized doctrine to an age that prefers a demythologized interpretation of the faith. Shifts toward a modern sensibility for time have subverted the eschatological notion of the end time that flourished throughout the medieval period.[2] Moreover, in traditional portrayals of the end time, the bodies of the dead are raised back to life and joined again to their souls so that the entire person may stand before the judgment seat of Christ. And yet, many contemporary Christians seem to be so poorly educated in the basic tenets of the faith that they imagine the afterlife not in traditional terms as the resurrection of the body but instead as the immortality of the soul alone. In light of that deficient belief, the universal miracle anticipated on the last day seems to be superfluous, to say nothing of incredible.

In this chapter I propose some ways in which the doctrine of the Last Judgment can still resonate theologically and spiritually with contemporary believers who, unlike apocalyptically minded fundamentalists, do not imagine the end of the world around the next temporal corner. There are elements of the tradition whose recovery could contribute to a contemporary appreciation of the Last Judgment, and so I spend some time considering how some lessons from the doctrinal past might enliven the doctrinal present. I will speculate too about the nature of the Last Judgment in light of our last chapter's conclusions about a possible novel development in the tradition. In what ways might a noncompetitive spirituality, itself an appreciation for the gifted power of divine grace, shape our imagination about the Last Judgment? Might a noncompetitive spirituality shed light on the kind of judgment that Christ will render at the end time, as well as on the character of the saintly community that is established by virtue of that judgment? Before I consider these questions and others in the constructive section of this chapter, I need to examine some traditional themes bearing on the Last Judgment that will inform my constructive efforts.

WHEN THE LAST JUDGMENT
IMAGINATIVELY MATTERED

Any visitor to the city of Florence, Italy, is happily forced to make both the Basilica of Santa Maria del Fiore and the Baptistery of San Giovanni the shared center of all of the wonderful sights to see there. Situated in the heart of the old medieval city, the Basilica, or Duomo as it is called, towers over every other Florentine structure. The immense dome of its famous cupola with its surface of striking orange tiles defines the space of Florence itself. The Baptistery is a much smaller structure, a kind of miniature in sacred space by comparison. Octagonal in shape and topped by a pointed cupola that extends each of its eight sides to its summit, the Baptistery stands directly in front of the Duomo, only a few short steps from the basilica's main doors. Although many contemporary tourists probably miss the point of this physical proximity, its meaning was clear to the medieval Christians who negotiated these spaces. The Christian life, itself the meaning of life, began in the Baptistery with the child's reception of the sacrament of initiation. And as life's journey continued, the sacred events in the basilica, all occasions for the believer's reception of sacramental grace, would conform the believer's life to the life of Christ, and prepare him or her to stand at the Savior's right hand on judgment day as a disciple worthy of heavenly joy. For our concerns here, these ecclesial spaces are important testimonies to the ways in which the Last Judgment resonated in late medieval Christian faith.

The Baptistery is believed to be one of the oldest buildings in Florence. In its origins, it may have been a Roman temple that dates from as early as the fifth century. The structure was rebuilt in its present form between the eleventh and thirteenth centuries, and its famous gilded bronze doors, which once decorated the exterior with biblical scenes in bas-relief, were fashioned by Andrea Pisano in the fourteenth century and by Lorenzo Ghiberti in the fifteenth century. As much as these exterior works of art enlivened the religious imagination of any pious circumambulator of the structure, entry into the sacred space of the Baptistery did so all the more. Upon entering the Baptistery, one's eyes are drawn upward to the elaborate Last Judgment mosaic that decorates the eight sides of the cupola, and that calls the believer to consider the culmination of the biblical narrative that is episodically presented on the exterior doors. Most prominent and striking among the many details of time's final event is the enormous rendition of the coming Son of Man, which fills nearly an entire octagonal ceiling panel (figure 1). Likely based on a drawing by the thirteenth-century Italian painter Cope do Marcovaldo, this Christ towers over the hundreds of smaller figures that populate the cupola and who, the scene assumes, reap the joys and pains of his judgment on their lives. Angels announce this drama by sounding trumpets just as the book of Revelation describes, and all the world stands before the Savior to receive its eschatological due. In the spaces of the cupola base, demons torment and even devour the damned, while in the cupola's higher rungs, the haloed saints stand serenely shoulder to shoulder, righteously anticipating heavenly reward.[3]

It is interesting that this mosaic decorates the cupola of a baptistery, and in a way that iconically overwhelms all who entered its space. The religious message that it conveyed was simple and direct. The sacrament of baptism initiates the believer into a journey that culminates in the events depicted in the mosaic. The child who typically received the sacrament in the Baptistery was not, of course, capable of discerning this meaning, or any other. But the medieval Florentine families who brought their newborns to be baptized in this place, just as they were as infants, could not miss the implications of the art for their own Christian responsibilities. All that a believer said and did in the course of life would be held accountable in an eschatological horizon, and at the end of historical time Christ himself would render a verdict on each life that would seal the believer's destiny for everlasting joy or everlasting misery. In an age in which the style of Christian faith was thoroughly Matthean, the theme of judgment loomed large in both the Christian imagination and the Christian conscience.

Nor, evidently, could the theme of judgment be overdone. Just a few short steps from the Baptistery, the Cathedral of Santa Maria del Fiore, begun in 1296, was consecrated in March 1436, and Brunelleschi's magnificent dome or cupola, a remarkable feat of medieval engineering, was completed five months later. The cupola was, and to this day still is, the largest dome in the world, stretching one hundred and forty-three feet at its base. Even in the midst of the sixteen years that it took to construct the cupola, Brunelleschi anticipated that one day its huge interior would be a plaster canvas for an immense painting, since, as construction progressed, he anchored "iron rings from which scaffolding could be hung . . . into the interior of the inner shell. The shell is also pierced by small windows through which a painter could crawl onto the hanging platform and begin work with his brushes."[4] It was not until 1572 that the artist Giorgio Vasari began the fresco that now fills this space. After Vasari's death in 1574, the project was assumed by Federico Zuccari and completed in 1579.

Without any concern for proximate redundancy, Vasari chose the theme of the "Last Judgment" for his fresco, which is painted in eight concentric strips that ascend from the base of the dome to the higher reaches of the cupola (figure 2). In the lowest and widest strip at the dome's base, the damned suffer infernal punishments at the hands of grotesque demons (figure 3). The strip above this hellish lowest level portrays the measure of judgment itself. Angels sit centered on eight individual clouds that circle the octagonal strip and, on each, the angel sits between two human figures. Each of these figures symbolizes a particular beatitude, virtue, or gift of the Holy Spirit that each of the saved accomplished or used responsibly to merit heavenly reward, and which each of the damned neglected or abused on the path to perdition. The two heavenly strips are defined by Christ seated on his judgment throne, double-haloed and radiating a golden light of heavenly glory. Unmistakably the center of eschatological attention, he is yet surrounded by all those who will share his heavenly glory, their number composed of popes, bishops, monks, kings, and all of humanity, who are represented by Adam and Eve, now redeemed, who themselves stand before the New Adam who has come in judgment.[5]

Clearly, the Vasari-Zuccari fresco was not judged to be duplicative of the Baptistery's own Last Judgment scene, even though both sacred spaces, just a few paces from each other, were dominated by ceiling art portraying exactly the same theme. Vasari obviously was unconcerned about the choice of content, as were those who commissioned the work. And given the popularity of this motif in the Christian art of the late medieval world, one must assume that the people of Florence who worshipped in these spaces never tired of the meaning that these Last Judgment scenes conveyed. Indeed, there is a real sense in which the Last Judgment theme in late medieval art possesses a narrative quality that captured the Christian imagination.

The Byzantine Last Judgment mosaic on the west wall of the Torcello Duomo Santa Maria Assunta near Venice expresses this narrative quality well. Dating from the eleventh century, the mosaic presents the events of the end time in five scenes that rise from the floor to the ceiling (figure 4).[6] In the lower register, Satan and condemning angels torment the damned in hell, who are depicted as naked bodies in shame burning in the subterranean fires or as fragmented bodies— severed heads, torsos, and limbs—suffering the same infernal fate. The middle scenes of the mosaic portray the response of all the dead to the trumpet blasts of angels who announce the day of reckoning. Shrouded bodies emerge whole and reconstituted from their tombs, and those unfortunate enough to have been graveless are miraculously regurgitated by the lions, leopards, dogs, and birds that consumed their dead bodies. Made whole, the worthy who pass Christ's judgment both stand and sit around his glorious presence which, as in all the other Last Judgment scenes we have considered, centers the eschatological spectacle. As in all the Last Judgment scenes too, the Torcello mosaic presents the narrative of all of history brought to judgment through the second coming of Christ. Caroline Walker Bynum has observed that a leitmotif in the Torcello mosaic's more particular version of the narrative is its "association of wholeness with salvation, fragmentation with hell." Risking the heterodox position that only the blessed and not the damned are eschatologically restored to bodily wholeness, the mosaic encouraged its medieval viewer to imagine the eternally horrible and fragmentary consequences of sin, and "salvation as the triumph of whole over part."[7]

Giotto's Last Judgment fresco renders this narrative quality of the genre in a different way. Dating from 1306 and painted on the wall of the Cappella Scrovegni in Padua, the fresco directs the viewer's attention to the classical motif of Christ centered in an oval halo of glorious light, where he is seated in judgment (figure 5).[8] Flanking him on each side are six seated figures; the twelve apostles, who are witnesses to his judgment; and symmetrical choirs of saints who frame the background of each of these sacred flanks. In the lowest register of Giotto's busy scene, which hovers just above a centering doorway and below the judging Christ, the saved and the damned are spatially juxtaposed. Those who have procured a favorable judgment fill the lower left quadrant, their numbers formed by men and women from all walks of life whose faces radiate both joy and expectation for the life to come. They stand to the right of the judging Christ. To the savior's left, in the lower right quadrant of the fresco, are the damned. Dizzyingly miserable, they swirl in various states of torment around a gargantuan Satan, who indulges himself by devouring their recently resurrected bodies. These two quadrants are separated by the cross of Christ. Empty now of Christ's body, which appears glorified directly above it, this cross was the redemptive site of everyone in the fresco. But since not all responded the same way to the grace that this cross unleashed in time, it now is presented in the fresco as a barrier that divides the saved and the damned. The narrative of the entire work is thus a history-long morality play in which the viewer is required to reflect on his or her inescapable role in the eschatological script. And that role requires making a choice for standing on one side of the cross or the other, among the saved or the damned.

The most famous Last Judgment scene graces the entire altar wall of the Sistine Chapel. Painted by Michelangelo in the 1530s, the work simply assumes and replicates the hierarchical character of judgment in the earlier renditions of the theme we have examined, but does so in a style of fluid representation that conveys the eventfulness of the end time (figure 6). In the lower left quadrant of the painting, the dead rise bodily from their graves, answering the trumpet calls of angels centered above. Ascending heavenward, those who have been judged favorably grapple to reach the embodied saints who ride the clouds above and who stand ready to haul the new arrivals into paradise. In the lower right quadrant, the damned suffer in hell. A demonic version of Charon, the boatman of classic myth who transports the damned across the river Styx, ferries the condemned from earth toward the fiery punishment.[9] Their arrival is attended by grotesque demons who greet the damned with unspeakable tortures. The few who venture escape by heavenly ascent are pummeled from above by muscular angels who, on this project alone, cooperate with airy demons who drag the bodies of the damned back to hell. One of the fresco's signature scenes captures the psychological horror of infernal judgment by depicting a man pulled down from the sky into hell by three demons, one a reptilian figure who gnaws on his thigh (figure 7). Naked and hunched into a fetal position, the man in despair covers the left side of his face with his hand, the exposed right side of his visage with its wide-eyed stare and parted lips expressing the terrible realization of eternal loss.

At the center of the scene is Michelangelo's remarkable Christ (figure 8). With the Virgin seated at his right side in supernatural analogy to his own heavenly place beside the Father, the Christ appears in judgment youthful and beardless. His body in glory yet bears the wounds of crucifixion. Quite unlike the Last Judgment Christs we have considered thus far, there is nothing static about his epiphany. Indeed, his posture is the most identifiable feature in Michelangelo's fresco. His left arm extends bent in front of his torso in a leading position while his right arm is angled behind and above his head, his fingers spread open-handed. In her study of the fresco, Bernadine Barnes sides with any number of critics in viewing the bodily posture of Michelangelo's Christ as a representation of his authority as eschatological judge. Specifically, she proposes, the "dual nature of the gesture—at once damning and blessing—is absolutely basic to the meaning of a Last Judgment,"[10] an interpretation that sees his left hand welcoming the saints by pointing to the saving wound in his side and his right hand raised in condemnation of the damned. That Christ's eyes are turned down toward his left, apparently gazing at the damned, seems to support this reading, since his visual bearing is consistent with the far more dramatic gesture of his right hand raised in condemnation.

This thematic understanding of Michelangelo's Christ, however, should not overlook the extent to which his gestures resonate with the movement that so palpably animates this Last Judgment, a style that was Michelangelo's original contribution to the genre. Michelangelo painted nearly all the bodies as nudes or seminudes so that the viewer could perceive in their muscled postures a tensive energy that conveys the eventfulness of the Last Judgment. The damned suffer the horrors of hell with a frightening realism. The saints number dozens of distinguishable figures who form concentric crescents around the judging Christ, evoking the petals of the heavenly rose that Dante's *Paradiso* depicted as the highest heaven and the scene of the Beatific Vision.[11] So unlike the orderly lines of the saints in the Florence Baptistery or the heavenly choirs standing in neat rows in the work of Giotto, Michelangelo's saints flourishingly radiate their end-time victory. Their eyes are riveted on their Savior's glory; their leaning bodies and outstretched arms express their ardent yearning for closeness to his graceful presence.

Once again, there is a narrative quality to this Last Judgment that appeals to the same sacred plot of all of the other works of art we have considered. In the space of the Sistine Chapel, though, this narration was more explicitly complete. The believing viewer's attention to the scenes of the painted ceiling is drawn inevitably to Michelangelo's famous portrayal of God's creation of Adam, the Father's outstretched fingers beckoning to the first begotten human son. And now, as the viewer's eyes move to the altar wall, they are riveted by the hands of the divine Son posed in judgment on all the sons and daughters of Adam among whom every viewer stands. And, even more, beyond the broad strokes of the Christian plot of all history set in the space of the entire chapel, the details of Michelangelo's Last Judgment fresco invite the viewer to participate imaginatively in the emotional drama of the eschaton by conveying through bodily movement and facial expressions the eternal consequences of the Christian life.

These late medieval Last Judgment scenes evince a Christian fascination with their religious content that is largely unknown to modern Christians, with the exception of fundamentalists whose faith is still charged with apocalyptic expectations. For modern Christians in the mainline churches, however, it is more than a little difficult to understand why the Last Judgment mattered so much to late medieval

Christians if only because the Last Judgment matters so little to their own religious lives.[12]

Why did the Last Judgment matter so much to late medieval Christians, and, we might reasonably assume, to so many Christians who lived before and after them? The most obvious answer to this question centers on the Matthean style of faith that has characterized so much of the Catholic tradition. I argued in the previous chapter that the gradual loss of Christian belief in Christ's imminent return led to the quotidianizing of judgment. Judgment saturated daily life as Christians measured their virtuous deeds against their sins and pondered their standing before God at a particular judgment that was as inevitable and imminent as their own death. My analysis of late medieval Last Judgment scenes has considered the various ways that artists chose to portray this eschatological event, though I noted that different representational styles are but variations on a consistent narrative theme that accentuates the believer's responsibility for living a Christian life and the eternal consequences of enacting this responsibility. The imaginative entry for the believer into these religious works of art was through the door of their personal anticipation of judgment at the moment of death. The Last Judgment was, at the very least, a confirmation of the believer's particular judgment. Even if the Last Judgment as an end-time event in this grand narrative offered a most comprehensive scenario for divine decision, it was a decision that had already been made for all but those still living when the Savior came out of the sky. And yet, though a reiteration of sorts, the Last Judgment represented and captured all the drama of the particular judgment, of God's final decision about the believer's eternal destiny. Medieval Christians found Last Judgment scenes to be captivating because they artistically rendered the believer's eschatological anxiety about facing God's decision, a decision that, unlike the Last Judgment, was never far off. At once a morality play, a cautionary tale, and a glimpse into the supernatural destinies between which the believer stood, the artistic rendition of the Last Judgment was an extraordinarily personal scene for all who took the Matthean style of faith seriously. For nearly all of the Catholic tradition, such seriousness was a simple trait of ordinary faith.

ESCHATOLOGICAL ANTICLIMAX

If the Last Judgment matters far less to mainline Christians today, then all the reasons considered thus far might serve as explanations. The most telling reason, however, is that so many contemporary believers do not possess the same anxiety before the prospect of divine judgment that medieval Christians did, and which the doctrine of the Last Judgment and its graphic rendering expressed so powerfully. For medieval Christians, the Last Judgment was the anticipated climax of an extended drama, one that traversed each and every individual life that would be lived in natural time. Although believers knew the general parameters of this event, they remained in suspense, and anxious, about its particular climax. Believers knew that at the end of the world, when God's plan for history had run its course, the Savior would descend from his seat at the right hand of the Father and appear in the world to judge the living and the dead. The dead would be raised bodily, their flesh miraculously reconstituted, and reunited with their souls which were summoned from their respective eschatological locales in heaven, hell, or purgatory. Those who were alive when the end arrived would not die but instead be transformed into bodily resurrected persons "in a moment, in the twinkling of an eye," as the Apostle Paul had promised long ago (1 Cor 15:52). Purgatory would pass away, its extended judgment no longer necessary as final judgment was passed on all. As medieval believers contemplated Last Judgment scenes, they could blatantly see how the end would end. The saved would amass at Christ's right hand and the damned at his left, all to enter personally whole into eternal bliss or eternal punishment.[13]

What these believers could not see, and what they could not know, were the actual faces of the saved and the damned, save those of the Apostles and the great saints who were already assured of their favorable judgment and whose exceptional achievement fueled the eschatological anxiety of all others in the hierarchy of discipleship. What they imagined, and ardently hoped to be true, was that on that last day, which they and everyone else would witness, their own visage would be visible among the group judged worthy of eternal reward. It was this unknown judgment that made the Last Judgment so full of suspense, energized by a climax that had yet personally to unfold and by the eschatological worth of a lifetime of actions that was yet in the process of unfolding. Indeed, the narrative quality of the Last Judgment scenes that mattered so much to medieval Christians was replete with the eschatological drama playing out in their own present lives, ever short of the climactic judgments—personal and then finally social—that would establish their eternal destinies.

Since medieval times, by contrast, the Last Judgment has become anticlimactic in a variety of Christian traditions at different points in their histories. The eschatological counterpoint of the traditional scene that had generated such suspense for so many Christians ceased to do so. And as the eventfulness of the Last Judgment has ceased to generate suspense in these traditions, the doctrine has ceased to matter. I would like to consider several examples of this postmedieval eschatological anticlimax. Since Lutheran Protestantism offers the most lucid example, we will spend some time exploring its version of anticlimax before moving on to the others.

In the previous chapter, I considered Reformation theology as a viable site for testing my hypothesis that where a strong doctrine of grace prevails, purgatory disappears. Reformation theology contested the legitimacy of the Matthean style of faith that gave rise to a competitive spirituality in the Catholic tradition's hierarchy of discipleship. The development of the doctrine of purgatory was an imaginative response to the eschatological anxiety engendered by this competition, as purgatory extended the time for judgment for the ordinary—nearly all—to compete with God's favorable judgment on the saints. As the Reformers reclaimed the Pauline style of faith as true Christianity, purgatory ceased to matter. Indeed, there is a sense in which Luther's objection to purgatory precipitated the Reformation, since it was his *Ninety-Five Theses or Disputation on the Power and Efficacy of Indulgences* (1517) that launched his theological claims into the public square.[14]

Unsurprisingly, the doctrine of the Last Judgment behaves at this Reformation site in much the same fashion as, even if not identically to, the doctrine of purgatory. The Reformers' strong doctrine of grace did not cause the doctrine of the Last Judgment to disappear, as it did the doctrine of purgatory. The doctrine of the Last Judgment in one

form or another is as old as the tradition and is affirmed as the orthodox faith in the ancient creeds that the Reformers readily embraced.
While the Reformers did not believe in purgatory and considered it to
be the worst kind of papist invention, they believed in the Last Judgment unquestioningly. They did not, however, believe in the Last
Judgment in the manner of medieval Catholics and the peculiar shape
of their belief made the Last Judgment anticlimactic to the point that
it mattered little in Reformation theology. We see this eschatological
anticlimax most clearly in Luther.

Scott H. Hendrix has catalogued Luther's career-long identification of the institution of the papacy and even the person of the pope
with the antichrist, and has noted that this rhetoric was consistent with
the apocalyptic currents of early sixteenth-century European culture.
Luther himself occasionally voiced his belief that papal corruption
evinced the extraordinary work of the devil and could be understood
as a sign of the imminent return of Christ.[15] Yet, Luther's apocalyptic identification of the papacy with the antichrist seems much more
bent on the criticism of Rome than on the elucidation of the Last Judgment. His theological commitment to a "magisterial" reform of the
Church, one that valorized the authority of the Gospel only alongside
the rightful and God-given authority of the civil magistrate, reflects
his more consistent expectation that a reformed Church is in the world
to stay and that the Last Judgment is an event distant in time. Moreover, Luther repudiated any end-time warrants for Christian reform.
He found Thomas Müntzer's incitement of the Peasant Rebellion
of 1525 by appeal to an apocalyptic reading of the Gospel to be the
worst kind of practical heresy. And he was utterly horrified by later
Anabaptist chiliasm, epitomized in the theocratic capture of Münster
in 1534–1535 by followers of Melchior Hoffman who claimed the city
as the New Jerusalem and the scene of Christ's imminent return.

Consistent with his views, Luther typically disavows exegetical
opportunities to elucidate the Last Judgment. In his extensive com-
mentaries on Scripture, he inclines toward historical readings of pas-
sages that could just as easily be read literally as accounts of the last
day. Luther's 1526 lectures on the book of Zechariah offer an interesting example. In the opening lines of the fourteenth chapter, the

minor Hebrew prophet describes a scene that any Christian would likely read as a reference to the Last Judgment:

> See, a day is coming for the Lord when the plunder taken from you will be divided in your midst. For I will gather all the nations against Jerusalem. . . . Then the Lord will go forth and fight against those nations as when he fights on a day of battle. . . . On that day living waters will flow out from Jerusalem. . . . And the Lord will become king over all the earth; on that day the Lord will be one and his name one. (Zec 14:1–9)

Luther, though, begins his commentary on this passage with the frustrated declaration "Here, in this chapter, I give up," and confesses that he is "not sure what the prophet is talking about." "Men," he continues, "have understood it to refer to the Antichrist and Judgment Day. But while this interpretation is to be found everywhere and is presented by many, I shall put it aside at present because it does not satisfy me."[16] Instead, Luther settles on a reading that makes the passage a prediction of the first-century fall of Jerusalem at the hands of Rome, and which understands the battle of the Lord as the power of the Gospel at work in the world daily.[17]

We find a similar eschatological avoidance in Luther's 1529 lectures on the book of Isaiah. Chapter 66 presents several images in which a Christian reading could readily find reference to the Last Judgment. But again, Luther is disinclined to such readings. Isaiah 66:15–16, for example, offers a rich opportunity for an eschatological hermeneutic: "For the Lord will come in fire, and his chariots like the whirlwind, to pay back his anger in fury, and his rebuke in flames of fire. For by fire will the Lord execute judgment, and by his sword, on all flesh; and those slain by the Lord shall be many." While acknowledging the possibility of finding the Last Judgment in these words, Luther prefers an historical interpretation. "It would seem," he concedes, "that this text is speaking of the Last Judgment, and I do not oppose it. . . . But we prefer to apply this text to the destruction of the Jews by the Romans, although I am not opposed to a general meaning."[18] The concluding words of the chapter, which end the book itself, convey Last Judgment imagery that points the Christian imagination to the powerful symbolism of the book of Revelation:

> For as the new heavens and the new earth, which I will make, shall remain before me, says the Lord; so shall your descendents and your name remain. From new moon to new moon, and from sabbath to sabbath, all flesh shall come to worship before me, says the Lord. And they shall go out and look at the dead bodies of the people who have rebelled against me; for their worm shall not die, their fire shall not be quenched, and they shall be an abhorrence to all flesh. (Is 66:22–24)

In Luther's reading, however, the "new heavens and the new earth" refer to the true Church's commitment to the doctrine of the priesthood of all believers, one of the mainstays of his theology. In much the same manner, the "dead bodies" of the rebellious do not refer to those about to be resurrected and damned, as medieval Catholic interpretation would be inclined, but instead to "all the ungodly [who] are dead bodies that have their existence without the Spirit and without faith, like our Enthusiasts and papists."[19]

Luther's doctrine of predestination, I propose, explains his avoidance of the Last Judgment in the texts we have considered. Luther had fully developed a theology of predestination by 1526 in his only book-length writing *The Bondage of the Will*. To his mind, predestination was not an ancillary Christian teaching about which believers might disagree, but instead expressed the heart of the Gospel itself. In humanity's fallen state, Luther insists, free will has no natural capacity at all to accomplish virtue worthy in God's eyes. As a consequence, an utterly sinful humanity deserves eternal condemnation. Yet God, not beholden to the canons of human justice, has willed that some be saved as a sheer exercise of divine love and goodness, and has determined the elect from all eternity. No person, Luther claims, "can be thoroughly humbled until he knows that his salvation is utterly beyond his own powers, devices, endeavors, will and works, and depends entirely on the choice, will, and work of another, namely, of God alone."[20] In Luther's recovery of ancient Pauline sensibilities,

God's eternal decision is not based on virtuous merit, since none exists in a thoroughly fallen humanity. Grace, and grace alone, brings the elect to salvation, and in a way that remains concealed in the secret and hidden will of God.

Luther wrote *The Bondage of the Will* as an attack on Erasmus of Rotterdam's *On Free Choice of the Will* (1524), a humanistic defense of the Matthean style of faith that insisted that eternal salvation required some degree of human responsibility measured by virtuous acts freely obedient to the divine will. In arguing this position, Erasmus had to confront the same problem faced by all medieval theologians who defended free choice: How could the human will truly be free if God possesses, as the eternal God must, a timeless and unchangeable foreknowledge of every act of the will in time? Erasmus addressed this problem in a most traditional way. God eternally foreknows the consequence of every volitional act. But since God, in the act of creation, has endowed the human will with the power of free choice, this same, unchanging foreknowledge of the results of free choice exerts no divine necessity upon the acts of the will that produce them.[21] Lu -ther judged this distinction between God's contingent foreknowledge of the effects of free choice and God's necessary forewilling of human deeds to be theologically baseless and contrary to the Christian gospel:

> Here, then, is something fundamentally necessary and salutary for a Christian, to know that God foreknows nothing contingently, but that he foresees and purposes and does all things by his immutable, eternal, and infallible will. Here is a thunderbolt by which free choice is completely prostrated and shattered, so that those who want free choice asserted must either deny or explain away the thunderbolt, or get rid of it by some other means.[22]

What we find in this Reformation controversy is a battle between two traditional Christian sensibilities, each of which laid claim to the orthodox tradition. Erasmus's position defended the most fundamental belief of the Matthean sensibility, which energized the medieval Catholic tradition. Luther's position defended a particular interpretation of the Pauline sensibility, and one that confronted the eschatological anxiety of the medieval hierarchy of discipleship. We might see Erasmus's Christian humanism, his confidence in the moral capacity of human nature, as his own effort to temper the eschatological anxiety otherwise engendered by the Matthean commitments he so ardently defended. But to Luther's mind, the Matthean tradition could not be interpretively negotiated but only condemned as false Christianity. Its most basic beliefs about the role of human responsibility before God inescapably made salvation competitive and stirred the eschatological anxiety from which Luther suffered so terribly in his early years as a monk. By contrast, the doctrine of God's predestinating will was a soothing balm to this anxiety, as Luther testified so emotionally in a well-known passage that deserves lengthy citation:

> For my own part, I frankly confess that even if it were possible, I should not wish to have free choice given to me, or to have anything left in my own hands by which I might strive toward salvation. For, on the one hand, I should be unable to stand firm and keep hold of it amid so many adversities and perils and so many assaults of demons, seeing that even one demon is mightier than all men, and no man at all could be saved; and on the other hand, even if there were no perils or adversities or demons, I should nevertheless have to labor under perpetual uncertainty and to fight as one beating the air, since even if I lived and worked to eternity, my conscience would never be assured and certain how much it ought to do to satisfy God. But whatever work might be accomplished, there would always remain an anxious doubt whether it pleased God or whether he required something more, as the experience of all self-justifiers proves, and as I myself learned to my bitter cost through so many years. But now, since God has taken my salvation out of my hands into his, making it depend on his choice and not mine, and has promised to save me, not by my own work or exertion but by his grace and mercy, I am assured and certain both that he is faithful and will not lie to me, and also that he is too great and powerful for any demons or any adversities to be able to break him or to snatch me from him.[23]

This comforting belief required Luther to imagine the Last Judgment quite differently from medieval Catholics—not as the climactic revelation of God's judgment on the eternal destiny of a life lived in this way or that but as the anticlimactic manifestation of God's predestinating will. What made Luther's regard for the Last Judgment anticlimactic was that the existential experience of faith, the believer's subjective affirmation of divine favor, had already confirmed one's eternal destiny and brought the emotional relief that Matthean sensibilities could not achieve this side of death or in the Last Judgment's doctrinal representation of a future eschatological climax.

Luther expresses this anticlimactic regard for the Last Judgment pointedly in his sermons on the Gospel of John, which date from 1538–1539. Here, in his commentary on John 3:19—"And this is the judgment, that the light has come into the world"—Luther consoles his congregation by asking them to imagine that Christ himself is assuring them that "'even if your sin and your conscience plague and oppress you and you stand in awe of God's judgment, you must realize that all has been changed and that judgment has been abolished. Instead of harboring fear of the Final Judgment you must yearn and long for it, since it does not denote your judgment at all but your redemption.'"[24] "This judgment," Luther continues, now in his own voice, "will draw you from the grave and deliver you from all evil. Therefore the Day of Judgment will be a time of rejoicing for you, far more so than the wedding day is for the bride; for this terrible Day has been converted into a happy and desirable Day for you."[25] For Luther, that conversion is the work of the predestinating God, and its eternal accomplishment gracefully defies the temporal categories of "first" and "last." Thus, nothing new happens judgmentally to the believer at the moment of death or on the last day, and everything old, and indeed eternally old, in God's judgment is utterly good news. "For the believer," Luther claims, "the thought of this Day is comforting, since condemnation and terrible judgment are gone."[26]

Eschatological anticlimax is affirmed from another angle in Luther's polemic treatise *Against Hanswurst* (1541). Railing against the papacy as a demonic institution, Luther finds support for his judgment in a very particular Last Judgment scene:

When the painters of old painted the Last Judgment, they pic-
tured hell as a great dragon's head with vast jaws, in the middle
of which, in the fire, stood the pope, cardinals, bishops, priests,
monks, emperors, kings, princes, all kinds of men and women,
but never a young child. I really do not know how one should, or
could, paint or describe the church of the pope better, more to
the point, or more clearly. It represents indeed the jaws of hell,
and through the mouth of the devil, that is, through its devilish
preaching and teaching, it swallows into the abyss of hell first and
foremost the pope himself, and then all the world.[27]

Interestingly, Luther interprets this Last Judgment scene by explaining the actual images of the painting and by noting too what the
painting omits.[28] The two images that he highlights—the one actually
present, the other meaningfully absent—convey, in his view, the effects of God's predestinating will. On the one hand, the painter represents the damned as the hierarchs of the Roman Church and all who
follow their heretical teaching. On the other hand, the absent child,
whom Luther introduces to elucidate the scene, represents the elect.
Luther assumes that this absent image, which never appears in the
jaws of hell, is a baptized Christian child. Such a child, who died at an
early age, "in his seventh or eighth year," could not yet be seduced by
the Roman teaching of self-salvation and, Luther asserts, "he has in
truth been saved and will be saved—of that we have no doubt."[29]

Luther, of course, would have no doubt about the salvation of anyone whom God had eternally predestined to eternal life. His appeal to
the image of the dead child may simply have been his consoling response to the theological conundrum posed by childhood death in a
merit religion. In any case, the two images convey Luther's anticlimactic regard for the Last Judgment, which in his view simply reiterates
both what God has eternally willed and what God has temporally fashioned in the graced works of the elect and in the utterly sinful works of
those from whom God has withheld his favor. For Luther, then, there
is no drama or suspense in the Last Judgment, anymore than there is
drama or suspense in a believer's particular judgment at the moment of
death or in the salvational effects of any person's words and deeds that

make for a life unfolding over time. The supposition of suspense in any of these events would be the source of an anxiety about eschatological outcome that Luther's entire theology was bent on quelling and that an anticlimactic regard for the Last Judgment was meant to soothe.

Luther's remarkable abilities did not extend to graphic art. Had they, it would have been interesting to see how he would have represented the Last Judgment to convey his desire for eschatological anticlimax. In some respects, though, we can see Luther's theology of eschatological anticlimax artistically captured in two woodcuts by Lucas Cranach the Younger (1515–1586). The first I consider is entitled *On the Difference between the True Religion of Christ and the False, Idolatrous Teaching of the Antichrist*, and dates from around the year 1545 (figure 9). This fine example of Reformation art was intended for viewing by a popular audience, and so functioned as graphic theology just like the medieval Last Judgment scenes examined earlier. In many respects, Cranach's woodcut reinscribes the medieval Last Judgment scene. Like the latter, the woodcut is divided down the middle, with the damned depicted on the right side of the entire scene and the saved on the left. Unlike the medieval Last Judgment scene, Christ is not the centered figure who divides the two groups. Rather, an ornate column rises from the bottom to the top center of the frame, dividing the woodcut into two panels and configuring a blatant antithesis between the two groups.

The left panel presents the "True Religion of Christ" as the Lutheran reform. In the right center of the panel, Luther preaches to a rapt congregation eager to hear him expound the words of the Bible open before him in the pulpit. The Holy Spirit, in the form of a dove, hovers above his head, validating the faithfulness of his message. Extending from Luther's upturned index finger is a banner that runs through a heavenly positioned Christ directly to the throne of God the Father in the upper reaches of the panel, and on the banner are inscribed several confessions of the Reformation faith that salvation is by Christ alone, and not, it is implied, by the agency of the Roman Church. In the panel of the elect, the only authentic sacraments are administered. A child is baptized and the Lord's Supper is celebrated for the true congregation as communion is distributed under both species.

The right panel presents the "Religion of the Antichrist" as Roman practice, and all who populate its space are the living damned. Back to back with Luther, in the left center of the panel, a rotund monk commands a pulpit antithetically juxtaposed to Luther's. There is no Bible before him, and a rat wearing a bishop's mitre sits on his shoulder pumping billows of air into his ear, a representation of his empty preaching. His fingers are pointed downward, signifying the worldly concerns of his words. His audience is composed of fellow clerics and the affluent. In the bottom right corner, the pope himself sits at a table collecting indulgence money. Catholic distortions of the true faith appear as well in the figure of a priest saying a mass for the dead by himself, Franciscan monks vesting a dying man in a monk's cowl to assure his entry into heaven, and pilgrims arriving at a shrine. The artist assumes that the viewer knows that money has changed hands from layperson to cleric in each of these "spiritual" scenes. An angry God the Father rains fire and brimstone from above on all this worldly corruption as Francis of Assisi, in heaven with God, pleads in vain for his mercy.[30]

It is important to note that this Reformation construal of the saved and the damned does not take place in any liminal time between history and eternity. It takes place in the day-to-day passing of ordinary time in which, Lutheran theology assumes, God's judgment has already been rendered. Christ does not descend from the heavens to pass a Last Judgment upon individual virtue and vice. All the scenes from daily religious life manifest either the graceful effects of predestination, God's primordially First Judgment, or the complete fallenness unleashed in the world by Adam's sin.

Cranach the Younger presents these same Lutheran sensibilities in a work from the same period that even more explicitly reinscribes the medieval Last Judgment scene. In an untitled woodcut that might be entitled *The True and the False Church*, Cranach Lutheranizes the Last Judgment motif by situating Luther in the place of the descending Christ (figure 10). At the top center of the woodcut, Luther preaches from an elaborate pulpit that divides the woodcut into two panels that present an antithesis, so common in Reformation propaganda art, between Roman and Reformation faith. A Bible is placed open on the lectern before Luther, whose arms are outstretched. His left hand points down toward his left to the figures in the right panel, who are all clerics: the pope, cardinals, bishops, and monks. All suffer the torment of infernal flames and smoke, which issue from the enormous mouth of a demonic beast in which they stand. Much in the manner of Catholic Last Judgment scenes, hell is portrayed in horrible, graphic detail, with devilish creatures contributing their share to the suffering endured there. Luther's right hand points toward his right to the figures in the left panel, and most directly at a stark image of the crucified Christ that hovers over a Lutheran community celebrating the Lord's Supper. The congregation is composed of laymen and laywomen whose piety is evinced by their kneeling postures as they receive the sacrament under both species, just as the minister does. The calm order of the evangelical congregation in the left panel offers a striking contrast to the entwined bodies suffering hellfire in the right panel.[31]

Three features of this woodcut confirm Cranach's specific intention to reconfigure the medieval Catholic Last Judgment scene. First, the artist not only places Luther at the top center of the scene in the traditional position of the descending Christ but also plays on the traditional Christian imagery of a condemning left-hand gesture and a saving right-hand gesture typically ascribed to the judging Christ in Catholic Last Judgment scenes. Second, the depiction of the damned in a surrealistic hell directly mimics the Catholic genre, with the exception that Cranach's hell is an exclusively clerical place. Third, Cranach exploits the propaganda genre of the antithesis in order to distinguish clearly between the damned and the saved, who are placed, respectively, to Luther's left and right, just as they would stand in biblical imagery (Mt 25:33). One might attribute arrogance to Cranach's setting Luther in the place of the judging Christ. Yet, Cranach's Luther points not to himself but to the crucified Christ in whom God's predestinating will has been revealed. And here, though the eternal destiny of the damned unfolds supernaturally in hellish torments, the saved dwell in the here-and-now, in ordinary time, grateful for a divine election they have not earned and comforted in the faith that God's eternal judgment cannot be undone. The Last Judgment has already happened, not as the reiteration of a particular judgment based on the deeds of a life lived, but rather as the reiteration of God's eternal decree willed before the beginning of time and creation.

All this evidence confirms, then, that where a strong doctrine of grace prevails, the doctrine of the Last Judgment becomes anticlimactic. We can see the same result in Calvin's theology, which makes the doctrine of predestination even more central. Calvin refers to the Last Judgment or the last day occasionally in his *Institutes*, but typically to make the point that all God's hidden ways will be revealed in that end-time event.[32] It is noteworthy that Calvin devotes twenty pages of his magnum opus to a discussion of "The Final Resurrection" and yet mentions the Last Judgment only in passing to comment on God's appropriate condemnation of the reprobate.[33] Calvin does take account of the doctrine of the Last Judgment in the *Institutes*'s commentary on the Apostles' Creed where he concludes his exposition of the doctrine with the observation: "Hence arises a wonderful consolation: that we perceive judgment to be in the hands of him who has already destined us to share with him the honor of judging . . . ! . . . Moreover, he who now promises eternal blessedness through the gospel will then fulfill his promise in judgment."[34] For Calvin too, the doctrine of the Last Judgment is rendered as anticlimax, as a function of the doctrine of predestination.

I have noted that the Last Judgment continues to flourish meaningfully in contemporary fundamentalist churches. Yet, this meaningful flourishing does not keep the Last Judgment from the same sort of anticlimactic regard seen in our previous examples. Contemporary fundamentalist fiction evinces this eschatological anticlimax well. The "Left Behind" series comprises twelve novels, published between 1995 and 2004, that narrate the final years of the world's end time, culminating in the Last Judgment. Thus far in this chapter, I have explored popular belief in the Last Judgment by weighing the evidence of visual imagery in what were largely the nonliterate cultures of Catholic medieval Europe and Reformation Germany. The imagery of the "Left Behind" series captures the beliefs of dispensationalist Christians in our largely literate culture. Indeed, the series has sold more than sixty-three million books.

In the very first scene of the first novel, the end times begin as a fraction of the world's population is instantly raptured, whisked away bodily into heavenly glory. Those "left behind" side with or struggle against the increasing power of the antichrist in the course of the next seven years, a time of tribulation that comes to a close with the second coming of Christ. This event occupies the last volume of the series entitled *Glorious Appearing: The End of Days*. The authors of the series, Tim LaHaye and Jerry B. Jenkins, see their project as a novelization of the book of Revelation, which serves as a precise template for character and circumstance. As *Glorious Appearing* opens, the exactly predicted moment for the second coming is imminent as the battle of Armaggedon rages in Israel. Jesus miraculously appears in the sky over the battle, and yet is visible everywhere at once in the world. All the words he speaks that bring the end time to completion are biblical. The Word speaks only the literal words of Scripture in which devoted readers of the series have placed their faith. It is interesting to see how the authors portray the terrible effects of Jesus' words on the armies of the antichrist:

> [Jesus says] "Come near, you nations, to hear; and heed, you people! . . . For the indignation of the Lord is against all nations, and His fury against all their armies; He has utterly destroyed them, He has given them over to the slaughter."
>
> Rayford [a Christian soldier fighting the armies of the antichrist] watched through the binocs as men and women soldiers and horses seemed to explode where they stood. It was as if the very words of the Lord had superheated their blood, causing it to burst through their veins and skin.
>
> [Jesus continues] "Also their slain shall be thrown out; their stench shall rise from their corpses, and the mountains shall be melted with their blood." . . .
>
> Tens of thousands of foot soldiers dropped their weapons, grabbed their heads or their chests, fell to their knees, and writhed as they were invisibly sliced asunder [by the power of Jesus' words]. Their innards and entrails gushed to the desert floor, and as those

around them turned to run, they too were slain, their blood pooling and rising in the unforgiving brightness of the glory of Christ.[35]

This scene might very well be interpreted as a postmodern literary version of the medieval Last Judgment depictions of hell, though here Jesus is cast not only in the role of judge but also in the role of eschatological warrior whose words confirm the salvation of believers with every horrific death that he wills on the unbeliever.

The Last Judgment itself takes place in the book's final pages. After Jesus has Michael the Archangel cast Satan into the sulfurous pit, all the survivors of Armaggedon who witness this event cheer his defeat. The true believers among the survivors, though, suspect that their number is much smaller than those who gleefully celebrate Christ's victory, and anticipate that the judgment of Christ has yet to be completed.

Closely following the book of Revelation, the authors assume that Jesus has just commenced his thousand-year reign on earth, after which Satan will be released from the pit for a while only to be finally and consummately defeated by Christ (Rev 20:1–3). Yet, the number of the saved who will live beyond death in that millennial reign has not yet been reached, as another winnowing is required. The day after Satan is cast into the pit, Jesus' voice is heard by each of the millions of persons still alive. His summons to join him in Jerusalem immediately causes their miraculous appearance there, and he instructs them to take their place either to his right or to his left. One of the deserving saints, Rayford, notices that "those assembling on Jesus' right were scant compared to those on His left."[36] As the angel Gabriel calls on those assembled to worship the Kings of Kings, "[t]hose on the left of Jesus began rising to their feet, while all around Rayford, everyone remained kneeling." Rayford knowingly observes to a friend who kneels with him among the saved, "'Clearly two different groups of people here, eh, Chaim?'"[37] In the very next scene, Jesus exacts eternal justice on the hypocritical worshippers:

> Rayford watched, horrified despite knowing this was coming, as the "goats" to Jesus' left beat their breasts and fell wailing to the desert

floor, gnashing their teeth and pulling their hair. Jesus merely raised one hand a few inches and a yawning chasm opened in the earth, stretching far and wide enough to swallow all of them. They tumbled in, howling and screeching, but their wailing was soon quashed and all was silent when the earth closed itself again.[38]

As Rayford, the believing protagonist, testifies, there was no surprise in the judgmental consequences of belief and unbelief. Indeed, these consequences are not simply expected now, late in the twelfth and final novel of the series, as the saved and the damned stand clearly divided at Jesus' right or left hand. Rather, the narrative in each and every novel conveys the belief, quite likely shared by the reader, that the confession of Jesus as Lord through a literally interpreted biblical faith defines the ranks of the saved, and that this exclusive circle concomitantly marks those outside of it as the damned. The final disposition of divine judgment is readily visible in any present moment. Eschatological anticlimax in this style is rooted in a self-assuredness on the part of believers that their faithful response to God's grace in a particular style of faith visibly manifests their salvation. Here, the strong doctrine of grace that causes eschatological anticlimax takes shape in a dualistic view of humanity. On the one hand, a certain kind of ecclesial community that perceives itself to be beleaguered by a godless, secular world imagines itself already to be an enclave of the elect. On the other hand, this same community imagines all outsiders who do not eventually convert to their presumed Christian exceptionalism to be on the sinister side of the Last Judgment. Thus, as we see in the novel *Glorious Appearing*, there is no suspense in the Last Judgment, only retributive spectacle whose terrible violence at the hand of the Prince of Peace himself strangely confirms the righteousness of those who find this narrative appealing.

Our final site of eschatological anticlimax is contemporary Roman Catholic belief. I have argued that the disappearance of purgatory in the aftermath of Vatican II could be attributed to the appearance of a novel style of faith that I described as a noncompetitive spirituality. This style of faith represents a shift among a significant number of postconciliar Catholics toward an appreciation of traditional Pauline sensibilities. Grace here is credited as the gifted cause of the believer's salvation much more than it is in the traditional Matthean style of faith, which places a premium on the believer's enacted response to the offer of grace. This noncompetitive spirituality rejects the sort of competition for salvation that flourishes in the hierarchy of discipleship so typical of Catholic belief to the eve of Vatican II. And with what I have argued is the productive loss of that competitive spirituality and the eschatological anxiety it engendered, not only has purgatory disappeared but also the Last Judgment has ceased to matter to contemporary Catholic believers.

Unlike purgatory, the Last Judgment has not disappeared for postconciliar Catholics, who continue to profess their belief in the doctrine with every faithful recitation of the Nicene Creed. The event of the Last Judgment is affirmed as the literal sense of the tradition, uncontested faith developing stolidly and uncontroversially in the life of the Church.[39] There is no doubting, though, that the Last Judgment has lost the drama that energized the doctrine in medieval belief. Post - conciliar Catholicism's distinctive belief in the efficacy of grace has made the Last Judgment anticlimactic in its own particular way, and so contributed to the postmedieval, and now post-Tridentine, eclipse of the doctrine. Unlike medieval Catholics, present-day Catholics tend not to contemplate Last Judgment scenes in their own contemporary church art, and, if they did, it seems quite unlikely that they would approach the scene with the suspense that medieval viewers brought to their images, eager to imagine their own faces among the saved and horrified at the thought of the alternative.

In the remaining pages of this chapter, I argue that, while there is good cause to applaud the loss of a competitive spirituality in Catho - lic belief, there is every reason to be concerned about the loss of suspense in the doctrine of the Last Judgment that in turn has led to the loss of its very meaningfulness. There is, I propose, a productive form of eschatological suspense that is compatible with a noncompetitive spirituality. An appreciation for this eschatological suspense might rescue the Last Judgment from its present oblivion and offer new ways for believers to have an emotional stake in the doctrine. Along these lines, I will offer a hermeneutical reconstruction of the Last Judgment that develops the arguments presented thus far and that leads to an eschatological consideration of the communion of the saints in our closing chapter.

A LAST JUDGMENT THAT MATTERS

I begin by clarifying my judgment that something is theologically amiss if the doctrine of the Last Judgment lacks suspense. This is not a universal judgment that applies to all Christian traditions but rather one that must be confessionally differentiated. The anticlimactic regard for the Last Judgment in the Lutheran and Reformed traditions expresses a theological consistency with the importance they place on the doctrine of predestination. In these mainline Protestant traditions, the eschatological anticlimax of the Last Judgment is simply a function of a certain kind of strong doctrine of grace pointedly conveyed in the belief that God graciously has chosen the elect from all eternity and, at least by an absence of saving volition, has set the number of the reprobate as well. There is nothing intraconfessionally problematic about eschatological anticlimax here, since anticlimax articulates the very sort of faithfulness that one would expect of a Christian tradition that finds solace in the doctrine of predestination. In this context, it is theologically appropriate that the Last Judgment lacks suspense.

I would be less than forthcoming if I did not express my concern that there is something troubling about the version of eschatological anticlimax that appears in the fundamentalist fiction we have explored. At this site, eschatological anticlimax issues from a sense of righteousness that a certain kind of faith brings to the believer and which in turn encourages the believer to see those who do not share this faith as the reprobate. At its worst, the "Left Behind" series conflates difference, even Christian difference, with the damned. Moreover, this same righteousness finds delight in the punishment of the reprobate that is all the more disturbing since such suffering serves to strengthen the confidence of those who count themselves redemptively secure at Jesus' right hand. Anticlimax here conveys the belief that the clarity of one's chosen status reflects the clarity of a literal reading of Scripture to which the believer has fully assented. Thus defined, anticlimax is not a matter of confessional inconsistency but the effect of a skewed reading of the Christian canon that accords a peculiar hermeneutical priority to the book of Revelation. So read, Scripture now glorifies divine vengeance and sanctions violence toward the other that has plagued Christian history and which, in my judgment, is inconsistent with a true canonical vision of how the kingdom of God achieves its ends in time. In this context, the loss of eschatological suspense is the necessary outcome of a canonical plot that ploddingly narrates a salvational dualism.

Contemporary Roman Catholicism's version of eschatological anticlimax is, I think, an excellent example of confessional inconsistency. The recent development of a stronger doctrine of grace and a noncompetitive spirituality in significant quarters of postconciliar Catholicism has resulted not in the disappearance of the Last Judgment but in the loss of its doctrinal meaning. I have argued that we would do well to understand this novel development as an authentic sign of the Spirit's presence in the life of the Church that may, with the passing of time, be embraced as truthful tradition.[40] I have cautioned that any effort to find theological warrant for a Catholic recovery of ancient Pauline sensibilities and a noncompetitive spirituality cannot simply lay claim to the way these Christian commitments take shape in the classical Protestant tradition. However much postconciliar Catholicism appreciates the efficacy of divine grace in bringing believers to redemption, it needs ever to affirm the cooperation of human agency in the redemptive process. Grace, in a properly Catholic understanding, does not eclipse human responsibility but perfects its freely willed virtuous acts as small but requisite contributions to the fulfillment of resurrected life.[41] By the same token, the integrity of human responsibility *coram gratia* means that free volitional acts may betray their authentically cooperative relationship with grace and so be guilty of sin that insidiously ruptures the fragile ties that bind the communion of the saints on this side of the end of time.

This confessional affirmation of human responsibility before grace, exercised in both virtuous and evil acts, means that the loss of Catholic suspense in the Last Judgment could very well issue from a self-satisfied complacency that the infinite reaches of God's grace necessarily obviate the need for human responsibility or from a naïve denial of the power of moral evil. The more recent Catholic appreciation for Pauline sensibilities may legitimately acknowledge and more truly fathom the boundless love that the Trinitarian God extends to all creation and especially to the creature who will "bear the image of the man of heaven" (1 Cor 15:49). But it should not do so at the cost of a sense of eschatological climax and the immanent suspense that its anticipation rightly brings to a believer who contemplates the meaning of resurrected life, personally and universally.

By "suspense" I do not mean a sense of excitement in the face of the unknown. Suspense is a literary category that describes how a narrative ending is anticipated in an unfolding plot. That anticipation is a sign of the coherence of the story. Narrative unity forms as storied beginnings develop into the meaningful actions of characters in circumstance and with the maturation of that meaning, for well or for ill, in some limited horizon of time. Suspense is a quality of this unity that offers an index of just how much the immanent actions of characters narratively matter. Although it may be tempting to think that suspense is always a function of the obscurity or indeterminacy of an ending, such is not the case. Endings that have not yet been consummated are, to be sure, indeterminate and their proleptic contingency naturally seeps into any present moment in an unfolding plot. Frank Kermode makes this point nicely, and in a way that indirectly passes judgment on the fundamentalist fiction we have considered above:

> We cannot, of course, be denied an end; it is one of the great charms of books that they have to end. But unless we are extremely naïve, as some apocalyptic sects still are, we do not ask that they progress towards that end precisely as we have been given to believe. In fact we should expect only the most trivial work to conform to pre-existent types.[42]

And yet, the obscurity of an ending is not the only source of narrative suspense. Suspense issues just as much from the ways that characters exercise choice, comically or tragically, and the even more complex ways these choices gradually reveal narrative meaning in the course of a time that culminates in an ending, however expected or unexpected. Indeed, the eventfulness of character action in circumstance is so much a source of suspense that a narrative could commence with an announcement of its ending and still generate suspense through its portrayal of the unfolding character actions that bring the ending to fruition.[43] Suspense, then, does not necessarily issue from a narrative stance short of an ending, though the obscurity of closure often partially accounts for the generation of suspense. Suspense, though, is always dependent on the contingency of character actions and their consequences in the movement of plot.

If we apply these narratological observations to a Catholic appropriation of the Last Judgment, we can see why it is crucially important that meaningful suspense about the end time ever accompany a Catholic eschatological faith. The denial of such suspense, which seems to be typical in much of contemporary Catholic belief, could reflect the assumption that God's judgment is a graciously foregone conclusion, and that the absence of judgmental hiddenness undercuts the very possibility of suspense. Yet, as we have seen, the revelation of an ending is not a necessary condition for the loss of narrative suspense. The contingency of character action is the necessary condition of narrative suspense. Thus, it seems far more likely that the Last Judgment's loss of suspense is attributable to a contemporary Catholic belief that virtuous and sinful agency account for little in the drama of salvation. These two beliefs are clearly related. The reason that the Last Judgment has become a foregone conclusion in the faith of contemporary Catholics is that the utterly predictable end has already been revealed in the way grace is imagined to overwhelm human responsibility for virtuous contribution to salvation and for the avoidance of sinful strides to perdition. As Hans Urs von Balthasar has argued eloquently, it is not at all contrary to Catholic belief to hope that all are saved[44]—that the Last Judgment will have a graceful singularity about it that would simply dash the eschatological imagination of our medieval artists, accustomed as they were to the divisive juxtaposition of the saved and the damned. It is, however, utterly contrary to

Catholic belief to maintain that human responsibility exercised in words and deeds matters little in the face of God's grace, even if the motivation for that belief is a deep appreciation for the infinity of God's love and mercy.

Another way in which to understand the suspense that I have argued needs to permeate a Catholic regard for the Last Judgment is that it is an expression of a certain kind of hope, specifically a hope that draws its tensive expectation from a keen sense that salvational consequence is invested in our ethical engagement. In the pages that follow, I will affirm this hope theologically by defending the integrity of the recent novel development of a noncompetitive spirituality in the Catholic tradition and yet insisting that within this noncompetitive sphere the believer's words and deeds do salvationally matter and so are subject to God's judgment, and even the Last Judgment as an eschatological event. The first step in this argument requires us to turn again to the doctrine of the resurrection of the body.

Christian faith was born in the experience that God raised Jesus from the dead. As the first Christian writings appeared in the middle and late first century, they increasingly portrayed the reality of this event by stressing the bodiliness of the risen Christ. The fullness of Jesus' person, they proclaimed, and not merely his invisible inner life, had been raised from the dead and had entered eternal life. Luke's resurrected Christ announces the consummate reality of his resurrected person in his first appearance to his gathered disciples by saying "'Look at my hands and my feet; see that it is I myself. Touch me and see; for a ghost does not have flesh and bones as you see that I have'" (Lk 24:39). Christians encountered Jesus' words as a testimony to the full personal reality of their own anticipated resurrection, and by the early Christian centuries had developed an explanation of how their personal integrity would be miraculously restored by God in the face of the obvious fragmentation that death brought to their bodily selves. Although body and soul parted at the moment of death and God's judgment on the individual's eternal destiny was passed immediately on the soul, body and soul would be joined again at the Last Judgment where the particular judgment at death would be universally repeated. For nearly all of eternity, then, heaven and hell would be embodied places where entire persons would enjoy or suffer the consequences of how they enacted the entirety of their personal existence in time.

This account of how the resurrection of the body would occur offered a rich variety of meaning for the Christian imagination to fathom. First and foremost, the notion of a bodily resurrection at the end time established an anthropology that conveyed the Christian belief in metaphysical holism. It at once explained how the undeniable reality of physical dissolution in time could be miraculously undone, and affirmed the anthropological consequences of Christian belief in the created goodness of all things, including and especially the body, which is an ontic dimension of the only being created in the image of God (Gen 1:27). Second, the notion of a bodily resurrection at the end time affirmed a social character to God's judgment. God's restoration of all bodies was a prelude, a necessary condition, to their all standing together before the judging Christ, all to witness together how all would be judged. Third, and most importantly for our concerns here, the notion of a bodily resurrection at the end time unified all meaningful times and all meaningful events by having them all appear again, so to speak, in the simultaneous resurrection of the bodies whose lives defined meaningful time and whose wills enacted meaningful events. In this respect, all of history stood before the judgment seat of Christ in the universal resurrection.

These perspectives are especially crucial for my argument. The doctrine of personal, bodily resurrection highlights the unity of our selves not only in our temporal lives in the world but also eschatologically, after the event of the Last Judgment. That the time of our lives in the world is riddled with suspense is a common human experience. The kind of self we have been and continue to become, our very character, unfolds and manifests itself in our enacted intentions, which become real in and through our bodily performance. The suspense we experience in becoming selves is simply a function of the degree to which we take the project of becoming selves seriously by assuming responsibility for our words and deeds, not only in relation to each other but also in relation to God. Certainly there are lives lived without this moral suspense. Sometimes this is so because overwhelming trauma or loss tragically has vitiated the very sense of a personal narrative and its moral emplotment, and so the possibility of its suspenseful development. Sometimes and indeed often, this is sinfully so because personal volition succumbs to the pitfalls of apathy that very well could have been avoided by the application of will. A religious version of this apathy is one in which this lack of suspense reflects the presumptuous judgment that God's infinite love eclipses human responsibility, rendering it happily meaningless in that judgment's complacent confidence in grace. A Catholic appreciation for the moral narrative of our lives needs to value the suspense that comes both from a real sense of the moral engagement that makes us the enacted persons we are and from the anticipation that in God's judgment we will have to face the consequences of these efforts. This suspense appears in every act of faith, hope, and love with which we venture the meaningfulness of our lives. It appears in our experience of anticipation that our faith will be founded, our hope consummated, and our love fulfilled, that our lives in the end will be made whole.

The doctrine of bodily resurrection as a social event at the end of time calls attention to another kind of moral suspense whose theological significance we are especially well positioned to appreciate. A relatively recent theological debate between two German theologians, Gisbert Greshake and Joseph Ratzinger, later Pope Benedict XVI, can make this point well. Finding the notion of an end-time, bodily resurrection far too mythologized and so incomprehensible for contemporary believers, Greshake proposed that personal resurrection is better imagined as an event that takes place immediately upon death. Greshake's argument against the traditional conception of the bodily resurrection of all as a prelude to the Last Judgment especially finds fault with the anthropology that it presupposes. Even though the traditional conception finally insists on the eschatological unity of body and soul after the universal resurrection, its account of an interim state in which body and soul are separated between personal death and the Last Judgment, he claims, violates the holistic anthropology in which the Christian tradition has always believed.[45] Greshake maintains that an immediate bodily resurrection upon death, which assumes the unbroken unity of the person, satisfies an existentialist perspective on the self that the ancient categories of body and soul simply cannot make intelligible today.[46]

Against this position, Ratzinger argued that the claim for a resurrection upon death rather individualistically overlooks the historical dimensions of salvation, particularly the ways in which a person's actions continue to have consequences in future history that are simply unimaginable at any person's biological death. "When we die," Ratzinger avers, "we step beyond history. In a preliminary fashion, history is concluded—for me. But this does not mean that we lose our relation to history: the network of human relationality belongs to human nature itself. History would be deprived of its seriousness if resurrection occurred at the moment of death."[47] Were we to explain Ratzinger's insight in narratological categories, we could say that all of history is a soteriological story in which character action multiplies in meaning in every passing moment in ways that could never be anticipated in any present time short of history's end. Suspense in this extensive narrative, an index of meaningful action as it develops into its future, is generated by character actions and circumstances so numerous and complexly entwined that no human person could ever begin to explain or judge their consummate historical meaning. As we find ourselves living in an increasingly globalized world, in which cultural meanings and causalities are thickly interwoven, we are able to appreciate this theological perspective in ways that previous generations simply could not.[48]

These two fields of theological meaning suggested by the traditional doctrine of bodily resurrection—the temporal horizon of an individual life and the temporal horizon of all of history—offer avenues for us to follow in considering the different kinds of suspense with which the Last Judgment might productively be anticipated. Let us begin with individual judgment.

A contemporary Catholic appropriation of Pauline sensibilities requires that Paul's own suggestive statements on judgment be read through the eyes of the later Gospels, which set a high standard for enacted discipleship. Paul ever insists that the believer's natural deeds are incapable of saving virtue. As a consequence, he claims, "whatever the law says, it speaks to those who are under the law, so that every mouth may be silenced, and the whole world may be held accountable to God. For 'no human being will be justified in his sight' by deeds prescribed by the law, for through the law comes the knowledge of sin" (Rom 3:19–20). And yet, later in the same letter to the Romans, Paul imagines another exercise of God's will that utterly reverses the judgment on sin that humanity so thoroughly deserves. "And the free gift [of grace]," Paul continues, "is not like the effect of the one man's [Adam's] sin. For the judgment following one trespass brought condemnation, but the free gift following many trespasses brings justification" (Rom 5:16). Imagining that God's free gift of grace trumps the entire history of sin and death, Paul proclaims that the good news of the Christ event is that God does not enact the judgment that human justice expects of God. Sin has no such power to constrain the divine will, since "where sin increased, grace abounded all the more" (Rom 5:20).

Paul recognizes that human fallenness is inclined to pervert this marvelous revelation, to see in it a self-serving excuse for moral laxity. "Should we continue in sin," he rhetorically asks, "in order that grace may abound? By no means! How can we who died to sin go on living in it?" (Rom 6:1–2). As always for Paul, Christ is the paradigm of the new creation in which humanity's bondage to sin has already been broken by the graceful power of eternal life. "We know that Christ, being raised from the dead, will never die again; death no longer has dominion over him. The death he died he died to sin, once for all; but the life he lives he lives to God. So you also must consider yourselves dead to sin and alive to God in Christ Jesus" (Rom 6:9–11). Even if Paul denies the moral capacity of the human will to achieve righteousness through the law and under God's judgment, he yet expects those who have entered into Christ's resurrected life in grace to share too in the sinless state of that new life, and to act in their graced lives in ways that begin to approximate that sinless state. A Catholic reading of Paul would understand this sinless life as an eschatological state achieved to some small degree by our own volitional power.

Here, in my Catholic reconstruction of judgment, I follow Paul in distinguishing between God's judgment and God's graceful gift of eternal life, even if I will not follow Paul in understanding God's judgment as a universal condemnation of the entire history of human agency as a tragic mass of sin and death. Thus, with Paul, we should not imagine that God's judgment upon our personal lives will assign to each and every one of us some eschatological destiny that our actions deserve, and in a way that is unchangeably set and merely reiterated at the Last Judgment. If the recent Catholic sensibility for the gracious dimensions of eternal life is true, then what contemporary believers have fathomed is that eternal life is not a consequence of judgment but utterly the gift that Paul insists it is. Like a gift it cannot be merited or earned but only gratefully received with a deep sense of unworthiness. Eternal life is not a prize won in a competition, and certainly not a competition in which believers vie for God's favor, anxious that there are limits to the ranks of the saints and anxious even more in the knowledge that there are accomplished moral performances that threaten the eschatological security of those less accomplished. Grace is neither a commodity with determinate proportions nor a property whose possession is exclusive to some. Whether we imagine grace as uncreated, and so as the divine life itself, or as created, and so as the divinely willed energy of eternal life, it remains a self-effusive gift that transcends the sphere of competitive life so typical of the cultures that human beings have made and in which contest all too often takes the form of hatred, discrimination, and sinful violence. If Paul is right that grace cannot be restrained by the history of sin, then God's judgment on sin is entirely different from God's gift of grace and believers have every cause to hope that the gifted, and so noncompetitive, quality of grace means that eternal life is God's gift to all.

Let us imagine, then, that God's judgment, whether particular or universal, is not a verdict to which an eschatological destiny is assigned. Let us imagine instead that God's judgment reveals something about what each and every one of our selves has been in time, as well as something about what these same selves might be eschatologically. God's judgment would be a judgment on sin and the many ways that persons show themselves to be unworthy of grace. All of God's power is devoted to the destruction of the death and deathliness that distort the goodness of creation and in which the divine agency plays no role at all.[49] God's particular judgment presses the sinner to face his or her own contributions to that history of death and deathliness, and so all the ways that the sinner has acted to thwart God's providential love. Given the human capacity for self-deception and self-justification, one might imagine the particular judgment as a time of struggle in which the person judged persists in the sinful refusal that served the denial of moral responsibility throughout life. If, though, God's judgment and the graceful gift of eternal life are not the same, then we might imagine that, much in the manner that Catherine of Genoa describes purgatorial fire as the power of God's love that inevitably brings the soul to redemptive worthiness,[50] God's own presence, and perhaps the irresistibility of the Beatific Vision itself in the midst of judgment, breaks through sinful resistance and gracefully causes an acceptance of judgment that is simply the truth of a person's character at this moment, at life's end.[51] This acceptance is not in any way a self-judgment, but the realization that God's judgment is utterly true. God's judgment in such a scenario would be noncompetitive. It would not measure one person by comparison with another but rather would measure each and every person by a vision of who he or she might be, redeemed from his or her sinful resistance to grace, and so standing in authentic relationship to the community of persons and to creation. Universally given, grace is a gift that defies the competitive contours of sinful resistance, especially the person's vain and egotistical competition with grace and for grace.

We might imagine too that this judgmental revelation of personal sin and its effects has heavenly consequences. I argued in chapter 2 that the doctrine of bodily resurrection requires us to imagine the blessed dead as actively engaged in the work of salvation. The doctrine of bodily resurrection insists that our entire self, in its created goodness, shares eschatologically in the eternal life of God. Since our personal integrity, our character, is shaped by the enactment of our intentions, saved persons must continue to act eschatologically in order to be themselves. I proposed that one activity in which we might imagine the blessed dead to be engaged is the task of forgiveness among the saints. Let us now imagine that activity as one of the fruits of the particular judgment.

Perhaps the generosity of God's grace, that we have assumed contemporary Catholic sensibilities have truthfully discerned, continues its work beyond the particular judgment by motivating the blessed dead to practice the truth of themselves revealed in the particular judgment, and to do so by seeking forgiveness as penance for their sin and by graciously offering forgiveness as a virtuous response to the judgment of others. This network of forgiving activity on the part of the blessed dead allows them to be themselves, and even more themselves, through the enactment of character in community. I have insisted that sin may not dwell in heavenly life, and yet the effects of sin truly must endure eschatologically, since those effects, from actions we committed as perpetrators and from actions we suffered as victims, have shaped our identity in ways that continue to make us the persons we are even in the afterlife. There may be a host of activities in which the blessed dead engage. But theologically it is only fruitful for us to speculate about those that have a redemptive resonance. At first glance, it may seem as though asking for and offering forgiveness are really purgatorial behaviors and so appropriate for a vestibule to heaven but not for heaven itself. Yet, if we imagine redemption not simply as a lot settled at judgment but as a development that continues in the afterlife so that we will increasingly come to "bear the image of the man of heaven" (1 Cor 15:49), then it would be difficult to identify a relational practice more redemptive and so more gracious than sincerely requesting, receiving, and offering forgiveness.

The particular judgment, I suggest, marks out a redemption that is eschatologically different for us all. Dante suggested much the same in the *Paradiso* when he imagined the saved dwelling in various levels of the heavenly hierarchy, each celestial rung further from or closer to the heights of the Empyrean and each heavenly station a testimony to the earthly actions of those who dwell there. For Dante, though, judgment and salvation have been fixed in a way that leaves little for the blessed dead to do, except for the wonderfully passive activity of seeing God and what certainly must be the rare conversation with a passing poet in which the heavenly dweller expresses satisfaction with his or her heavenly lot. Instead, I have proposed that just as there is cause for suspense in anticipation of the particular judgment upon death, so too is there cause to imagine heavenly life as suspenseful.

Suspense attends the anticipation of the particular judgment because it will reveal the state of our character as it has been shaped by actions that continue to unfold meaningfully in the present moment. The time of our lives now has every reason to be held in suspense as we struggle to fill it with words and deeds that shape our relations to others and to God. Suspense attends our expectation of the particular judgment since that act of God will reveal how we have or have not been responsible to grace, and will do so in a way that likely will shatter the unrealistic self-judgments we offer ourselves on life's way. But if heavenly life is at all the eventful reconciliation that I have imagined it to be, then suspense too must characterize the eschatological busyness that continues to be enacted in the communion of the saints. This suspense does not derive, of course, from any sense that redemption could be undone in the course of the heavenly activity of forgiveness, but rather from an appreciation for the mystery that eschatological persons are in themselves and even more in the relations they form with each other, in this case through their reconciling actions.[52] Karl Rahner has offered the speculation on heavenly experience that God's incomprehensibility and mystery increase rather than diminish in the Beatific Vision enjoyed by the saints.[53] Perhaps, in finite analogy with his proposal, we might consider that one of the joys of heavenly life is that we will experience more profoundly the mystery of ourselves and other persons, and especially the mystery of how our meaningful relationships unfold in reconciling actions that continue to make us who we are, and that develop us into who we yet might be. Eschatological suspense would attend these events, arising in the experience of the saints as they ever encounter the determinate ways that reconciliation mysteriously transpires in their efforts to negotiate God's judgment under the graceful auspices of eternal life.

This same suspense can also be imagined to issue from an eschatological anticipation of the Last Judgment, which is shared by the saints on either side of the particular judgment. I have proposed, in effect, that the particular judgment is partial because the saints continue to engage in virtuous action that reconciles the effects of sin that linger in their very identities. There is another sense, however, in which the particular judgment is partial that can be inferred from the Greshake–Ratzinger debate on bodily resurrection.

Certainly Ratzinger is correct that the Last Judgment is theologically momentous because it comprises all of history, and so capitulates every particular judgment in ways that simply could not be known or even credibly imagined by any person in his or her particular judgment. Even though God omnisciently comprehends the redemption of history and the ways in which every individual's actions are causally implicated in that redemption beyond the scope of his or her life, the particular judgment remains just that, a person's confrontation with the moral truth of his or her life as it has unfolded only to a certain point within a never-ending trajectory. The particular judgment is partial not only because the blessed dead continue to exercise virtue and so eschatologically do not remain the selves that they were judged to be at death but also because the judgment before which they exercise virtue is not historically complete and will only be so as all of history comes to an end. The doctrine of the Last Judgment affirms the social nature of judgment, and an appreciation for the myriad ways that all of our lives are bound together across time and space that elude individual perception. No doubt, this judgment will reveal all the virtue that the saints have accomplished in their earthly lives and the ways in which their actions resonated beyond their worldly time to achieve the ends of the kingdom of God in history. It will reveal too the eschatological virtue of the blessed dead and their redemptive response to their partial judgment in the communion of the saints. Yet, this virtue, I have suggested, will continue throughout eternity in a heavenly kingdom in which the saints continue to be their holistically enacted selves. What will be truly "last" about the Last Judgment will be its revelation of the insidious finality of sin in all its historical proportions.

This judgment applies especially to social sin, which is the consequence of our collective moral failure and for that very reason so easy to misrepresent as beyond anyone's individual moral responsibility. In our own day, we have become more theologically aware of the inescapable power of social sin in the critiques of patriarchy, racism, structural poverty, ethnocentrism, colonialism, and environmental predation advanced by liberation theologies.[54] This heightened consciousness of social sin has been evinced as well, though more cautiously, in the magisterial teaching of John Paul II, which ever stresses that the root of sin lies in the human will rather than in social structures, however much social structures manifest the effects of personal volition.[55] While liberationist critiques rightly highlight a kind of sinfulness that the Christian tradition has ignored, the concern of John Paul II that social sin never be divorced from its cause in the actions of persons best serves our theological reconstruction of the Last Judgment. We can imagine the Last Judgment will make known all the hidden, ambiguous, self-excused, and self-justified ways in which our personal actions, by commission and omission, served the history of sin and so contributed to the historical legacy of sinfulness that the tradition calls original sin. This judgment will be a judgment about our actions as individuals, and about the ways the sins of our earthly lives continued to ripple out through history. But this judgment will also reveal the complex ways in which personal acts, consciously and unconsciously, so readily enter into partnership with evil in order to thwart God's graceful purposes, and so all the peculiar ways in which individuals are responsible for the horrors of history that, in history, would seem disconnected from their agency.

Perhaps we should describe the eschatological suspense that should be stirred by the believer's anticipation of the end time as a "guilty" suspense, a sensibility prompted by the recognition that the Last Judgment will both reveal and condemn all the dimensions of social sin to which each individual has certainly contributed, even if, in time here and now, these dimensions are beyond the grasp of even the most scrupulous conscience. Indeed, this guilty suspense should itself be the cause of judgmental anxiety, though rightly an anxiety about ethical failure in the face of grace, God's blessed alternative to judgment. No competition among the saints incites this anxiety since all are inescapably guilty in the vast, temporal reaches of this sinful history. The proper response to this guilty suspense is a hopeful suspense that derives from the belief that our actions are implicated in the judgment of all of history—not only sinfully but also virtuously—and that in spite of the inevitability of social sin, our personal actions can indeed have some role to play in countering the sinful structures that we make and by which we often seem to be overwhelmed. For the blessed dead in heaven, the Last Judgment is not simply a reiteration of the particular judgment but its completion, which, in its finely detailed revelation of the history of virtue and sin, deepens the mystery of personal relations in the communion of the saints as they continue to be reconciled in the gracious task of mutual forgiveness. Heavenly suspense short of the Last Judgment derives from the expectation that this event will manifest the resurrected integrity of all who have lived, both as individuals and in the otherwise unseen ways that our lives intersect across time and space. We might imagine that the Last Judgment stirs a sense of guilty suspense among the blessed dead too, indeed a guilty suspense that is all the more pointed since those who have passed through the particular judgment have come to see their culpability with a clarity that those in earthly life simply lack. In this regard, the blessed dead anticipate the Last Judgment as the fullest revelation of the effects of sin, theirs and others, that their eschatological virtue must continue to engage. And as we saw in the case of those on this side of death, guilty suspense before the Last Judgment properly incites a hopeful suspense on the part of the blessed dead that their heavenly virtue will testify to God's gracious providence at history's final act and in some small way work toward the realization of his kingdom.[56]

Finally, there is a sense of suspense toward the Last Judgment that all the saints should share, whether they dwell in this world or the next. It is a suspense born of hope, but not the tensive hope we have described thus far which issues from the Catholic belief that our actions are responsible to grace. Rather, this is a suspense generated by God's infinite love alone and the hope that God's grace and mercy will extend to all. If God's judgment and God's grace are not the same, as Paul insists, then this hope is authentically Christian and at once an ardent act of faith in a God who is believed to be so gracious toward creation and so intent on the subversion of evil that this God would not allow any creature to be lost when eternal life offers an infinite horizon for one's redemptive response to judgment to be enacted.[57]

This utterly noncompetitive hope, that is at once an act of faith, delights in the prospect that God's judgment on every life and on all of history will not bring the eschatological consequences imagined by the medieval artists who represented the Last Judgment, and indeed by Catholic believers throughout the tradition until our most recent days.

There is a profound symbolism in the Catholic imaginary's portrayal of the Last Judgment as the prerogative of Christ, even though it sees God in the role of judge at the particular judgment. This reservation of judgment on the last day to the Son certainly has its historical roots in the apocalyptic faith of the very first Christians and their expectation that the last day, and the appearance of their Savior, would soon be upon them. But even though this symbolism began then and there, its power and beauty lie even more in its capacity to develop traditionally. The most ardent Christian hope, I propose, will see in the image of the judging Christ the prospect of apocatastasis, and will find in his incarnated presence a living testimony to the difference between God's judgment and the eschatological destiny of those who yet stand under that judgment. Such a hope will hope that just as the divine Word shared in the humanity of all, so too will all share in the eternal life of the divine Word.[58] Although the Last Judgment has stirred suspense throughout most of the Catholic tradition, it has done so in an anxious pitch that has resonated throughout the hierarchy of discipleship. Imagining the Last Judgment as I have proposed offers contemporary Catholic sensibilities a different kind of eschatological suspense that I hope will enable the Last Judgment to matter for us, and in a way that is theologically faithful to the noncompetitive reality of God's grace.

CHAPTER 5

Forgiveness in the Communion of the Saints

Eschatology in a Noncompetitive Key

As much as the saints have served as paradigms of discipleship, as inspiring role models for Christic imitation, and as eschatological beacons for the Christian journey to the fullness of God's kingdom, their powerful presence in the tradition also has created an effect that I have called the hierarchy of discipleship. Hierarchy, of course, is one of the traditional features of the communion of the saints. Dante in the *Para - diso* depicts heaven as a saintly hierarchy even for those who have passed from the Church militant to the Church triumphant. In his poetic description, heaven below its highest heights—from the realm of the fixed stars to the lowest celestial rung of the moon—is differentiated not only by distance from the elevated reaches of the Empyrean but also according to the merits of the saved, each heavenly inhabitant assigned his or her proper place by divine judgment at death.

Recently, Elizabeth Johnson has criticized this hierarchy in what she calls a "patrons–petitioners" understanding of the communion of the saints that has flourished throughout nearly all Catholic history.

Based on the social stratification of the early medieval feudal system, this model of the communion sees believers as the needy supplicants of morally accomplished saints who dispense spiritual gifts from beyond the grave, much in the manner of worldly lords doling out material favors to their powerless clients. Inequality permeates this exchange, which assumes that the effects of redemption issue from the saintly patron's hierarchical distance from the worldly petitioner. Johnson judges this hierarchy to compromise a more authentic and deeply traditional understanding and practice of the communion of the saints that she calls the "companionship of friends" model, one that stresses the egalitarian nature of the one saintly community that stretches from earth to heaven. For Johnson, the "companionship of friends" model counters the hierarchical structure of the traditional saintly communion, which, she argues, so easily reifies the sinful propensity to distinguish between superior and inferior persons by seizing on human differences of all sorts—including gender—to warrant such marginalizing judgments.[1]

My own concern with the hierarchy of discipleship appreciates Johnson's perspective, but offers a somewhat different account of the hierarchy and its consequences. The hierarchy of discipleship, I have argued, is a function of the Matthean style of faith, the traditional Catholic sensibility that human works—words and deeds—contribute in some significant way to one's eschatological destiny fixed by God's judgment at death. The hierarchy of discipleship is a way of configuring relationships in this Catholic imaginary, and issues from the perception of believers that some, and to be sure, only a few, of their number are such accomplished imitators of Christ that God's favorable judgment upon their lives is beyond doubt. Their stellar example of discipleship establishes the apex of the hierarchy. It produces an emotional response in all its lower reaches that I have called eschatological anxiety about the prospects for favorable judgment, an anxiety generated by the unavoidable comparison that those lower in the hierarchy make between their judgment by God and what they presume is God's blatantly favorable judgment of the spiritually accomplished. This perception gravitates around the Catholic ascetical tradition. The martyr's consummate example of discipleship fuels eschatological anxiety in, and at the very least in the representation of, the lives of the tradition's greatest ascetical saints like Antony and Francis, just as the great ascetical saints stir the anxiety of ordinary ascetics. The vowed lives of ordinary ascetics, in turn, offer an anxious measure to the lives of laypersons whose worldly attentions seem to falter in comparison with the lifelong dedication of monks, nuns, and priests to the Matthean path to heaven.

This eschatological anxiety is the consequence of what I have called a competitive spirituality that has dominated the Catholic tradition from its earliest beginnings until Vatican II. I have argued that the rise of this competitive spirituality through the medieval valorization of ascetical practice gave birth to the doctrine of purgatory, as ascetical and lay believers both sought ways of imagining a greater span of time than a single, earthly life in order to compete with whatever more successful competitors they marked out—martyrs, ascetical saints, or simply ascetics—as their standards of certain heavenly reward. Purgatory, then, developed doctrinally in order to comfort the eschatological anxiety that saturated a Catholic culture shaped by Matthean sensibilities. I have suggested that the disappearance of purgatory from much of postconciliar belief and practice can be attributed to the novel development of a noncompetitive spirituality in the recent Catholic tradition, a spirituality that appreciates the ancient Pauline sensibility of faith, which has been all but obscured in the tradition's commitment to Matthean emphases.

In the previous chapter, I began the task of thinking through the implications of a noncompetitive spirituality for eschatology. My efforts to imagine God's judgment in a noncompetitive way appreciated the Pauline distinction between God's judgment and God's grace. That distinction in turn supported my proposal that the particular judgment might not be God's assignment of eschatological destiny to earthly merit, but instead a revelation of what we sinfully have been and what we redemptively might yet become in the divine plan. My noncompetitive regard for the Last Judgment allowed the expression of the Christian hope that not only God's love but also God's salvation extends to all, and to attempt a recovery of the tradition's minority theology of universal salvation. It also enabled me to reprise my earlier proposal that the blessed dead in heaven be imagined as ever engaged in the work of mutual forgiveness so that judgment could be configured as an eschatological project, one with both personal and social dimensions.

Here, in our concluding chapter, I bring this argument one step further by considering what the traditional Catholic doctrine of the communion of the saints might look like from the perspective of the noncompetitive spirituality that has been sketched thus far. There are many paths that might be pursued toward this end. The moral task of forgiveness has been a fruitful one to follow thus far, and its further pursuit will end this book-length reflection on the "last things," a speculative project that I have argued is very much worth the believer's while. This noncompetitive path, like all the others I might have pursued, will be suspicious of the communion of the saints conceived along the lines of the traditional hierarchy of discipleship and its consequences for the life of faith and the Church.

THE PROBLEM OF FORGIVENESS

As we have seen, the ancient profession of faith, the Apostles' Creed, closely links the Catholic beliefs in the "communion of the saints," the "forgiveness of sins," and resurrected life. After ending its confessional narrative of the redemptive events of the Savior's life with the assertion that "He will come again to judge the living and the dead," the Creed concludes by professing the common faith of the Church expressed as the words of the individual believer: "I believe in the Holy Spirit, the holy catholic Church, the communion of saints, the forgiveness of sins, the resurrection of the body, and the life everlasting."[2] These words of the time-honored symbol, closely reiterated in the closing lines of the Nicene Creed, envisage redemption as forgiveness, infer that forgiveness transpires in the communion of the saints, and suggest that eternal life is the consequence of the redemption that forgiveness brings. In a plain-sense understanding of the Creed, though, forgiveness is typically understood as an act of God's infinite love. It is God's forgiveness of the sins of the world that brings about the redemption of humanity, and this act of forgiveness unfolds in the event of the cross in which, paradoxically, God's forgiving love encounters the merciless violence of the world.[3] It is God's forgiveness that brings humanity beyond the consequences of its guilt, from the deathliness that it so predictably makes in the world to the miraculous gift of eternal life. Here, though, I wish to reflect a bit more on the redemptive power of forgiveness not only in God's forgiveness of sins but also as an ongoing activity in the communion of the saints, as we find that community in this world and in the next.

Perhaps it is not surprising that Christians are inclined to think of forgiveness nearly entirely as the divine act of redemption itself. If forgiveness is something that God does, then no creaturely will or thought need trouble very much about the remarkable difficulty that authentic forgiveness otherwise seems to pose for the person who might approach forgiveness as a moral obligation. Indeed, there are strains in contemporary philosophical thought that seriously question whether forgiveness is humanly possible. We can see this perspective articulated in the work of Jacques Derrida and John Milbank.

In his essay "On Forgiveness," Derrida portrays forgiveness as such an anomalous act that its appearance in time would shatter the ordinary and expected ties of human relationship. "Forgiveness," he maintains, "is not, it *should not be*, normal, normative, normalizing. It *should* remain exceptional and extraordinary, in the face of the impossible: as if it interrupted the ordinary course of historical temporality."[4] Derrida does not claim that forgiveness *is* impossible, though neither does he affirm its possibility. Rather, his insistence that forgiveness, to be such, must take place in the face of the impossible acknowledges that forgiveness, to be forgiveness, must be a response to evil of such proportions that forgiveness would present itself as an impossible act. Derrida makes this point strikingly in the following passage:

> It is necessary, it seems to me, to begin from the fact that, yes, there is the unforgivable. Is this not, in truth, the only thing to forgive? The only thing that *calls* for forgiveness? If one is only prepared to forgive what appears forgivable, what the church calls 'venial sin,' then the very idea of forgiveness would disappear.

> If there is something to forgive, it would be what in religious language is called mortal sin, the worst, the unforgivable crime or harm. From which comes the aporia, which can be described in its dry and implacable formality, without mercy: forgiveness forgives only the unforgivable. One cannot, or should not, forgive; there is only forgiveness, if there is any, where there is the unforgivable. That is to say that forgiveness must announce itself as impossibility itself. It can only be possible in doing the impossible.[5]

Construed by Derrida not as impossible but as "the impossible," forgiveness, were it truly to occur, would spring from that extraordinarily rare human possibility in which evil's vicious cycle of violence is rebuffed by a moral response that refuses participation in evil's tragically predictable, ongoing effects and that does so simply for the sake of doing so, without self-interest or the accounting of consequence.

Clearly, Derrida is not imagining forgiveness as the acceptance of an apology in the face of a personal slight. That kind of reconciliation is ordinary and common, and in many respects a daily event. Since Derrida offers philosophical interpretation apart from any theistic commitment, forgiveness in his view is something like a secular miracle. In its motivational purity, it transcends all terms or any hint of reciprocity. More than amnesty or reconciliation, which involve transaction and mediation, forgiveness is unconditional, eschewing any recognition of guilt on the part of the guilty or any benefit whatsoever on the part of the victim forgiving the unforgivable. Thus, for Derrida, the paradox of forgiveness is that the "conditions" of its possibility seem to be the impossible, and all the more so as Derrida weighs this paradox against the tragic history of atrocities and intractable conflicts between peoples and nations. In light of this account, it is no wonder that he insists that "pure and unconditional forgiveness, in order to have its own meaning, must have no 'meaning,' no finality, even no intelligibility." "It is," he asserts, "a madness of the impossible."[6]

John Milbank too has argued that forgiveness between human persons explained reasonably is beset by standards that seem to conspire against its actual occurrence. There are, he claims, several aporias—logical dead-ends—that call into question the coherence of a purely human act of forgiveness. First, there is the problem of "who" forgives. Only the victim can forgive, and the victims of history are too numerous and their victimization too intertwined for anyone to account for the practically infinite burden of what needs to be forgiven. Moreover, he observes, "the true victims do not survive at all in order to proffer pardon."[7] Second, time presents insuperable difficulties to the act of forgiveness since acts of evil cannot be expunged from the past. They endure as matters of fact, just as do the initial hatred and desire for revenge that they stir on the part of the victim. Even if the passing of time allows forgiveness to emerge from an alternate perspective on the evil done, it is questionable whether the mitigated memory now seemingly capable of forgiveness truly represents the guilty perpetrator or the evil done, thus calling into question the reality of the forgiveness offered. With the passing of more time, of course, the victim who might forgive disappears in his or her death.[8]

A third obstacle concerns the act of forgetting that forgiveness would seem to require. If the past remains the past, and, a fortiori, the evil past remains the evil past, then forgetting as a precondition to forgiveness would require the dissolution of a continuous moral memory in time, a requirement that would dissolve moral agency itself. Were we to posit that dissolution as a thought-experiment, then an actually forgotten evil would transcend moral response since nothing would lie in one's actual experience to prompt the challenge of forgiveness.[9] Yet a fourth difficulty to the possibility of forgiveness attends the common assumption that forgiveness possesses finality in the closure it is expected to bring to the evil forgiven. Even though this desire for forgiving closure is emotionally understandable, it remains, for Milbank, a chimaera, "an illusory eschaton" as he strikingly puts it. Were such closure achieved in the negative acts of forgetting the evil perpetrated or leaving behind hatred and indignation, then, once again, a contradiction ensues. For if, he notes, "one should not harbour resentment, then equally one should not forget injustice, not only in order to honour the memories of its victims, but also in order to remind oneself of possible future danger."[10] The very closure that aims to restore peace and stability becomes itself the seed of a future evil.

A fifth and final obstacle to forgiveness concerns an issue that Derrida placed at the heart of his understanding of forgiveness as the impossible, that is, the purity of motive that true forgiveness, as unconditional, would seem to require. Here we must remind ourselves that Milbank's account of these aporias, including the one we are about to consider, addresses the problem of forgiveness considered as an interhuman act, in an immanentist setting, apart from belief in, and so the assumption of relationship to, God. Indeed, Milbank affirms that within Christian assumptions a creaturely act of forgiveness escapes the reasonable obstacles he enumerates, since, Christianly understood, forgiveness is a finite extension of the infinite divine love that one has already received. In such a theological frame of reference, the issue of purity of motive in forgiving does not arise, since the human forgiver already stands in the giftedness of the divine forgiveness in which God has healed the relationship broken by sin, and in that grace—nothing less than infinite love—there is nothing more to receive. The believer's forgiveness of others, then, like all forms of giving, "is not enacted in order to achieve purity of motive" but rather "to re-establish a reciprocity only possible as the attainment of a mysterious harmony through its participation in the divine infinite harmony."[11] Beyond the assumptions of such a theological field of explanation, though, forgiveness runs aground on the shoals of self-interest. Within the frailty of human desire, the offer of forgiveness cannot help but be an exchange or trade that barters for the false security of an illusory peace, for the lie that suffering and death have not taken their toll, or for the grandiose status of one who, through the forgiving interruption of justice, anarchically stands above the law. As an interhuman calculation, Milbank concludes, "forgiveness never can be offered for its own sake."[12]

Like Derrida, Milbank wishes to problematize forgiveness explained exclusively "from below," as a considered human act that generates moral ideals, expectations, discourse, and commitment in the realm of personal relations, but which, under the scrutiny of reasoned analysis, fails to escape incoherence, contradiction, and the vagaries of self-interest, all of which subvert its volitional integrity. True to his philosophical claim that meaning proliferates infinitely, always giving rise to a supplement that questions its predecessor, Derrida is unwilling to say that forgiveness exists as an accomplishable act. Human forgiveness is his sole frame of reference, and he is content to catalogue the overwhelming obstacles that would need to be overcome were someone to forgive with the unconditional purity that forgiveness would require. To invoke an analogy that I suggested before, he wishes to describe what a natural miracle would be were it to occur, but is quite unwilling to say that one ever has. Milbank despairs of human forgiveness as the work of humanity's natural powers, fallen as he believes them to be. But he affirms human forgiveness as a graced act that extends the reconciliation with which God has gifted humanity. God has no need to forgive humanity, since God cannot be aggrieved or victimized. It is, he claims, the humanity of Christ, brutally victimized by the world's sinful violence, that forgives fallen humanity and which, through its incarnational union with the divine Logos, gracefully enables humanity to participate in this divine practice of reconciliation. "Therefore," Milbank concludes, "divine redemption is not God's forgiving us, but rather his giving us the gift of the capacity for forgiveness."[13]

As different as they are in their positions, Derrida and Milbank share a common assumption that true forgiveness is an act of "grace." This is an expected assumption for a Christian thinker like Milbank who explains forgiveness as a positive act that in its giftedness cannot be an exchange between mutual beneficiaries, since the divine nature transcends need. Derrida, proceeding from an atheistic stance, surprisingly offers us a secular analogue for grace in his expectation that forgiveness, like his understanding of a gift, is utterly unconditional, and then, unsurprisingly, wonders if such grace really exists, since the accomplishment of such moral purity presents the impossible. This tension enables Derrida to deconstruct moral intention, which, considered in its historical proportions, allows him in turn to envisage the apparent failure of forgiveness as a secular analogue of original sin.

It seems correct to me to judge forgiveness to be a gifted act that defies the ordinary economy of exchange. I will argue, though, following Milbank, that the giftedness of forgiveness does not preclude the expectation of response and so what Derrida would regard as the unacceptable condition of reciprocity.[14] This argument, I hope, will elucidate my previous discussion of eschatological forgiveness and its bearing on the Catholic belief in the communion of the saints.

FORGIVENESS IN CATHOLIC ANTHROPOLOGY

Derrida, indirectly and in spite of his atheistic assumptions, and Milbank, quite explicitly, explain forgiveness by appeal to a Christian understanding of grace. For both thinkers, forgiveness is fundamentally a divine act, whether or not God exists. Both too elucidate this "graceful" character of forgiveness by appealing to the category of "gift," and it is here that we are able to appreciate the differences between their respective interpretations. For Derrida, a gift, by its very nature, is unconditional and purely so. To understand forgiveness as gift requires that forgiveness transcend any condition, including, and perhaps even especially, the condition of reciprocity. Derrida so affirms the purity of gift, and so the purity of forgiveness as an instance of gift, that only the finality of death, which precludes the very possibility of exchange, can meet the measure of purity, and so integrity, that he expects of gift.[15] Milbank too thinks that reciprocity subverts forgiveness in an utterly reasonable account of interhuman forgiveness, though he does not think that merely interhuman forgiveness at all exhausts the realm in which forgiveness might transpire. Thus, he rejects Derrida's notion of "pure gift" for a host of reasons, and most basically for the reason that Derrida's immanentist account cannot be true to the reality of God and God's creation. Milbank maintains that forgiveness is unconditional in the sense that its appearance in the incarnation is an expression of God's eternal love which, as grace, is unconditional. In the redemption that God works and reveals in the incarnation, God gives to humanity the gift of the capacity to forgive. Redemption embraces sinful humanity into a "participation" in this divine act, enabling graced persons to enter into restored relationship with God. The divine gift, and its expression in forgiveness, does not obliterate the conditional, for to do so would destroy the very terms of relationship that forgiveness restores. Milbank, in explicit opposition to Derrida, thus affirms the existence of reciprocity within the dynamics of the gift, as he has argued to much effect in his earlier work on the "gift-exchange" that his reflections on forgiveness presuppose. Reciprocity, he insists, "is as much as a condition for the gift as gift is for reciprocity." Envisaged theologically, this observation leads him to affirm that "the one given condition of the gift . . . [is] that we love God because God first loved us."[16]

I find Milbank's refutation of the Derridian notion of "pure gift," and thus "pure forgiveness," to be a helpful first step in our continuing attention to eschatological forgiveness. At the very least, Milbank's objection to Derrida's deconstructive stance is an expression of his belief that forgiveness, as an article of faith, cannot be "the impossible" in a Christian frame of explanation. In Milbank's judgment, forgiveness apart from the condition of reciprocity would vitiate the relationship that faith affirms toward God, and that authentic forgiveness, affirmed in faith, must be. It matters not, for Milbank, that faith, its redemptive experience of forgiveness, and its extension to others in forgiveness are forms of reciprocity that are themselves gifted, for this is true of all conditions that appear in the realm of creation where existence itself is a gift. Reciprocity in relationship to God must be indescribably unequal given the nature of God and the nature of the creature. Perhaps Milbank tries modestly to capture this indescribability when he speaks of the believer's forgiveness of others as "a reciprocity only possible as the attainment of a mysterious harmony through its participation in the divine infinite harmony."[17] As Sarah Coakley has pointed out, Milbank does not explain in any detail, or perhaps even at all, what this participation in God is that rescues reciprocity from worldly economy.[18] A generous reading would understand "participation" to express the graced quality of the reciprocity that Milbank affirms in the gift exchange with God, or, even more simply, his claim that authentic relationship always transpires through God's prevenient grace.

As much as Milbank's notion of the gracefully purified gift exchange enables us to appreciate the limitations of Derrida's understanding of gift and forgiveness as unconditional and the impossible, I believe that his reflections do not bring us far enough in appreciating the workings of forgiveness. One important limitation is that Milbank's difference with Derrida causes him to pay very little attention to the workings of graced human forgiveness. He is content to account theologically for the conditions of its possibility and remains largely unconcerned about how human forgiveness actually transpires. Here, I propose another template for understanding the conditions of forgiveness that I hope will advance our appreciation for how human forgiveness occurs in practice, namely, the Tridentine teaching on justification.

The Tridentine doctrine has already informed my Catholic recovery of a Pauline anthropology of grace in the previous chapter on judgment. According to the Council of Trent's "Decree on Justification," God's grace is the source of the justification that brings the human person to eternal life, and the offer of this grace is not merited. Justification, though founded in grace, yet requires the human person's freely willed assent and cooperation. These forms of reciprocity, though minimal and not at all causative, are necessary in order for justification to be brought to completion. Grace is an "invitation" that must be answered, an offer that must be accepted. The person touched by God's saving grace stands under responsibility to grace, a responsibility that requires the enacted embrace of the divine gift. This response has an integrity of its own. Through it, Trent teaches, those who are aided by God's grace "turn towards their own justification by giving free assent to and co-operating with this same grace."[19] From this reciprocity come the benefits of eternal life. While Trent's teaching could be understood to affirm the same reciprocity *coram gratia* on which Milbank insists, the conciliar decree does not invoke the language of "participation" in order to express this reciprocity. Human agency, even though under the auspices of grace, is clearly distinguished from divine agency, and through this distinction human agency's inherent power and soteriological obligation to God are just as clearly defined. Were we to imagine the divine offer of justification as the forgiveness of sins, then just as clearly God's offer of forgiveness in Catholic teaching could not be unconditional or one-sided. Forgiveness would require the freely willed cooperation of the forgiven, at the very least through the acceptance of the grace of the forgiveness offered. Trent, we might say, by implication calls for reciprocity in the relationship between the divine forgiver and the forgiven in order for forgiveness to be brought to completion.

Thus far in my argument, I have proposed an eschatological soteriology that stresses the role of forgiveness as an ongoing activity in the communion of the saints. To this point, though, I have considered forgiveness as an activity of the blessed dead in the heavenly dimensions of that communion, an activity of sufficient significance—and no doubt there are many more—to justify the pursuit of a speculative approach to theological interpretation. Now, let us consider the relationship between forgiveness in the Church militant and in the Church triumphant, directed by Trent's teaching on justification and its implications for forgiveness.

If Trent's teaching on justification infers something about the workings of divine forgiveness, then, by analogy, it may also suggest something important about interhuman forgiveness explained not within the limits of reason alone, but theologically. In articulating my position on the often vexing matter of just what forgiveness is, I begin by affirming that forgiveness is a personal relationship that by definition entails reciprocity, in this case, in the giving and accepting of forgiveness. For Derrida, personal relationship is a fundamental quality of forgiveness, though, paradoxically, the very quality that places it in the circumstance of the impossible. Forgiveness, in his view, must, but can never, transcend the conditions of exchange that relationship requires, thus setting forgiveness in a bind from which it can never be rescued. Finally, Derrida's sophisticated skepticism holds that forgiveness should be a personal relationship but may not be. A far more common view that in effect denies the reciprocal nature of forgiveness maintains that the victim may grant forgiveness to the offender irrespective of the offender's remorse, acceptance, or even knowledge of the forgiveness granted. Forgiveness so imagined is unilateral, an unconditionally generous act that overlooks the need for reciprocity in order to bring forgiveness to consummation. Often, though not always, this view emerges from Christian commitments in which the believer judges that he or she is obliged to enact Jesus' command to forgive ceaselessly (Mt 18:22). Were forgiveness necessarily a personal relationship entailing reciprocity, then this command could not be obeyed consistently in the realm of offense, since reciprocity between victim and victimizer so rarely occurs. Considered from the perspective of forgiveness as reciprocity, this unilateral act is better understood as an expression of the victim's ability to pass beyond the suffering and anger caused by the actions of the offender. Although offered as forgiveness, this act is better understood as a healing gesture that rebuffs evil not by the positive act of reconciliation but by the negative act of dismissing the emotional burden of the past. As the defeat of anger and the desire for revenge, it is virtue even if not forgiveness.[20]

Forgiveness as a personal relationship presupposes an engaged reciprocity. In anthropological analogy to Trent's teaching on justification, interhuman forgiveness requires both graceful offer and responsible, free acceptance. Unlike the relationship between God and creature, however, creaturely forgiveness does not necessarily occur in that sequence, which in the act of divine forgiveness is fixed by God's eternity and so the timeless prevenience of grace. So many initiatives offered in a variety of sequence might venture forgiveness between finite persons. Human forgiveness can begin with the guilt and remorse of the perpetrator, the perpetrator's recognition of the need for forgiveness, and the request for forgiveness. This request in turn could break into the world of the victim as a gracious surprise or as a monstrous assault that attempts to deny the victim's suffering. Or, the initiative to forgiving relationship could begin with the victim's offer of forgiveness that fails to break through the perpetrator's self-justifying denial of wrongdoing or that, in its remarkable graciousness, begins the conversion of the perpetrator that authentic forgiveness will achieve in some way. However the dynamics of encounter occur, forgiveness eventually requires the offer of forgiveness on the part of the victim and the acceptance of forgiveness on the part of the perpetrator. Forgiveness is a personal relationship and to be so it must transpire in a meaningful reciprocity that unfolds in reconciling words and deeds that restore communion between the victim and the victimizer.

Theologically explained, forgiving reciprocity always occurs under the economy of grace, as do all good things. Neither the forgiving offer of the victim nor the acceptance of forgiveness by the perpetrator could contribute to their moral partnership unless their energies were buoyed by grace. This sort of economy does involve exchange, though not the kind of exchange that typically occurs in the economies that cultures have constructed in order to secure goods and services required by instinct and self-interested desire. Nor would it be correct to say that forgiveness is aneconomic since grace is its source and the setting for its moral exchange. Grace itself is aneconomic but its workings in redemption are not. Moreover, grace does not nullify sin or the effects of sin, which continue to be tragic matters of fact in our common and personal histories. The economy of grace conducts its business in the environs of sin. Thus, an act of grace that enables forgiveness does not bring forgiveness to a purity that transcends every dimension of sinful exchange involving self-interest and the expectation of consequence. Such an idealized standard, as set by Derrida, finally despairs of forgiveness by imagining it as a hypothetical divine act in a godless world. However much an act of forgiveness unfolds in the midst of sinful self-interest always already in the ambit of grace, it requires both the offer and the acceptance of forgiveness by graced natural powers exercised in the creaturely conditions of personal freedom.

Forgiveness understood along the lines of a Catholic anthropology does not present us with the impossible. But neither should we be sanguine about the task of forgiveness. Derrida's sensibilities on the prospect of forgiveness are not at all strange, even if we finally judge them to be overstated. Forgiveness happens, but happens rarely if only because the moral partnership through which it comes to be is so difficult to achieve. So often, the perpetrator fails to recognize the need for forgiveness, instead living the lie of self-righteousness or hiding in the grotesque defense that the victim is actually the guilty perpetrator. Or, the perpetrator recognizes personal guilt and so the need for forgiveness, but fails to request it, since doing so would lead to the loss of moral face. Or yet still, the perpetrator could recognize the need for forgiveness and request it, only to find the victim unable to respond generously because the request is judged to be a mockery of the evil suffered, or because the evil committed has damaged the character of the victim that might previously have been capable of moral heroism, or simply because the need for forgiveness itself is a sign of a lack of trust between the parties encountering the possibility of reconciliation.

So often, the victim fails to offer the perpetrator forgiveness for all the reasons considered above and uncountable reasons we have not. Or, the victim offers forgiveness only to find that the act of astonishing generosity is neither needed nor wanted, since the offer itself presupposes a truthful self-regard that the perpetrator lacks or a willingness on the part of the perpetrator to accept the responsibility of forgiveness in the difficult moral work of conversion and reconciliation. Forgiveness is so rare precisely because the relationship in which it is established requires the rejection of the ordinary terms of human judgment, defined as they are by the circumstances of sin and into which grace enters only as a difficult struggle.

The thick history of human sinfulness calls for forgiveness of seemingly infinite proportions, and only grace is up to the task set by the tragic power of sin. The infinite love of God timelessly accomplishes what human initiative most often even fails to begin. The reciprocity that grace expects is not grace, even if it is graced. Yet, forgiveness enacted by human energies imitates the divine act of redemption and so extends the effects of redemption into the realm of human persons that the Catholic tradition calls the communion of the saints. That human forgiveness happens rarely has no bearing on the power of grace. Nevertheless, the failure of its remarkable economy on the part of its recipients continues to form rifts in the communion of the saints as this failure in graceful cooperation causes sin to abound all the more.

If this analysis of the virtue of forgiveness and the prevalence of its moral failure in life rings true, then the many rifts in the communion of the saints carved by the failure of forgiveness pass into the heavenly dimensions of the communion unhealed. These rifts endure not as sin but as the effects of sin that continue to define the identities of perpetrator and victim. They are the redeemed, and yet unreconciled, breaches between and among persons that continue to echo even in the afterlife beyond the judgment of God. The traditional Catholic imaginary requires that sin, and presumably its effects, be obliterated in purgatorial suffering before the redeemed person is worthy of heavenly entry and the vision of God. In this rendering of the distinction between the sacred and the profane, human fallenness is relegated to one side of a line drawn along the horizon of purgatory's punishments, and separating the reconciled purity of heavenly life from the still guilty and unreconciled realms of sin's effective history. Let us imagine this line and the crossing of it differently.

In the previous chapter I proposed that we imagine the particular judgment as the person's moment of encounter with the Beatific Vision, and that encounter as so overwhelmingly graceful that before it all resistance to the truth of God's judgment gradually collapses. Here, the Beatific Vision itself conquers sin through an act of forgiveness whose infinite love is irresistible, engendering the acceptance that the offer of grace requires. My Catholic efforts to develop a Pauline sensibility on judgment distinguished sharply between God's grace and God's judgment. God's judgment, I argued, is not a verdict to which an eschatological destiny is assigned, but instead a revelation of the person's unworthiness of grace through lifelong participation in the history of sin and the failure of forgiveness, nothing less, we might say, than the failure of the acceptance of redemption.

It may seem to some that this conception of the particular judgment has compromised the freedom of the personal act of accepting God's offer, since I have highlighted the power of grace in effecting the conversion of the sinner and have hoped that God's grace is universally irresistible. Ironically, such a powerful rendition of grace might seem to cheapen it, since it seems to come at little cost. Grace itself, of course, costs nothing, since it is a gift. The acceptance of the gift, however, implicitly brings responsibilities that proliferate into the lives of the blessed dead. As grace opens the person under judgment to the truth of judgment, the revelation of fallen character exposes all the ways in which the person so judged failed to imitate the forgiveness of God in his or her life, through offering and accepting forgiveness. The revelation of sin in judgment concomitantly reveals the effects of sin that shape the identity of the person who, by grace, enters heavenly life. The acceptance of grace is itself a commitment to the eschatological project of offering and accepting forgiveness, and thus to the task of healing the rifts that linger in the communion of the saints even in its heavenly dimensions. That project, we should recall, entails no small expense of emotional and moral energy since the effects of sin in any individual life are extensive, and both actively and passively so. They multiply further as one remembers that these effects are relational and abound even more as the consequences of these broken relationships increase across all of history until the event of the Last Judgment. Cooperation in divine judgment and forgiveness is a communal endeavor in which much is required by the actions of all the saints who in so many instances would be unable even to see the guilty need for forgiveness prior to the Last Judgment.

This portrait of eschatological forgiveness might be judged by some to diminish personal responsibility for forgiveness existentially, in the world in which our lives transpire now. If heavenly life offers an endless time for reconciliation, then why would one be motivated to attend to the responsibility of forgiveness on this side of death? At first glance, this criticism might seem to be a specific version of the more general critique of belief in God and life after death offered by many modern atheists, from Feuerbach to Marx to Freud to the recent new atheists like Sam Harris, Daniel Dennett, and Christopher Hitchens. All these critics of theism hold that affirming the existence of the supernatural in any way diminishes the integrity of the natural order— whether it be this world as such, the value of human life, the truth of reason, or morality defined by naturalistic ends. Actually, though, there is a specifically theological version of this criticism. From this perspective, if redemptive responsibility does not lie exclusively in the words and deeds that transpire in this life, then what motivation would there be for believers to respond to the call of grace in anticipation of their particular judgment by God? Furthermore, if heavenly life presents an endless time for forgiveness to be offered and accepted, on what basis could the particular judgment be made? To pose the question even more pointedly, on what basis could God distinguish in judgment between the saved and the damned, between those who stand in the communion of the saints and those who, through their final and freely willed rejection of divine love, stand outside of it?

These Christian concerns, of course, issue from the sensibilities of the Matthean style of faith. They presume an atmosphere of anxiety about eschatological destiny, and measure judgment comparatively in the hierarchy of discipleship. A Catholic appropriation of the Pauline style of faith reconfigures the particular Christian assumptions that prompt these concerns. From the perspective of Pauline sensibilities, judgment is not an assignment of supernatural destiny but a delineation of the contours of human fallenness in a particular life and finally in all of history. Eternal life is an overwhelming gift that requires graceful acceptance in order to establish the relationship that redemptive forgiveness is. This acceptance on the part of the one graced and forgiven, I have suggested, assumes the responsibility of eschatological forgiveness, the task of healing the rifts that linger in the communion of the saints as the effects of sin. This eschatological forgiveness is not a disincentive to forgiveness in our lives on this side of God's judgment. Indeed, imagining the consequences of redemption in this way, as a cooperative task that ensues throughout heavenly life, heightens the sense of moral obligation to forgive and to acknowledge the need to be forgiven in our lives now. If the forgiveness that binds human persons extends the very redemption that issues from God's act of forgiveness, then those who have encountered the power of God's grace in their lives have every motivation, to say nothing of the obligation, to anticipate the heavenly features of forgiving redemption here and now. That the tragedy of human sinfulness consistently thwarts the existential enactment of this responsibility should disparage neither the portrait of eschatological forgiveness offered here nor the principled obligation to forgive in the midst of this historical failure.

ALL THE SAINTS

Our Pauline understanding of the communion of the saints asks us to imagine the consequences of not drawing a line in the supernatural realm that separates the reconciled purity of resurrected life from the effects of sin that continue to be purged in purgatory and from the sins of the world and their effects prior to the particular judgment. In the traditional Catholic imaginary, this purity, beyond the contamination of sin, is a quality of creaturely holiness that the vision of God presupposes. This purity is reflected in the passivity of the resurrected person before the Beatific Vision. Since redemption has itself achieved reconciliation, there is nothing for the blessed dead to do. The reconciliation that redemption causes is utterly the work of grace, which brings about a heavenly peace that is enjoyed, but not accomplished in any way, by the saints. This disjunctive way of thinking about resurrected life and the effects of sin has held sway in the Catholic tradition from the twelfth century, with the birth of purgatory, to the present, even though its details have been filled in imaginatively in various ways. Interestingly, this imaginary expects that entry into the heavenly dimensions of the communion of the saints requires the rendering of the resurrected person to a prelapsarian state before both sin and its effects, a personal state that all born in original sin could never claim as their own. This, I have suggested, is one of several ways in which the traditional Catholic conception of life after death works at cross purposes to the doctrine of bodily resurrection.

Sin, of course, may not flourish in resurrected life. If it could, then God's redemption could be undone. Were we, though, to erase the line that separates the heavenly dimensions of the communion of the saints from the *effects* of sin that mark the identity of each and every person, both perpetrator and victim, then a theological opportunity appears for imagining our actual personal histories in heavenly life, by envisaging the saints ardently devoted to the graceful task of reconciliation. Heaven does not remain aloof from all things lapsed, but instead, to invoke Jonathan Edwards's compelling image, heaven is a "world of love" that embraces the unforgiven, a world where God's grace empowers human wills to forge the forgiving relationships that establish the communion of the saints. This redemptive work begins in the earthly dimensions of the communion of the saints but it can only be completed eschatologically, not only because forgiveness is so rare in life and humanity so sinfully broken but also because the reconciliation that brings about the fullness of God's kingdom is an activity that fi -nally requires the cooperation of all the saints. In this way, the eschatology presented here is a "realized" or "inaugurated" eschatology. Earthly forgiveness may need to overcome seemingly insuperable obstacles in order to occur. But it does, however rarely in the midst of human failure. When forgiveness happens in history, its occurrence is a manifestation of grace, the small beginning of a future eschatological reconciliation in which God will be all in all (1 Cor 15:28).

Imagining the effects of grace countering the effects of sin in an inaugurated eschatology of the communion of the saints situates us squarely in the practice of a noncompetitive spirituality. Forgiveness, by its very nature, is a noncompetitive practice that, when it succeeds, establishes a noncompetitive relationship. It defies the sinful parameters of competition that define all sorts of exchange in the world of the unforgiven and the unreconciled. Forgiveness transcends the contest of power that fills the world with victims. Forgiveness rejects the competition for moral righteousness that immediately ensues in the broken relationship between victim and victimizer. It refuses the competition of narratives between the aggrieved parties to own the truth of being the one truly aggrieved. Forgiveness renounces the competition for greater complacency in the face of estrangement, and has no interest in the competition within one's self to defeat conscience's call for a reconciling gesture. As an imitation and extension of the divine forgiveness, forgiveness in the communion of the saints is an act of love, which like any act of love recognizes the competitive desires of pride and selfish ego as contrary to the grace of authentic relationship. The relationship of forgiveness, shaped in the offer and acceptance of the gift of reconciliation, flourishes only when humility, the most noncompetitive of the virtues, is practiced not merely once, as forgiveness initially bridges unforgiven estrangement, but again and again as an integrated dimension of ongoing reconciliation.

As the enacted fruit of redemption, forgiveness on either side of God's judgment is a saintly activity, though one that does not give rise to a hierarchy of discipleship. The grace that empowers forgiveness is the divine love itself, which in its infinite gratuity has no hierarchy of dispensation. The kind of graceful cooperation that forgiveness requires obviates the notion of competitive merit, since the act of forgiveness leaves no room for individual achievement. Forgiveness is a remarkable moral partnership in which merit, if it exists at all, appears not competitively, in which one party is more and another less in the offering and accepting of forgiveness, but rather reciprocally in the shared cooperation of forgiver and forgiven. As this network of forgiveness proliferates eschatologically to accommodate the sins of history, what merit there is in forgiveness is shared all the more throughout the saintly community. No doubt, in any historical moment, some persons are more open to the saintly activity of forgiveness, and some persons are tragically resistant to it. And yet, openness to forgiveness, while saintly comportment, is not individual saintly merit precisely because forgiveness and the reconciliation it brings cannot be accomplished by individuals acting on their own. A saintly *habitus* begins in a selfless gratitude for the gift of forgiveness that God's grace has offered to all, in the desire that the human response to this grace bring the effects of forgiveness into every quarter of the communion of the saints, and in a willingness to devote oneself to this most challenging and frustrating task of offering and accepting forgiveness. The more the saints together cooperate with the grace of forgiveness, both in this world and in the next, the more any kind of hierarchy of discipleship loses definition in the reconciliation that binds the saintly communion.

I appreciate very much Elizabeth Johnson's feminist reconstruction of the doctrine of the communion of the saints, and her ardent efforts to expose and criticize the sinful manifestations of hierarchy that have damaged its practice through the centuries. Even though I have tried to sketch a theological portrait of the communion of the saints as a noncompetitive and nonhierarchical society, I would be reluctant to describe this understanding as egalitarian, as Johnson does in her description of the reconstructed communion as a "companionship of friends."[21] Equality is a noble political virtue that, when practiced in history, diminishes the effects of sinful violence. The practice of political equality thus has consequences for the communion of the saints that stretch beyond history into its eschatological dimensions. But like hierarchy, which distinguishes superior and inferior statuses in the relationships of persons, equality simply is not a quality of forgiving relationship. There is nothing equal in the relationship between perpetrator and victim, and the reconciliation that forgiveness achieves need not at all be the restoration of a lost equality or the creation of an equality that never existed before, even when forgiveness forgives the evil violation of equality. The graced reciprocity of reconciliation may very well lead to friendship, and this expression of saving hope is one of the many reasons that Johnson's argument for understanding the communion of the saints as a companionship of friends is so compelling. But our attention to forgiveness as the redemptive resonance of this companionship simply pushes to the side the importance of equality as a necessary feature of that holy society.

By the same token, my efforts to think the communion of saints apart from the traditional notion of the hierarchy of discipleship do not require the abandonment of the traditional practice of supplication in which believers pray for saintly intercession. The doctrine of the communion of the saints imagines that the distance between heaven and earth is negligible and this spatial homology enables believers to act in a way that presupposes the ongoing presence of the blessed dead in their lives, even in specific actions that aid believers in their own path to resurrected life. Once again, engaging Elizabeth Johnson's work offers a helpful point of comparison.

Johnson, we have seen, is most suspicious of what she calls the "patrons–petitioners" model of the communion. This understanding valorizes the moral accomplishments of Christians whose exceptional discipleship achieves paradigmatic saintly status. These saints in turn, acting as patrons from their privileged state in the hierarchy of heavenly reward, are able to grant spiritual favors to the living who in their need call upon these powerful friends for aid. Johnson, I believe, is rightly concerned that the "patrons–petitioners" model all too easily instantiates the harmful imbalance of social power relations, laden as they are with the terrible effects of discrimination. Her feminist concern is prompted by a gender imbalance in the Church's canonization process that has produced an inordinate number of male saints whom believers invoke as patrons in times of need.[22] Yet, as we have seen, the task of imagining the communion of saints as a community of forgiveness does not entail the privileging of equality as a dimension of reconciled relationship. Forgiving activity in the very unequal relationship between perpetrator and victim may actually require that in practice one of these persons serve as a patron in the work of reconciliation, the patron by graceful persistence leading the other toward a forgiveness that initially was regarded as neither needed nor wanted, to say nothing of redemptive. There is a host of ways in which relationships unequal in power can be remarkable settings for the workings of grace, and the forgiving relationship often exemplifies this well.

This kind of supplication and intercession in the communion of the saints can happen in all sorts of ways in the redemptive community that we are imagining the communion of the saints to be. Supplication and intercession can happen between and among the saints who dwell in history as they take up the difficult work of responding to grace by offering and accepting forgiveness. Their task can be aided by their petition to or by the free initiative of the heavenly dimensions of the communion, whose members' prayers are faithful expressions of faith and hope in the efficacy of grace, the source of forgiveness that finally brings its difficult task to completion. Or, supplication and intercession can happen between and among the blessed dead in heaven as they engage in the much more complex task of forgiving in the eschatological expanse of the communion that the particular judgment and finally the Last Judgment reveal. Their heavenly task can be aided by the prayers of the earthly dimension of the communion, since every yearning for redemption is a desire for the reconciling co-operation of the entire communion of the saints in bringing the kingdom of God to fulfillment. Or, supplication and intercession can ensue between those whose estrangement spans heaven and earth. The need for forgiveness may appear in a supplicative request on the part of the guilty party in this broken relationship who, on this side of death, petitions his or her innocent victim in heaven. Or, the need for forgiveness may appear in an intercessory gesture on the part of a victim on this side of death who offers forgiveness to the offender who has died, and now stands among the blessed dead. Since these acts of supplication and intercession extend across the reaches of death and judgment, they may not directly culminate in forgiveness for all the reasons we have considered thus far. Forgiveness by its very nature is a relationship that requires reciprocity, and creaturely reciprocity cannot take place across the rupture to engaged relationship that death makes in the communion of the saints. Supplication and intercession in the face of this kind of estrangement may be proleptic of forgiveness, but these reconciling works await their eschatological exercise in order to be brought to completion.

Our efforts to imagine the communion of the saints beyond the assumptions of the hierarchy of discipleship and energized by a non-competitive spirituality raise a question about the possibility of truly exceptional saints, saints like Stephen, the first martyr, Francis of Assisi, Catherine of Siena, and Blessed Teresa of Calcutta. As much as these great saints have been inspiring models of holiness throughout the Catholic tradition, the interpretation of their lives in the Matthean style of faith has also been a source of eschatological anxiety prompted by the judgment that lives of such extraordinary holiness mark a pinnacle of merited salvation in comparison with which the merits of more ordinary believers simply pale. This competitive spirituality, in which ethical cooperation threatens to outrun grace, is certainly at odds with the Catholic imaginary developed in these pages. But what of the exceptional saints around whom this competitive spirituality has gravitated? Might their achievements appear in our Catholic imaginary in a way that will honor their holiness without the creation of a hierarchy of discipleship, and thus a stratified understanding of the communion of the saints?

Nothing in the noncompetitive spirituality I have developed here suggests that the communion of the saints is devoid of extraordinary saints. I have, though, seized every opportunity to argue against a particular understanding of extraordinary saints that gives rise to the Matthean hierarchy of discipleship. If openness to, and a willingness to offer, forgiveness are saintly actions, then certainly there are some members of the communion of the saints in its earthly and heavenly dimensions who are extraordinary saints by virtue of their forgiving cooperation with grace. Moreover, the difficult moral work of forgiveness does not emerge from the human will as something utterly new, but instead presupposes a change of heart, a moral conversion that itself suggests a broader development of virtuous character. This is especially true of the person who takes the initiative in the forgiving relationship. Forgiveness may be a virtuous act that is especially resonant with grace, since in forgiving the human person offers to another what

God has offered to every person. Yet, forgiveness is an act of love that is nurtured and strengthened by so many other virtuous acts of love practiced throughout a lifetime, and even, I have proposed, throughout resurrected lifetimes. These are the virtues that the Catholic tradition has recognized and celebrated in the lives of the great saints.

Even though we would be hard-pressed to find one of the tradition's recognized saints especially distinguished for the virtue of forgiveness,[23] it would not be difficult for us to imagine the martyrs and the ascetical saints lovingly engaged in this activity—in forgiving and in seeking forgiveness—in the largely unknown moments of their earthly lives and eschatologically. One of the advantages of my proposal, of course, is that what I have just suggested we might imagine of the recognized saints, we might just as easily imagine of seemingly ordinary persons whose virtuous lives provide a context of character for their own extraordinary contributions to eschatological reconciliation. Occasionally, albeit rarely, their extraordinary acts of forgiveness take place in this life without much fanfare or even notice. Yet, however rare forgiveness may be in its existential appearance, the unheralded saints who accomplish it far outnumber the saints who are officially recognized. There is ever hope in the communion of the saints too that the number of those accomplished in bringing reconciliation to the communion will increase eschatologically as more and eventually all face the burden of sin revealed in the particular judgment and the Last Judgment.

The Pauline sensibility at work in a noncompetitive spirituality does not expect that all the saints are the same in their moral response to God's grace. But neither does it expect that differences in moral response will lead to an understanding of the communion as a hierarchy in which authentic discipleship is defined by the ascetical virtue of the few, in comparison with which the virtuous discipleship of the many always falls short. The Pauline sensibility in its Catholic style will credit God's grace as the power enabling virtue of all sorts in the communion of the saints, including the virtue of forgiveness. The appropriate response to grace is gratitude, just as gratitude is the appropriate response to all forms of virtuous, and always graced, cooperation with

God's generous gift of redemption. Gratitude too is the appropriate response to reconciliation that takes the form of forgiveness in the communion of the saints, and this same response is a gratitude for the initiative of all the saints struggling both in this world and in the next to bring their lives and their relationships to a state of communal holiness worthy and reflective of God's limitless love.

In the traditional Catholic imaginary, the exceptional saints possess a paradigmatic status whose effects ripple throughout all the regions of the supernatural and natural hierarchy below the Beatific Vision. It is not surprising that in this worldview the truly exceptional would be capable of such efficacy. By comparison, though, it is interesting to see the degree to which the seemingly least exceptional possess astonishing efficacy in the conception of the communion of the saints developed here.

Earlier in my argument, I proposed that the outcome of the Last Judgment remains in a state of suspense even for the blessed dead, and that this suspense is generated by the hope that God's grace is universally efficacious, that all are saved. Matthean sensibilities would be uncomfortable with this graceful efficacy, and understandably so. Universal salvation seems to undercut genuine responsibility for cooperation with God's grace that Trent defines as necessary for justification. Since even a quick glance at any moment in history reveals sin of overwhelming proportions, the hope for universal salvation suggests that such sin, which in so many instances is blatantly unrepentant, is held to no account at all in the court of divine judgment. A consequence of such apparent disregard for sin, and human responsibility for it, is that the gift of grace that would bring about universal salvation would seem to be an empty parody of justice. Grace in such a scenario would not be offered to be received by an enacted cooperation but instead, it seems, distributed freely with a complete disregard for the sin that permeates human lives and indeed all of history. If sin matters not, neither, it seems, does grace. If the most terrible sinners could enter eternal life so easily and in spite of their evil deeds, then salvation would come at no cost, with no struggle, and with no acknowledgment at all of the remarkable differences between an accomplished saintly life and a horrendously sinful life. To some degree, and perhaps to a great degree, the exemplary life of the extraordinary saint in the hierarchy of discipleship intensifies these legitimate Catholic concerns.

Were we to follow Catholicly Pauline sensibilities in contemplating universal redemption, then we would need to enter this imaginary not through the door of the Matthean paradigmatic saint, whose life of exceptional discipleship, as a reflection of Christ's sinless life, measures the virtues of the saved and the failures of the damned, but instead through the door of the most scandalous life of sin, through the door of the Matthean imaginary's damned. The medieval artists whose work we have considered had no difficulty at all imagining a densely populated hell. As one views their paintings, mosaics, and frescoes, however, the tormented faces of the damned in the midst of hellish punishments tell one nothing about their particular sins and the personal histories through which their eternal failures came to pass. The medieval artists expected that those who approached their work would bring their own narratives to these Last Judgment scenes, and use them to imagine the merits of eternal joy and the perdition of eternal suffering. Doing so is not difficult out of the mixed moral resources that most lives typically offer. Neither is it difficult to imagine by both abstraction and concrete example the few who are extraordinarily virtuous and the few who are extraordinarily sinful. Let us consider the latter.

History offers us so many examples of human lives that were so egregiously sinful that, presuming they were unrepentant, could readily be imagined as deserving of eternal condemnation in the traditional Catholic imaginary. The architects of the Holocaust and all their willing minions, the perpetrators of the many genocides that have punctuated global history in only the last century, to say nothing of the previous millennia, the entrepreneurs of the modern slave trade and the many slave owners who understood the consequences of their racist actions and delighted in their violence and the suffering it caused, and the most recent murderer of an innocent child who, at the sentencing segment of his trial, responded to the parents' plaintive call for a reason by describing in graphic detail the terrified screams of their child on the brink of death are just a few of the literally uncountable examples of those whom the Matthean imaginary would consign to the ranks of the damned. Something about that placement seems so eschatologically right, not only because it could be understood as the enactment of divine justice but also because it would be so difficult to imagine being in the company of such persons for all eternity. This is precisely what universal salvation asks us to imagine: a communion of the saints in which persons who are responsible for the most heinous acts of evil yet stand for all eternity in the company of all the saints. This is not at all an easy conception of salvation, capriciously generous in its generalization of the joys of heaven, but one that is emotionally demanding. For if evil persons are members of the communion of the saints in its heavenly dimensions, then they are members of the communion of the saints here and now, in its earthly dimensions as well. And if the egregiously sinful can be reconciled eschatologically, then responsibility falls on all the saints on this side of the particular judgment to forgive them and to work on forging the bonds of reconciliation in a saintly communion that includes and embraces them too.[24]

The traditional Catholic imaginary draws a line along the contours of purgatory that separates the effects of sin from the purity of heaven. But this line is the shadow of an eschatologically indelible line along the contours of God's judgment that separates the saved from the damned, the eternal happiness of heaven from the eternal pains of hell. Both lines define the gates of heaven, which keep at bay the evil things people do and finally the evil persons that some willfully become. Theologically, these lines fix the consummate supernatural difference between good and evil in its eternal, eschatological trajectory. There are so many ways in which these lines too are drawn in this world, on this side of divine judgment, as human persons perversely venture an idolatrous imitation of the divine judgment, seizing on all kinds of difference in order to imagine a worldly version of the eschatological divide that reflects it and, in their judgment, anticipates it. Differences in race, ethnicity, and gender often occasion this judgment, as do the differences between the rich and the poor, the healthy and the ill, the free and the incarcerated, those on either side of a national border, or individuals in conflict. This idolatrous judgment consigns the other to hell, where, of course, in Dante's well-known description, all hope is abandoned because the condemned are beyond God's forgiveness.[25] This mentality surrounding the commission of sin helps to explain why forgiveness is so rare in human lives on this side of the particular judgment. The line that separates heaven from hell not only excludes the worst sinners from paradise but also falsely justifies the sinful ruptures that ever multiply in the communion of the saints.

The paucity of worldly forgiveness encourages us to imagine that forgiveness is the cooperative work of all the saints eschatologically so that the effects of grace might contribute to the justification of the effects of sin. If we truly are committed to the Christian belief in resurrected life and take seriously the Catholic belief in human responsibility to God's grace, then the saints' engagement in supernatural forgiveness is not an escapist alternative to this-worldly obligation but instead offers a way of imagining a continuity in achieved solidarity in the communion that surpasses a solidarity of mere intention or hope. Eliminating the line that separates the effects of sin from heavenly life enables the saints who work at forgiveness eschatologically to be who they are, in grace and in the heritage of sin, redeemed and being reconciled. The indelible line separating heaven from hell, however, may not be eliminated, since hell, as the rejection of God, is always a possibility if human freedom is real. But even if this indelible line remains in the Catholicly Pauline imaginary proposed here, we may yet affirm that the divine judgment it so sharply defines is not at all the same as divine grace, and ardently hope that God's grace is so universally effective that, when the Last Judgment is rendered, no persons will stand separated from each other across this line for all eternity. This hopeful prospect is itself a paradoxically graceful judgment on all the ways that human sin spuriously creates its own divides between "heaven" and "hell" in consigning marginalized others of all sorts to perdition.[26] This hopeful, but difficult and troubling, prospect also calls on us not to marginalize even the most egregious sinners, to imagine even those guilty of monstrous acts of overwhelming evil to be capable of eschatological conversion and the benefits of reconciliation that, in such cases, would seem to require the extraordinary heavenly energies of all the saints. This hopeful prospect, which the desire for vengeance regards as folly or even madness, asks us to imagine that, in whatever ways possible, this consummate heavenly reconciliation be the standard of Christian discipleship for all in the earthly dimensions of the communion of the saints, so that the reconciliation that issues from God's redemption will begin without exception "on earth, as it is in heaven" (Mt 6:10).

THE CROSS AND RESURRECTION IN
THE COMMUNION OF THE SAINTS

Traditionally interpreted, the cross of Christ is the central symbol of God's forgiveness. The cross is the scene of forgiving exchange in which God responds to the violence and betrayal of worldly sin with the loving sacrifice of his Son, and through this sacrifice the sins of the world are forgiven and redeemed. Paul articulated this redemptive motif very early in the tradition when he urged the Corinthian Christians to affirm the faith he had handed on to them "that Christ died for our sins in accordance with the scriptures" (1 Cor 15:3). Luke explicitly highlighted the cross as the scene of eschatological forgiveness in Jesus' gift of eternal life in paradise to the criminal crucified with him who had acknowledged his guilt and Jesus' innocence (Lk 23:43). Anselm of Canterbury (c. 1033–1109) dramatically influenced the reception of this redemptive motif in the later tradition by highlighting how fitting it was for God to forgive the sins of the world in the way his providence chose, through the sacrifice of his Son on the cross. For Anselm, who draws on Chalcedon's definition of the person of Christ for his explanation, the human nature of Jesus represents the humanity of all who in their fallenness are obliged, but unable, to make amends for sin, while his divine nature alone possesses the power to cancel the human debt of sin by paying the infinitely exorbitant price of his death on the cross. The punishment incurred by sin is borne by the Son of God so that God's forgiveness might extend to humanity.[27] This motif has been criticized from many quarters of modern theology for its close identification of suffering and redemption, an identification that could easily encourage the victims of history to understand their suffering as willed by God, much in the manner that Anselm's account has God will the sufferings of the cross to save the world.[28] Understood at its best, though, Anselm's theology of atonement expresses the reciprocity between parties that any act of forgiveness entails, the fittingness of Jesus' sacrifice on the cross through the cooperation of his divine and human natures serving as a profound expression of both the giftedness of the offer of forgiveness and the need for its meaningful acceptance.

I conclude by calling attention to the theological value of a minority tradition in the theology of the cross as an expression of the eschatology developed here, namely, a small strain in Christian imagery that portrays the abiding presence of the cross in heaven. Even if the traditional Catholic imaginary has assumed the existence of a line that keeps the effects of sin from tainting the purity of heaven as the necessary ambit of the Beatific Vision, there have been some symbolically powerful exceptions to this conception. I have already considered the earliest example in the resurrection appearances in Luke and John in which Jesus offers the wounds of his crucifixion as proof of his identity, and so as proof of the reality of his resurrection, to his astonished and disbelieving disciples (Lk 24:36–43; Jn 20:24–29). The effects of sin accompany Jesus into his glorified life. In a sense, his cross appears in his afterlife, and after his ascension, one would presume, in heaven. On this point, Dante is even more explicit. In the fourteenth-century verses of the *Paradiso*, Dante's ascent through the fourth heaven in the company of Beatrice culminates in a vision of the cross radiant with the redeeming sacrifice of Christ. Upon his encounter with "two rays" whose splendors appeared overwhelming, Dante observes:

> As . . . the Milky Way so gleams as to cause even the wise to question, so did those beams, thus constellated, make in the depth of Mars the venerable sign which joinings of quadrants make in a circle. Here my memory outstrips my wit, for that Cross so flashed forth Christ that I can find for it no fit comparison; but he that takes up his cross and follows Christ shall yet forgive me for what I leave untold when he sees Christ flash in that dawn.[29]

Even though the glory of Christ eludes his poetic ability, Dante finds comfort in his expectation that all who have shared in the sufferings of discipleship will one day themselves appreciate the ineffability of this heavenly vision when they cross its path in their own heavenly ascent.

We find this same motif represented vividly in a painting by Albrecht Dürer (1471–1528) entitled *Adoration of the Trinity* (1511) (figure 11). In this painting on wood, Dürer presents a heavenly scene in which the blessed dead stand above the clouds fully embodied in their resurrection. Their clothing marks their social status and among the heavenly throng are popes and religious, kings and queens, peasants and choirs of angels. All adore the Trinity that commands the painting's center. The Father is portrayed familiarly in Christian medieval art—as an old, bearded man wearing regal robes—as is the Holy Spirit, who hovers above the Father's head as a radiant dove whose wings have just caught a heavenly breeze. Surprisingly, and even somewhat shockingly, the Son appears before the Father's outstretched arms crucified, and represented exactly as he would have been had this been a painting of Golgotha. Since the blessed dead who worship the Triune God are embodied, one presumes that this scene takes place after the Last Judgment. Thus the artist suggests that Jesus is crucified in heaven for all eternity.[30]

At face value, these images of the cross and crucifixion in heaven are powerful symbolic testimonies to the incarnational price of redemption, to the remarkable suffering of the Savior that brings eternal life to the world as a graceful gift. So understood, these provocative images, whether on page or on graphic surface, are expressions of Christian memory that issue from the believer's appreciation of the depths of God's love that brings redemption at such a cost. They all make much of the suffering of Christ's humanity in this salvation, just as Anselm insisted was theologically appropriate. But interpreted further, these images express a willingness to imagine the effects of sin in heaven in order to contemplate an eternal life that consummately embraces and transforms the deathliness that all encounter in their earthly lives. These images of the cross in heaven make Jesus utterly paradigmatic in this regard. They reserve the heavenly contemplation of the effects of sin *only* to the effects of sin that appear in his suffering, undoubtedly because this occasional image sees the cross in heaven as an eternal echo of an earthly event whose resonance alone brings the harmony and peace of God's kingdom to the communion of the saints. I have proposed that we extend this imaginary so that the effects of sin in humanity as such, in the lives of all the saints, continue to echo guiltily throughout all eternity so that the saints may be eternally at work at the cooperative reconciliation that this very eschatological harmony and peace require in order to be responsibly accepted.[31] The cross, we might say, continues to dwell in heaven in the sinful burden of broken relationships which, though redeemed, yet are in need of healing.

The doctrine of the Last Judgment in the traditional Catholic imaginary is a profound reminder that the resurrection is not something that occurs individually but socially, that resurrection brings to embodiment again all of our relationships in their virtuous integrity and in their fallen brokenness. Finally, the icons of hope presented in these pages offer a way of imagining resurrection, not only as the wholeness of ourselves as individuals but also as the wholeness of ourselves in our relationships—in relationships that shape our immediate personal histories and in relationships to those in our pasts and in our futures that could never be known in life but that nevertheless are in need of reconciliation. I have intimated that the heavenly existence of this need means that a kind of sadness continues to course in eternal life along with the happiness of redemption and the happiness occasioned by all the virtuous and loving relationships that began in history and continue unbroken into eternity. This eschatological sadness is prompted by the guilty burden of the effects of sin that continue to be borne by all in the communion of the saints as they work toward an eschatological solidarity that is both universal and fulfilled in every imaginable way.[32]

It is interesting to notice how important it was in the traditional Christian imaginary to keep the sadness of sin and its effects utterly distant from the joys of heaven. Thomas Aquinas and Jonathan Edwards, who served our study earlier in their different visions of the blessed dead in heaven, may again come to our exemplary aid, though now as partners in theological agreement. In considering whether the blessed in heaven will witness the sufferings of the damned, Thomas maintains that they will, and much to the increase of their heavenly happiness. "Wherefore in order that the happiness of the saints may be more delightful to them and that they may render more copious thanks to God for it," he insists, "they are allowed to see perfectly the sufferings of the damned."[33] Much in the same manner, Jonathan Edwards exclaims in a 1739 sermon that

> the sight of hell torments will exalt the happiness of the saints forever. It will not only make them more sensible of the greatness and freeness of the grace of God in their happiness, but it will really make their happiness the greater, as it will make them more sensible of their own happiness. It will give them a more lively relish of it: it will make them prize it more.[34]

Both Aquinas and Edwards imagine an eternity in which happiness and sadness stand in polar opposition, eschatologically at odds in a way that redounds to the greater happiness of the saints in heaven. Neither can imagine a heaven in which the actual presence of sadness in our shared lives together has the effect of increasing joy, just as it does in our lives together here and now. Both find it crucial that even the sadness of the effects of sin be banished from heaven so that its joys will be unburdened by our actual sinful histories.

Nothing, though, produces true joy more than does the reconciliation that follows upon forgiveness and repentance, as the gospel parables of the lost sheep and the lost coin testify (Lk 15:1–10). The bliss of heavenly life is caused by the vision of God who is Truth, Beauty, and Goodness itself. But the happiness of heaven, I have suggested, ever increases as the divine truth, goodness, and beauty are embraced actively more and more in the communion of the saints in the face of the sadness of sin's lingering effects. This increase is not a consequence of any deficiency in the Beatific Vision, but is instead a function of our own created capacities, of our ability to be or not to be faithful as persons to the divine image in which we were created. This increase in happiness, which comes through the practice of forgiveness, reflects a saintly growth in the work of love, the very Love that

God is, that became incarnate in the world to bring its estrangement to reconciliation, and that permeates the communion of the saints as the presence of the Holy Spirit. Both the sadness and joys of heaven begin in our lives now, though, tragically, the power of sin in history ever threatens the energy of joy. Hope is the virtue, and indeed a kind of faith, that urges our constancy in the face of all this sadness. Hope is the expectant faith that God's grace and our communal response to it will prevail eschatologically so that the joy of reconciliation will eclipse the tragedy of division in our shared lives together on both sides of God's judgment.

NOTES

Chapter 1. *For What May We Hope?*

1. Christoph Schwöbel, "Last Things First? The Century of Eschatology in Retrospect," in *The Future as God's Gift: Explorations in Christian Eschatology*, ed. D. Fergusson and M. Sarot (Edinburgh: T. & T. Clark, 2000), 217.

2. Albert Schweitzer, *The Quest of the Historical Jesus: A Critical Study of Its Progress from Reimarus to Wrede*, trans. W. Montgomery (New York: Macmillan, 1968).

3. Johannes Weiss, *Jesus' Proclamation of the Kingdom of God*, trans. R. H. Hiers and D. L. Holland (Philadelphia: Fortress Press, 1971).

4. The most recent survey is *The Oxford Handbook of Eschatology*, ed. J. L. Walls (New York: Oxford University Press, 2008).

5. Immanuel Kant, *Critique of Pure Reason*, trans. N. K. Smith (New York: St. Martin's Press, 1965), 635 (B833).

6. Ibid., 639 (B839).

7. Charles Péguy, *The Portal of the Mystery of Hope*, trans. D. Schindler, Jr. (Grand Rapids, MI: W. B. Eerdmanns, 1996).

8. Immanuel Kant, "The End of All Things," in *On History*, ed. L. W. Beck, trans. R. E. Anchor (Indianapolis, IN: Bobbs-Merrill, 1963), 79.

9. Ibid.

10. Cyril O'Regan has categorized various forms of recent apocalyptic thought that he describes as the pleromatic, the kenomatic, and the metaxic. The first draws thickly on traditional Christian imagery; the second pursues philosophical criticism to empty eschatological imagery of its traditional meaning; and the third ventures interpretation "between" these extremes to negotiate a critical hermeneutics of the tradition. What I have described as modern, critical, apologetical theologies would find their home in O'Regan's third category. See Cyril O'Regan, *Theology and the Spaces of Apocalyptic*, Père Marquette Lecture in Theology, 2009 (Milwaukee: Marquette University Press, 2009).

11. David Tracy, "The Return of God in Contemporary Theology," in *Why Theology?* (*Concilium*, 1994–1996), ed. C. Geffré and W. Jeanrond (Maryknoll, NY: Orbis Books, 1994), 42.

12. Karl Rahner, "The Hermeneutics of Eschatological Assertions," in *Theological Investigations*, vol. 4, trans. K. Smyth (Baltimore: Helicon Press, 1966), 323–46.

13. Ibid., 324.

14. Ibid., 328.

15. Ibid., 329.

16. Ibid., 331.

17. Ibid., 337.

18. Ibid., 332.

19. Karl Rahner, "The Concept of Mystery in Catholic Theology," in *Theological Investigations*, 4.50.

20. Karl Rahner, "The Life of the Dead," in *Theological Investigations*, 4.349.

21. Ibid., 353, 352.

22. Ibid., 352.

23. Ibid., 353–54.

24. There are many examples. A good one is Kathryn Tanner, *Jesus, Humanity and the Trinity: A Brief Systematic Theology* (Minneapolis: Fortress Press, 2001), 97–124.

25. Barth makes this point nicely in his discussion of heaven in the *Church Dogmatics*: "Heaven is the boundary which is clearly and distinctly marked off for man [*sic*]. It exists. But in distinction from earth it exists as invisible creaturely reality. It is invisible and therefore incomprehensible and inaccessible, outside the limits of human capacity. . . . It is not merely God who is incomprehensible; the same can also be said of heaven within the creaturely world" (Karl Barth, *Church Dogmatics*, 3.3, ed. G. W. Bromiley and T. F. Torrance, trans. G. W. Bromiley and R. J. Ehrlich [Edinburgh: T. & T. Clark, 1960], 424–25).

26. The classical locus is Karl Rahner, *Spirit in the World*, trans. W. Dych (London: Sheed & Ward, 1968).

27. I would be willing to concede that there may be no direct connection between Rahner's regard for the Kantian rule and his constructive position on the life of the dead. It may be that the consistency between the two positions is simply a matter of coincidence, that his theological construction of the life of the dead is not the consequence of his epistemological assumptions, and that I have committed the logical error of post hoc ergo propter hoc. But if that were so, it would seem to imply Rahner's own inconsistency in applying his special hermeneutics of eschatological assertions.

28. There is no better articulation of this most important scriptural sensibility in an eschatological key than Christopher Morse, *The Difference Heaven Makes: Rehearing the Gospel as News* (London: T. & T. Clark, 2010).

29. This understanding of idolatry as a perversion of sacramentality is suggested in the work of Marion and Chauvet. See Jean-Luc Marion, *God without Being*, trans. T. A. Carlson (Chicago: University of Chicago Press, 1991), 163–69; Louis-Marie Chauvet, *Symbol and Sacrament*, trans. P. Madigan, S.J., and M. Beaumont (Collegeville, MN: Liturgical Press, 1995), 216–20.

30. Steven Ozment's helpful distinction between a Latin or Christo-centric mysticism and a Germanic or theocentric mysticism in late medieval Christianity highlights the prevalence of the former and the virtual identifi-cation of the latter category with Eckhart. See Steven Ozment, *The Age of Reform, 1250–1550: An Intellectual and Religious History of Late Medieval and Reformation Europe* (New Haven, CT: Yale University Press, 1980), 115–16. Cyril O'Regan's unfolding scholarly project explores the heterodox-critical varieties of Gnosticism. See Cyril O'Regan, *Gnostic Return in Modernity* (Albany, NY: SUNY Press, 2001); idem, *Gnostic Apocalypse: Jacob Boehme's Haunted Narrative* (Albany, NY: SUNY Press, 2002).

31. For discussions of Jewish understandings of resurrection, see Neil Gillman, *The Death of Death: Resurrection and Immortality in Jewish Thought* (Woodstock, VT: Jewish Lights Publishing, 1997); Claudia Setzer, *Resurrec-tion of the Body in Early Judaism and Early Christianity: Doctrine, Community, and Self-Definition* (Leiden: Brill, 2004); Jon Levenson, *Resurrection and the Restoration of Israel: The Ultimate Victory of the God of Life* (New Haven, CT: Yale University Press, 2006).

32. Martin Luther, *Heidelberg Disputation*, in *Luther's Works*, vol. 31, ed. and trans. H. J. Grimm (Philadelphia: Fortress Press, 1957), 39–70, espe-cially theses 19–22.

33. The position of "realized" eschatology was developed by C. H. Dodd. See, for example, C. H. Dodd, *The Parables of the Kingdom* (New York: Scribner, 1961). "Inaugurated" eschatology, which corrects the "this-worldly" weighting of eschatological symbols in Dodd's approach, was developed by Jürgen Moltmann and Wolfhart Pannenberg. See Jürgen Moltmann, *Theology of Hope*, trans. M. Kohl (New York: HarperCollins, 1991); idem, *The Coming of God: Christian Eschatology*, trans. M. Kohl (Minneapolis: Fortress Press, 1996); Wolfhart Pannenberg, *Theology and the Kingdom of God* (Philadelphia: Westminster Press, 1969).

34. The 1979 teaching of the Congregation for the Doctrine of the Faith (CDF) "Letter on Certain Questions Concerning Eschatology" states: "When dealing with man's situation after death, one must especially beware of arbitrary imaginative representations: excess of this kind is a major cause

of the difficulties that Christian faith often encounters. Respect must however be given to the images employed in the Scriptures. Their profound meaning must be discerned, while avoiding the risk of over-attenuating them, since
this often empties of substance the realities designated by the images" ("Letter
on Certain Questions Concerning Eschatology," 7 [http://www.doctrinafidei
.va/documents/rc_con_cfaith_doc_19790517_escatologia_en.html]). Since
there are uncountable descriptions of the supernatural landscapes of heaven,
hell, and purgatory by authoritative Christian writers and respected Christian artists throughout the Catholic tradition, this wise teaching of the CDF
cannot be read as a warning against the project of eschatological thick description itself. Rather, it cautions against trivial performance, and the doctrinal errors to which it can lead.

Chapter 2. *Imagining the Life of the Blessed Dead*

1. Thomas Aquinas, *Summa Contra Gentiles, Book Four: Salvation*, trans.
C. J. O'Neil (Notre Dame, IN: University of Notre Dame Press, 1975), 301
(IV.80.4).
2. Ibid. (IV.80.5).
3. Ibid., 306 (IV.81.12).
4. Ibid., 307 (IV.82.13).
5. Ibid., 299 (IV.79.10).
6. Ibid., 323 (IV.85.1).
7. Ibid., 312 (IV.83.3).
8. Ibid. (IV.83.4).
9. Ibid., 313 (IV.83.6).
10. Ibid., 313–14 (IV.83.7).
11. Thomas Aquinas, *Summa Contra Gentiles, Book Three: Providence, Part 1*, trans. V. J. Bourke (Notre Dame, IN: University of Notre Dame Press, 1975), 206–9 (III.63).
12. Aquinas, *Summa Contra Gentiles, Book Four*, 314–15 (IV.83.10).
13. Ibid., 315 (IV.83.12).
14. Ibid., 319 (IV.83.24).
15. Thomas Aquinas, *Summa Theologiae*, vol. 46, trans. J. Aumann, O.P. (New York: McGraw-Hill, 1966), 67–77 (2a2ae, q. 182, art. 1–2).
16. Ibid., 81 (2a2ae, q. 182, art. 4).
17. Aquinas, *Summa Contra Gentiles, Book Three, Part 1*, 123–25 (III.37).
18. Jonathan Edwards, "Heaven Is a World of Love," in *The Works of Jonathan Edwards: Ethical Writings*, vol. 8, ed. P. Ramsey (New Haven, CT: Yale University Press, 1989), 369.
19. Ibid., 370.

No

20. Ibid., 370–71. For a discussion of the place of the Trinity in Edwards's speculation about heaven, see Amy Plantinga Pauw, "'Heaven Is a World of Love': Edwards on Heaven and the Trinity," *Calvin Theological Journal* 30 (1995): 392–401.

21. Edwards, "Heaven Is a World of Love," in *The Works of Jonathan Edwards: Ethical Writings*, 8.371–72.

22. Ibid., 377.

23. Ibid., 375.

24. Ibid., 377.

25. Ibid., 378.

26. Ibid., 383. Edwards develops this view in "Happiness of Heaven Is Progressive" (Miscellany #777) in Jonathan Edwards, *The Works of Jonathan Edwards: The "Miscellanies," Entries Nos. 501–832*, vol. 18, ed. A. Chamberlain (New Haven, CT: Yale University Press, 2000), 427–34.

27. Edwards, "Heaven Is a World of Love," in *The Works of Jonathan Edwards: Ethical Writings*, 8.384.

28. Cf. "Heaven" (Miscellany #639) in Edwards, *The Works of Jonathan Edwards: The "Miscellanies," Entries Nos. 501–832*, 18.170–73.

29. Jonathan Edwards, "Serving God in Heaven," in *The Works of Jonathan Edwards: Sermons and Discourses, 1730–1733*, vol. 17, ed. M. Valeri (New Haven, CT: Yale University Press, 1999), 254.

30. Ibid., 255.

31. Ibid., 257.

32. Ibid., 258.

33. Ibid., 258–59.

34. Ibid., 259.

35. Both Aquinas and Edwards are later representatives of ancient traditions that classically articulated the quiescent and the activist understandings of the afterlife. The former was expressed above all by Augustine in the final book of the *City of God*: "How great will be that felicity, where there will be no evil, where no good will be withheld, where there will be leisure for the praises of God, who will be all in all! What other occupation could there be, in a state where there will be no inactivity of idleness, and yet no toil constrained by want? I can think of none" (Augustine, *City of God*, trans. H. Bettenson [New York: Penguin Books, 1984], 1087 [XXII.30]). The latter, a minority tradition, was expressed above all in the work of Gregory of Nyssa, in his notion of *epektasis* as infinite spiritual progress. Consider, for example, his account in the *Life of Moses*: "Made to desire and not to abandon the transcendent height by the things already attained, it [the soul after its release from the body] makes its way upward without ceasing, ever through its prior accomplishments renewing its intensity for the flight. Activity directed toward virtue causes its capacity to grow through exertion; this kind of activity

alone does not slacken its intensity by the effort, but increases it" (Gregory of Nyssa, *Gregory of Nyssa: The Life of Moses*, trans. A. J. Malherbe [New York: Paulist Press, 1978], 113). Cf. Theodoros Alexopoulos, "Das unendliche Sichausstrecken (Epektasis) zum Guten bei Gregor von Nyssa und Plotin: Eine vergleichende Untersuchung," *Zeitschrift für antikes Christentum* 10 (2007): 302–12.

36. Colleen McDannell and Bernhard Lang, *Heaven: A History* (New Haven, CT: Yale University Press, 1988), 177–80, 303–6.

37. Caroline Walker Bynum, "Material Continuity, Personal Survival and the Resurrection of the Body: A Scholastic Discussion in Its Medieval and Modern Contexts," in *Fragmentation and Redemption: Essays on Gender and the Human Body in Medieval Religion* (New York: Zone Books, 1991), 239.

38. See Caroline Walker Bynum, *The Resurrection of the Body in Western Christianity, 200–1336* (New York: Columbia University Press, 1995).

39. *Enchiridion Symbolorum Definitionum et Declarationum de Rebus Fidei et Morum*, ed. H. Denzinger and A. Schönmetzer, S.J. (Freiburg im Briesgau: Herder, 1967), 28 (no. 30); 66–67 (no. 150).

40. On the sacramentality of Scripture, see Louis-Marie Chauvet, *Symbol and Sacrament: A Sacramental Reinterpretation of Christian Existence*, trans. P. Madigan, S.J., and M. Beaumont (Collegeville, MN: Liturgical Press, 1995), 213–27. One might object that the resurrection appearances of Jesus in the Gospels are themselves exercises of the theological imagination and so are poor warrants for the theological speculation offered here on the life of the blessed dead. I agree that the appearance stories in Scripture are acts of theological imagination in narrative form. Yet their canonical status authorizes these imaginative acts as God's inspired Word. Imagination and authority need not be disjunctively posed in the life of faith.

41. I have developed this theological motif at length in John E. Thiel, *God, Evil, and Innocent Suffering: A Theological Reflection* (New York: Crossroad, 2002). This same motif is developed from another angle in James Alison, *Raising Abel: The Recovery of the Eschatological Imagination* (New York: Crossroad, 1996).

42. Rowan Williams makes this same scene the cornerstone for his reflections on the meaning of forgiveness in light of Jesus' resurrection. See Rowan Williams, *Resurrection: Interpreting the Easter Gospel* (Cleveland, OH: Pilgrim Press, 2002), 23–44.

43. Hans W. Frei, *The Identity of Jesus Christ: The Hermeneutical Bases of Dogmatic Theology* (Philadelphia: Fortress Press, 1975), 139–52.

44. Ibid., 145.

45. With respect to modern theological interpretation of this belief, I find myself in complete agreement with Joseph Ratzinger, who resists all attempts to interpret bodily resurrection as an event that occurs individually

and immediately upon death. See Joseph Ratzinger, *Eschatology: Death and Eternal Life*, trans. M. Waldstein (Washington, DC: The Catholic University of America Press, 1988), 241–60. The importance of the classical belief in the resurrection of the body at the Last Judgment will be developed further in chapter 4.

46. For a good summary of this controversy, see Bynum, *The Resurrection of the Body in Western Christianity, 200–1336*, 283–91.

47. In an effort to resist the modern and postmodern reduction of the body to a biological factum, Anthony Godzieba proposes the application of the medieval "four senses" of Scripture to the body. Here I am proposing something akin to his "anagogic sense" of the body, "God's promise for our embodied selves made manifest in the glorified body of the Lord" (Anthony J. Godzieba, "Bodies and Persons, Resurrected and Postmodern: Towards a Relational Eschatology," in *Theology and Conversation: Towards a Relational Theology*, ed. J. Haers and P. De Mey [Leuven: Leuven University Press, 2003], 220). Like Godzieba, I want to respect the tradition's meaningful distinction between body and soul in accounting for the integrity of the self, while not being constrained by a false literalism on either side of the distinction.

48. Margaret A. Farley, *Personal Commitments: Beginning, Keeping, Changing* (San Francisco: Harper & Row, 1986).

49. Martin Buber, *I and Thou*, trans. R. G. Smith (New York: Macmillan, 1987), 6, 75. David Kelsey insightfully employs the motif of promise keeping for imagining redemption in David H. Kelsey, *Imagining Redemption* (Louisville, KY: Westminster John Knox Press, 2005), 21–41. Kelsey's focus is on the graceful encounter with Jesus' redemptive power in this life.

50. Bradford Hinze has written convincingly of our theological reticence to speak of sinful dimensions of the communion of the saints, and of the need to do so in order to acknowledge the reality of human fallenness, which is not annulled by saintly virtue. Hinze makes this point ecclesiologically, with regard to the sin of the Church. I propose here that his important insight applies eschatologically as well. See Bradford E. Hinze, "Ecclesial Repentance and the Demands of Dialogue," *Theological Studies* 61 (2000): 232–33.

Chapter 3. *Time, Judgment, and Competitive Spirituality*

1. Jacques Le Goff, *The Birth of Purgatory*, trans. A. Goldhammer (Chicago: University of Chicago Press, 1984). For critical assessments of this work, see Graham Robert Edwards, "Purgatory: 'Birth' or Evolution?," *Journal of Ecclesiastical History* 36 (1985): 634–46; and Brian Patrick McGuire, "Purgatory, the Communion of the Saints, and Medieval Change," *Viator* 20 (1989): 61–84.

2. Le Goff, *The Birth of Purgatory*, 4.

3. The most extensive study of the motif of the otherworldly journey is Claude Carozzi, *Le Voyage de l'Âme dans l'Au-Delà d'après la Littérature latine (Ve–XIIIe Siècle)* (Rome: École Francaise de Rome, 1994).

4. Le Goff, of course, has his critics on the dating of a developed doctrine of purgatory. Isabel Moreira, for example, makes much of a theology of purgatory in the early eighth-century writings of Bede and Boniface. See Isabel Moreira, *Heaven's Purge: Purgatory in Late Antiquity* (New York: Oxford University Press, 2010), esp. 147–76.

5. Le Goff, *The Birth of Purgatory*, 357.

6. Ibid., 226.

7. Ibid.

8. Ibid., 358.

9. Ibid., 359.

10. Ibid., 358.

11. Ibid., 357. For a comprehensive account of purgatorial belief in historical perspective, see A. Michel, "Purgatoire," in *Dictionnaire de Théologie Catholique*, ed. A. Vacant and E. Mangenot, vol. 13/1 (Paris: Librairie Letouzey et Ané, 1936), 1163–326.

12. Augustine, *City of God*, trans. H. Bettenson (New York: Penguin Books, 1984), 990–91 (21.13). In book 21.26, Augustine speaks of a purifying fire as the cause of the otherworldly pain of purgation, an idea he mentions in several of his works. See Joseph Ntedika, *L'évolution de la doctrine du purgatoire chez Saint Augustin* (Paris: Études Augustiniennes, 1966).

13. Paul, of course, assumes that undeserved grace brings the believer to ethical responsibility that flourishes in virtuous deeds. See, for example, 1 Cor 9:24–27; 2 Cor 5:9–10; Gal 6:7–10. I do not wish here to take a stand amid the various positions in the "new perspective on Paul" debate, though I do agree with E. P. Sanders's view that Judaism, contrary to Christian stereotype and scholarly misinterpretation (which may overlap), is a religion of grace and that the Pauline accent on grace is consistent with Paul's Palestinian Jewish background. I especially agree with his reading of Paul, which maintains that, for Paul, God's grace and God's judgment are not the same. God's salvation is by grace and God's judgment is according to works. In chapters 4 and 5 I will develop this distinction in the Pauline style of faith to constructive ends in reimagining the traditional Christian imaginary of the particular judgment and the Last Judgment. See E. P. Sanders, *Paul and Palestinian Judaism: A Comparison of Patterns of Religion* (Minneapolis: Fortress Press, 1977), 515–18, 543–56. For a discussion of the "new perspective on Paul" debate, see James D. G. Dunn, "The New Perspective: Whence, What, Whither?," in *The New Perspective on Paul: Collected Essays* (Tübingen: Mohr Siebeck, 2005), 1–88.

14. All the talk here of Paul and Matthew as representative of two styles of early Christian faith raises questions about how the Gospel of John compares. There are, of course, many styles of first-century Christian faith. The literary evidence suggests that there are at least as many as there are texts. The Gospel of John is one important example that had a prominent influence on the later tradition, especially through its Christology of preexistence. The Gospel of John, however, was far less influential on the later tradition than the Gospel of Matthew with respect to the issues of discipleship and judgment. Like Paul, John highlights the power of God's grace in a way that draws his attention away from the theme of virtuous responsibility. On this point, see Alan E. Bernstein, *The Formation of Hell: Death and Retribution in the Ancient and Early Christian Worlds* (Ithaca, NY: Cornell University Press, 1993), 224–27. John's theology of grace thus tended to obviate a rigorous ethic of discipleship, the likes of which we find in the Gospel of Matthew. Much in the manner that the Christologies of the Synoptic Gospels were absorbed into John's high Christology of preexistence in the tradition's later, uncritical readings of the New Testament, John was absorbed into the Matthean theology of discipleship and divine judgment. I have distinguished only two styles of Christian faith—Pauline and Matthean—on the basis of their history of effects on the Christian tradition's understandings of judgment. There are, of course, many more.

15. Peter Brown, "The Decline of the Empire of God: Amnesty, Penance, and the Afterlife from Late Antiquity to the Middle Ages," in *Last Things: Death and the Apocalypse in the Middle Ages*, ed. C. W. Bynum and P. Freedman (Philadelphia: University of Pennsylvania Press, 2000), 58. This essay develops the argument Brown makes in his earlier "Vers la Naissance du Purgatoire: Amnistie et pénitence dans le christianisme occidental de l'Antiquité tardive au Haut Moyen Age," *Annales HSS* 52 (1997): 1247–61.

16. Brown, "The Decline of the Empire of God," 43. Unlike Le Goff, Andreas Merkt is willing to consider the origins of purgatory in a host of Late Antique Christian beliefs, among them Brown's notion of the *peccata levia*. Merkt finds this idea first in Cyprian's willingness to conceive the Church not simply as a community of the perfect but as a community that embraced the repentant sinner. This ecclesiology defined a category of Christians who were neither certainly saved nor certainly lost, and which Augustine came to call the "not very good and not very bad." Merkt argues that this third category of believers, perched in the salvational hierarchy between the martyrs and the damned, provided a seedbed for the growth of purgatory. See Andreas Merkt, *Das Fegfeuer: Entstehung und Funktion einer Idee* (Darmstadt: Wissenschaft - liche Buchgesellschaft, 2005), 65–68.

17. Brown, "The Decline of the Empire of God," 47.

18. Ibid., 44, 45. Here, Brown is supported by the work of Éric Rebillard. Rebillard acknowledges that the fear of death and judgment was absent in writings from the earliest Christian centuries. Yet, "au tournant des IVe et Ve siècles, la prédication chrétienne cesse peu à peu d'ignorer, ou de sublimer, les craintes de l'homme face à la mort" (Éric Rebillard, *In Hora Mortis: Évolution de la pastorale chrétienne de la mort aux IVe et Ve siècles dans l'occident latin* [Rome: École française de Rome, 1994], 229). Brown sees the moment of death in early Christian belief as a reflection of the Last Judgment. On this point he seems to disagree with Philippe Ariès, who argues that the interval between personal death and the Last Judgment in early Christian belief diminished the importance of the former and valorized the latter. The moment of death, he claims, gathered importance as the scene of judgment only with the rise of a sense of individuality in the late Middle Ages and in the early modern period. See Philippe Ariès, *The Hour of Our Death*, trans. H. Weaver (New York: Alfred A. Knopf, 1981), 99–110. Rebillard's important study cited above suggests that Ariès's position requires qualification, if not complete revision.

19. Brian Daley concludes that this eschatological imaginary of a particular judgment at death, followed by an "interim state" of a disembodied soul dwelling in its place of judgment, culminating in a Last Judgment at which the soul and the resurrected body would be rejoined to enjoy heaven or suffer hell endlessly dates from the time of Tertullian in the late second century. See Brian E. Daley, S.J., *The Hope of the Early Church: A Handbook of Patristic Eschatology* (Cambridge: Cambridge University Press, 1991), 220.

20. Brown, "The Decline of the Empire of God," 44.

21. Peter Brown, *The Cult of the Saints: Its Rise and Function in Latin Christianity* (Chicago: University of Chicago Press, 1981). From the critical perspective of systematic theology, see Elizabeth A. Johnson, *Friends of God and Prophets: A Feminist Theological Reading of the Communion of the Saints* (New York: Continuum, 1998), 86–92.

22. Brown, *The Cult of the Saints*, 35.

23. See Yvette Duval, *Auprès des Saints Corps et Âme: L'inhumation "ad sanctos" dans la chrétienté d'Orient et d'Occident du IIIe au VIIe siècle* (Paris: Études augustiniennes, 1988), 51–98, 203–23.

24. Athanasius, "The Life of Antony," in *Athansius: The Life of Antony and the Letter to Marcellinus*, trans. R. C. Gregg (New York: Paulist Press, 1980), 42.

25. Ibid.

26. Ibid., 66.

27. Ibid.

28. Bonaventure, "The Life of Francis," in *Bonaventure: The Soul's Journey into God, The Tree of Life, The Life of Francis*, trans. E. Cousins (New York: Paulist Press, 1978), 181.

29. Ibid., 225–26.

30. Ibid., 263–64.

31. Ibid., 244.

32. Ibid., 266–67.

33. Ibid., 266.

34. Ibid., 267.

35. Ibid., 268.

36. Ibid., 304.

37. Ibid., 304–5.

38. Ibid., 305–6.

39. Ariès, *The Hour of Our Death*, 151–54.

40. Barbara Newman, "On the Threshold of the Dead: Purgatory, Hell, and Religious Women," in *From Virile Woman to WomanChrist: Studies in Medieval Religion and Literature* (Philadelphia: University of Pennsylvania Press, 1995), 108–36.

41. Le Goff, *The Birth of Purgatory*, 359.

42. Pierre Chaunau, *La Mort à Paris: XVIe, XVIIe et XVIIIe siècles* (Paris: Librairie Arthème Fayard, 1978), 83–112.

43. Patrick Geary, *Living with the Dead in the Middle Ages* (Ithaca, NY: Cornell University Press, 1995), 95.

44. A pious instructional book from the early twentieth century explains the duration of purgatory in relation to the martyr's instantaneous judgment: "With God's grace and man's faithful labour, all these mischiefs can be undone in the end. But we cannot wonder if it takes a very long time, and is still un-completed when death comes. To our seeing, the new making of our souls is a task for a thousand years. But the power and the mercy of God can do it in an instant. The Church sings of the martyrs fitted for heaven Mortis sacrae compendio, by the crowded action of their holy death. For what God does slowly through our years of prayer and self-denial and suffering is still God's work, not ours" (J. B. McLaughlin, O. S. B., *Purgatory or the Church Suffering* [London: Burns, Oates & Washbourne, 1929], 8). And, in a similar vein: "The soul's love for [God] could be raised to such intensity as to burn out instantly all other loves, desires, attractions. This we believe God does in the souls of his martyrs, who lay down their lives for him with a love than which no man hath greater. But in other souls there is no reason to suppose such a miracle of grace. It is fitting that they should go through the long agony of painfully de-taching their souls from the wrong affections to creatures which they have willfully and persistently encouraged to take root in their souls" (Ibid., 29–30).

45. Marie de France, *Saint Patrick's Purgatory: A Poem by Marie de France*, trans. M. J. Curley (Binghamton, NY: Center for Medieval and Early Renaissance Texts, 1993), 127.

46. Hildegard of Bingen, *The Letters of Hildegard of Bingen*, vol. 3, trans. J. L. Baird and R. K. Ehrman (New York: Oxford University Press, 2004), 163–64.

47. Dante Alighieri, *The Divine Comedy*, 6 vols. in 3, trans. C. S. Singleton, Bollingen 80 (Princeton, NJ: Princeton University Press, 1973), *Purgatorio*, part 1, 197 (canto 18I, 88–127).

48. Ibid., 209 (canto 19, 98–145).

49. *A Revelation of Purgatory by an Unknown, Fifteenth-Century Woman Visionary: Introduction, Critical Text, and Translation*, trans. M. P. Harley (Lewiston, NY: Edwin Mellen Press, 1985), 129.

50. Ibid.

51. Ibid., 113.

52. Ibid.

53. Ibid., 113–14.

54. Ibid., 123.

55. Ibid., 125–26.

56. Ibid., 126.

57. Michel Vovelle argues that the flourishing of belief in purgatory truly takes place in the late fourteenth and fifteenth centuries, when images of the third place begin to proliferate in art. Several images that he cites as evidence express this hierarchical inversion by depicting the purgatorial suffering of clerics. The late fourteenth-century "Le Brévaire parisien" is a decorated letter that portrays a bishop sharing the pain of purgatorial fire with laypersons. The eighteenth-century Spanish altarpiece from San Pedro da Mezquita includes sculptures of a bishop and a priest, each in his own bouquet of purgatorial flames. See Michel Vovelle, *Les âmes du purgatoire, ou le travail du deuil* (Paris: Gallimard, 1996), 47, 182.

58. Marie de France, *Saint Patrick's Purgatory*, 75.

59. Ibid., 71.

60. Ibid, 81. Clearly *"wandiches"* refers to physical features or trimmings in the palace, but the exact referent of the word is unknown. See ibid., n. 9.

61. Ibid., 83.

62. Ibid., 133.

63. Ibid., 132.

64. Catherine of Genoa, *Purgation and Purgatory*, in *Purgation and Purgatory, The Spiritual Dialogue*, trans. S. Hughes (New York: Paulist Press, 1979), 71.

65. Ibid., 72. It is interesting to see this same motif affirmed in a theological treatise of the early twentieth century, as it largely was from Catherine of Genoa to the eve of Vatican II. See Bernhard Bartmann, *Purgatory: A Book of Christian Comfort*, trans. Dom Ernest Graf, O. S. B. (London: Burns, Oates & Washbourne, 1936), 228–41. Just as interesting, though, is Bartmann's sus-

picion of imaginative accounts of purgatory offered by the likes of Catherine of Genoa and Marie de France. He dismisses private revelations as bearing too "striking a resemblance to pathological hallucinations" and strives for a doctrinally based theology of purgatory (Ibid., 14). To the contrary, the argument presented here for the asceticization of purgatory finds the rich imagery of these late medieval accounts to be especially revealing.

66. Maria Maddalena de' Pazzi, *Probation*, in *Tutte le opera di Santa Maria Maddalena de' Pazzi dai manoscritti originali*, vol. 1 (Florence: Nardini, 1960), 51, quoted in Armando Maggi, "Walking in the Garden of Purgatory: The Discourse of the Mind in the *Probation* of St. Maria Maddalena de' Pazzi," *Satan's Rhetoric: A Study of Renaissance Demonology* (Chicago: University of Chicago Press, 2001), 170.

67. Catherine of Genoa, *Purgation and Purgatory*, 82. We find similar testimony to the joys of purgatorial suffering in a tract from the early seventeenth century by the French Jesuit Etienne Binet: "Wherefore under the notion of the Paradice of Purgatory, I understand, the excessive joyes of these captive souls, the incomparable acts of their will and understanding, and the continual favours shour'd down upon them from Heaven, even amidst their most cruel torments" (Etienne Binet, *Purgatory Surveyed, or, A Particular Accompt of the Happy and Yet Thrice Unhappy State of the Souls There: Also of the Singular Charity and Wayes We Have to Relieve Them*, trans. R. Thimelly [London, 1663], 82–83). In addition to enlisting an ascetical paradigm to portray the joyful sufferings of purgatory, Binet invokes the highest standard of competition by comparing these sufferings to the martyrs' pains: "Now will you clearly see, how the souls can at the same instant, swim in a paradise of delights, and yet be overwhelmed with the hellish torments of Purgatory? cast your eyes upon the holy Martyrs of Gods Church, and observe their behaviour. They were torn, mangled, dismembered, flead [flayed] alive, rakt, broyled, burnt, and tell me, was not this to live in a kind of Hell, and yet in the very height of their torments, their hearts and souls, were ready to leape for joy; you would have taken them, to be already transported into heaven" (Ibid., 85–86).

68. Catherine of Genoa, *Purgation and Purgatory*, 85.

69. Ibid.

70. Ibid., 71.

71. For example, P. W. von Keppler, *The Poor Souls in Purgatory: A Homiletic Treatise*, trans. S. Landolt (St. Louis, MO: B. Herder, 1923), 65: "these Holy Souls enter upon their sufferings entirely of their own free will and persevere in them joyfully."

72. An interesting example of this monastic authority in purgatory can be found in the work of Mechthild of Magdeburg (c. 1208–c.1282/94), who barters successfully with God for the release of its suffering souls. Mechthild's

power over purgatory as a worthy ascetic is sufficient to secure the release of one thousand souls at once. On another occasion, she wins the release of seventy thousand souls by offering herself as ransom to God. See Mechthild of Magdeburg, *The Flowering Light of the Godhead*, trans. F. Tobin (New York: Paulist Press, 1998), 77–78, 123–24. The same motif is present in the work of Gertrude of Helfta (1256–c.1301/02), who requests of God the release of suffering souls as numerous as the pieces of the fragmented communion wafer in her mouth. God grants her more. See Gertrude of Helfta, *The Herald of Divine Love*, trans. M. Winkworth (New York: Paulist Press, 1993), 183–84.

73. Any number of studies are instructive on this point, but especially helpful are Jacques Le Goff, *Your Money or Your Life: Economy and Religion in the Middle Ages*, trans. P. Ranum (Chicago: Zone Books, 1990), 65–84; Carlos M. N. Eire, *From Madrid to Purgatory: The Art and Craft of Dying in Sixteenth-Century Spain* (Cambridge: Cambridge University Press, 1995); Michelle Bastard-Fournié, "Le purgatoire dans la région toulousaine au XIVe et au début du XVe siècle," *Annales du Midi* (1980): 5–34.

74. Carlos Eire offers an interesting illustration in his study of sixteenth-century Spanish bequests for the souls in purgatory: "No testator showed a more profound mixture of anxiety over the afterlife and confidence in the power of masses than Father Gregorio de Oviedo. Calling himself an 'unworthy priest,' this curate sat down with a notary while he was still healthy . . . to write an obsessively detailed will . . . , focusing entirely on the business of saving his soul from punishment. . . . Father Gregorio left his soul as *heredera universal*, requesting at least 875 masses . . . , plus certain other clusters of masses. In addition, he asked with customary redundance that after all the appropriate fees had been paid for these, the remainder of his estate 'all be spent in pious works and alms for my soul. . . . I want it all spent on masses, sacrifices, and pious works'" (Eire, *From Madrid to Purgatory*, 193).

75. Thomas Aquinas, *Summa Contra Gentiles: Book 4: Salvation*, trans. C. J. O'Neil (Notre Dame, IN: University of Notre Dame Press, 1975), 344.

76. Ibid., 342.

77. Catherine of Genoa, *Purgation and Purgatory*, 71.

78. Ibid., 72, 75.

79. Ibid., 71.

80. Ibid., 78.

81. Ibid., 79.

82. Ibid., 81. This stance on the passivity of the suffering souls is affirmed in another sixteenth-century treatise by William Cardinal Allen, originally published in 1565: "Let us be circumspect therefore, and work while the day is here; for in the night or the next world sinners cannot help themselves, nor work one moment towards their own delivery or release" (Cardi-

nal Allen, *Souls Departed: Being a Defence and Declaration of the Catholic Church's Doctrine Touching Purgatory and Prayers for the Dead*, ed. T. E. Bridgett, C. Ss. R. [London: Burns & Oates, 1886], 160).

83. Von Keppler, *The Poor Souls in Purgatory*, 76. The counterposition is clearly expressed in an earlier work by Henry James Coleridge, S. J., that is much closer to the typical view of passivity: "This calm and peace [of those who die in a state of grace] is not, in the case of the Holy Souls, a passing, but a permanent state, it lasts as long as they remain in the holy prison of Purgatory. . . . This peace of the holy state of Purgatory is as true and real an element in the condition of those souls . . . as is the pain which they suffer and the length of time for which it may last" (Henry James Coleridge, *Prisoners of the King: Thoughts on the Catholic Doctrine of Purgatory* [London: Burns & Oates, 1878], 164).

84. Von Keppler, *The Poor Souls in Purgatory*, 78.

85. Martin Jugie, *Purgatory and the Means to Avoid It*, trans. M. G. Carroll (Westminster, MD: Newman Press, 1950), ii, 2.

86. Ibid., 11.

87. Ibid., 41.

88. Ibid., 42. A pious book from the early twentieth century shows this same tension between the passivity and activity of the suffering souls. The French Marianist H. Faure portrays purgatory as a place of the "most profound, the most absolute peace" and its inhabitants as souls "in pressing need . . . [who] cannot help themselves." And yet, he tells many stories of the souls interceding in earthly life on behalf of their devotees. Faure assumes, though, that these supernatural deeds are what we might call "passively" charitable actions, since they gain no merit. See H. Faure, *The Consolations of Purgatory*, trans. W. H. Page (New York: Benziger Brothers, 1912), 81, 136, 165–71.

89. "The Decree on Justification, Council of Trent," in *Decrees of the Ecumenical Councils*, vol. 2, ed. N. P. Tanner, S. J. (Washington, DC: Georgetown University Press, 1990), 676 (chap. 12), 672 (chap. 5).

90. This disdain for purgatory, however, does not mean that the mainline Reformation churches did not have their own version of eschatological anxiety, one peculiar to a "grace alone" style of faith and attended by its own kind of competition. The Reformation of sixteenth-century Zürich and Geneva are likely sites for evidence of Protestant versions, as is the theological and cultural evidence Max Weber enlists in his classic work *The Protestant Ethic and the Spirit of Capitalism*, trans. T. Parsons (New York: Charles Scribner's Sons, 1958).

91. Martin Luther, "Smalcald Articles," in *The Book of Concord: The Confessions of the Evangelical Lutheran Church*, trans. T. G. Tappert (Philadelphia: Fortress Press, 1959), 295 (2.2).

92. John Calvin, *Institutes of the Christian Religion*, Library of Christian Classics 20, vol. 1, trans. F. L. Battles (Philadelphia: Westminster Press, 1977), 676 (3.5.6).

93. Guillaume Cuchet documents an interesting rise in purgatorial devotions in France from the nineteenth century to the First World War, after which the same practices wane considerably. The title of his book portrays the waning as the "twilight" of purgatory, which may be appropriate as a metaphor if the virtual loss of purgatorial belief and practice after Vatican II is conceived as a far more advanced nightfall. See Guillaume Cuchet, *La crépuscule du purgatoire* (Paris: Armand Colin, 2005).

Yet, documenting the disappearance of the belief in purgatory is rather difficult. Sociological and historical studies of Catholic belief and practice since the council so completely assume its disappearance that it is not considered to be an illuminating site of investigation. The Gallup Poll Index from 1935 to 1997 makes no mention of purgatory (Alec M. Gallup, *The Gallup Poll Cumulative Index, Public Opinion 1935–1997* [Wilmington, DE: Scholarly Resources, Inc., 1999], 82–84). No mention of purgatory appears in the following excellent studies of postconciliar American Catholicism: Chester Gillis, *Roman Catholicism in America* (New York: Columbia University Press, 1999); Dean R. Hoge et al., *Young Adult Catholics: Religion in the Culture of Choice* (Notre Dame, IN: University of Notre Dame Press, 2001); James M. O'Toole, ed., *Habits of Devotion: Catholic Religious Practice in Twentieth-Century America* (Ithaca, NY: Cornell University Press, 2004). A personal story here might illustrate the experience of late middle-age Catholics who can still remember the power of purgatory in the preconciliar Church. In the year 2000, my parish church in Trumbull, Connecticut, was designated one of several churches in the diocese where one could fulfill the conditions of a plenary indulgence to celebrate the Jubilee Year. The indulgence, of course, is meaningful in Catholic belief only as a remission of purgatorial punishment. And yet, there had been no homiletical talk of purgatory in the parish for decades. An explanation of the Jubilee Year indulgence from the pulpit made every effort to affirm its earning as a good and virtuous thing without saying what it was exactly or mentioning its connection to purgatory at all. The assumption on the part of the homilist, I believe, was that younger members of the congregation would not know what purgatory was and that older members had long left it behind.

As interesting as I find Richard Fenn's thesis that purgatory has not disappeared but has become quotidian in secularized American life, I think that he has stretched the purgatorial metaphor to the breaking point. See Richard K. Fenn, *The Persistence of Purgatory* (Cambridge: Cambridge University Press, 1995). My judgment that the belief in purgatory has disappeared in the life of the Church is a sociological one. I have no qualms about believing in the reality of the "third place."

94. "Dogmatic Constitution on the Church" (*Lumen gentium*), in *Vatican Council II: The Conciliar and Post Conciliar Documents*, ed. A. Flannery, O.P. (Northport, NY: Costello Publishing Company, 1987), 359–69 (*LG*, 9–17).

95. A possible third historical site to test the eclipse of purgatory by grace is the long-held suspicion of belief in purgatory in Eastern Christianity. Here, though, it would be correct to speak of the absence of the doctrine of purgatory rather than of its disappearance. Perhaps the Eastern doctrine of uncreated grace and the image of salvation as divinization are avenues to pursue in explaining the Eastern suspicion of the belief. For a historical account of the theological differences between East and West on purgatory, see G. Dagron, "La perception d'une différence: Les débuts de la 'Querelle du Purgatoire,'" *Actes du XV. Congrès International d'Études Byzantines: Athènes, Septembre 1976* (1980): 84–92.

96. Kathryn Tanner, *Jesus, Humanity, and the Trinity: A Brief Systematic Theology* (Minneapolis: Fortress Press, 2001), 85.

97. Ibid., 90, 91.

98. Ibid., 91.

99. Ibid., 93.

100. Ibid.

101. Tanner develops the specifically economic implications of this theological motif in her *Economy of Grace* (Minneapolis: Fortress Press, 2005).

102. Tanner, *Jesus, Humanity, and the Trinity*, 89.

Chapter 4. *Imagining the Last Judgment*

1. Carlos Eire notes that by the sixteenth century a commonly accepted formula for imagining purgatorial time as lengthy was that one day of suffering on earth was equivalent to a thousand years of purgatorial suffering. See Carlos Eire, *A Very Brief History of Eternity* (Princeton, NJ: Princeton University Press), 110–11.

2. See Reinhart Koselleck, *Futures Past: On the Semantics of Historical Time*, trans. K. Tribe (New York: Columbia University Press, 2004).

3. Giuseppe Marchini, *The Baptistery, the Cathedral and the Museum of the Opera del Duomo* (Florence: Becocci Editore, 1980), 20–25.

4. Ross King, *Brunelleschi's Dome: How a Renaissance Genius Reinvented Architecture* (New York: Walker & Company, 2000), 161.

5. These figures are presented in fine detail in a work on the recent restoration of the Duomo cupola. See Cristina Acidini Luchinat and Riccardo

Dalla Negra, *Cupola di Santa Maria del Fiore: Il Cantiere di Restauro, 1980–1995* (Rome: Instituto Poligrafico e Zecca Dello Stato, 1995).

6. See Renato Polacco, *Cattedrale di Torcello* (Venice: L'Altra Riva, 1984).

7. Caroline Walker Bynum, *The Resurrection of the Body in Western Christianity, 200–1336* (New York: Columbia University Press, 1995), 190.

8. See Francesco Cessi, *Giotto: La Cappella degli Scrovegni* (Florence: Editoriale Asuna, 1978); Giuseppe Basile, *Giotto: The Arena Chapel Frescoes* (London: Thames & Hudson, 1993).

9. Marcia Hall, *Michelangelo and the Frescoes of the Sistine Chapel* (New York: Harry N. Abrams, 2002), 218.

10. Bernadine Barnes, *Michelangelo's "The Last Judgment": The Renaissance Response* (Berkeley and Los Angeles: University of California Press, 1998), 34–35.

11. Dante Alighieri, *The Divine Comedy*, 6 vols. in 3, trans. C. S. Singleton, Bollingen Series 80 (Princeton, NJ: Princeton University Press, 1975), *Paradiso*: part 1, 334–45 (canto 30).

12. For a comprehensive art-historical study of the Last Judgment theme, see Martin Zlatohlávek, *Das Jüngste Gericht: Fresken, Bilder und Gemälde* (Düsseldorf: Benziger Verlag, 2001).

13. Although belief in the Last Judgment was the ancient faith of the Church and appeared as a creedal teaching as early as the Eleventh Council of Toledo (675), its eventfulness was not defined specifically until the Second Council of Lyons in 1274. See *Enchiridion Symbolorum Definitionum et Declarationum de Rebus Fidei et Morum*, 34th ed., ed. H. Denzinger and A. Schönmetzer (Freiburg im Breisgau: Herder, 1965), 276–77, par. 856.

14. Martin Luther, "Ninety-five Theses or Disputation on the Power and Efficacy of Indulgences," in *Luther's Works*, vol. 31, ed. H. J. Grimm (Philadelphia: Fortress Press, 1957), 25–33.

15. Scott H. Hendrix, *Luther and the Papacy: Stages in a Reformation Conflict* (Philadelphia: Fortress Press, 1981), 150–51.

16. Martin Luther, "Lectures on Zechariah," in *Luther's Works*, vol. 20, ed. H. C. Oswald (St. Louis, MO: Concordia Publishing House, 1973), 337.

17. Ibid., 337–38.

18. Martin Luther, "Lectures on Isaiah, Chapters 40–66," in *Luther's Works*, vol. 17, ed. H. C. Hilton (St. Louis, MO: Concordia Publishing, 1972), 411.

19. Ibid., 415.

20. Martin Luther, *The Bondage of the Will*, in *Luther's Works*, vol. 33, ed. P. S. Watson (Philadelphia: Fortress Press, 1972), 62.

21. Erasmus, *On the Freedom of the Will*, in *Luther and Erasmus: Free Will and Salvation*, Library of Christian Classics, ed. and trans. E. G. Rupp (Philadelphia: Westminster Press, 1969), 66–74.

22. Luther, *The Bondage of the Will*, 37.

23. Ibid., 288–89.

24. Martin Luther, "Sermons on the Gospel of St. John, Chapters 1–4," in *Luther's Works*, vol. 22, ed. J. Pelikan (St. Louis, MO: Concordia Publishing House, 1957), 384–85.

25. Ibid., 385.

26. Ibid. John Headley highlights Luther's concern for an existential theology that eschews speculation about divine mystery: "Luther emphasizes the reality of God's presence to the believer. He deplores the fact that people devote excessive attention to the doctrines concerning the past and future actions of God such as the Creation, Incarnation, the Last Judgment, and hell, while remaining insensitive to His present activity which manifests itself through His mercy in the sacraments, His forgiveness, and His grace" (John M. Headley, *Luther's View of Church History* [New Haven, CT: Yale University Press, 1963], 60).

27. Martin Luther, *Against Hanswurst*, in *Luther's Works*, vol. 41, ed. E. W. Gritsch (Philadelphia: Fortress Press 1966), 206.

28. It is not clear, though, what specific artwork Luther has in mind. It was certainly not typical for Church painters "of old" to represent a hell rife with clerics, including the pope. And yet the motif did exist in northern Germany. A good example is Stefan Lochner's altarpiece painting *The Last Judgment* (c. 1435), which configures hell as a grotesque chamber of horrors in which dwell an identifiable pope, cardinal, and bishop. Yet, the date of Lochner's painting suggests that his more likely intention was to portray the eschatological fate of the pretender pope and clerics of the Great Schism, which ended at the Council of Constance (1414–1418). With respect to Luther's interpretation, it would be wise to heed the suggestion of Christian Rogge, that Luther read the religious crisis of his day into the artistic motif of the Last Judgment: "Sinnend stand er [Luther] wohl vor den jene Zeit so ergreifenden Darstellungen des jüngsten Gerichts. . . . Dann sah er in seiner Art zu schauen in solchen Bildern den ganzen Jammer seiner Zeit, und sie wurden ihm zu einer furchtbaren Anklage der herrschenden Papstkirche" (Christian Rogge, "Luther und die Kirchenbilder seiner Zeit," in *Schriften des Vereins für Reformationsgeschichte* 29 [1912]: 27).

29. Luther, *Against Hanswurst*, 207.

30. I have found three analyses of this woodcut to be especially helpful: Steven Ozment, *The Age of Reform, 1250–1550: An Intellectual and Religious History of Late Medieval and Reformation Europe* (New Haven, CT: Yale University Press, 1980), 214–15; R. W. Scribner, *For the Sake of Simple Folk: Popular Propaganda for the German Reformation* (Cambridge: Cambridge University Press, 1981), 204–5; Eire, *A Very Brief History of Eternity*, 127.

31. Scribner, *For the Sake of Simple Folk*, 205–6.

32. See, for example, John Calvin, *Institutes of the Christian Religion,* Library of Christian Classics, vol. 1, ed. J. T. McNeill (Philadelphia: Westminster Press, 1977), 169 (1.14.8); vol. 2, 919 (3.20.52), 1447 (4.18.20).

33. Calvin, *Institutes of the Christian Religion,* vol. 2, 1004 (3.24.9).

34. Calvin, *Institutes of the Christian Religion,* vol. 1, 526 (2.16.18).

35. Tim LaHaye and Jerry B. Jenkins, *Glorious Appearing: The End of Days* (Wheaton, IL: Tyndale House, 2004), 225–26.

36. Ibid., 375.

37. Ibid., 375–76.

38. Ibid., 380.

39. For a discussion of the literal sense of tradition, see John E. Thiel, *Senses of Tradition: Continuity and Development in Catholic Faith* (New York: Oxford University Press, 2000), 31–55.

40. On the role of novel development in the truthful continuity of tradition, see Ibid., 129–60.

41. This Catholic doctrine is defined in the Council of Trent's "Decree on Justification (1546)." See *The Decrees of the Ecumenical Councils,* vol. 2, ed. N. Tanner, S.J. (Washington, DC: Georgetown University Press, 1990), 671–79, chaps. 1–16.

42. Frank Kermode, *The Sense of an Ending: Studies in the Theory of Fiction* (New York: Oxford University Press, 1967; reprint 2000), 23–24.

43. A fine example from modern fiction is Nabokov's novel *Laughter in the Dark* (1938), which begins: "Once upon a time there lived in Berlin, Germany, a man called Albinus. He was rich, respectable, happy; one day he abandoned his wife for the sake of a youthful mistress; he loved; he was not loved; and his life ended in disaster.

This is the whole of the story and we might have left it at that had there not been profit and pleasure in the telling; and although there is plenty of space on a gravestone to contain, bound in moss, the abridged version of a man's life, detail is always welcome" (Vladimir Nabokov, *Laughter in the Dark* [New York: New Directions Publishing, 1966], 7). Another example is Toni Morrison's *Beloved,* which reveals its terrible climax in the book's opening pages; see Toni Morrison, *Beloved* (New York: Penguin Books, 1987), 3–5.

44. Hans Urs von Balthasar, *Dare We Hope "That All Men Be Saved"?,* trans. D. Kipp and L. Krauth (San Francisco: Ignatius Press, 1987).

45. Gisbert Greshake, "Das Verhältnis 'Unsterblichkeit der Seele' und 'Auferstehung des Leibes' in problemgeschichtlicher Sicht," in Gisbert Greshake and Gerhard Lohfink, *Naherwartung, Auferstehung, Unsterblichkeit: Untersuchungen zur christlichen Eschatologie* (Freiburg: Herder, 1976), 92–97.

46. Ibid., 113–20.

47. Joseph Ratzinger, *Eschatology: Death and Eternal Life,* trans. M. Waldstein (Washington, DC: The Catholic University of America Press, 1988), 184.

48. Long before the Greshake–Ratzinger debate, though, Jonathan Edwards imagined a Last Judgment of transcultural and transhistorical proportions: "Thus all the nations of Europe have dealings one with another continually, and these European nations have some dealings with almost all other nations upon earth, in Asia, Africa and America. . . . 'Tis therefore necessary that all nations should be gathered together before the judgment seat of the supreme lawgiver and judge, that he by his judgment may determine between them and settle all things by his wise, righteous and infallible decision. . . . Posterity is concerned in the actions of their ancestors or predecessors in families, nations and most communities of men, as standing in some respect in their stead. And so some particular persons may by their actions injure, not only great part of the world that are contemporary with them, but injure and undo all future generations. So that men that live now on the earth may have an action against those that lived a thousand years ago, or there may be a cause that needs to be decided betwixt them by the Judge of the world" (Jonathan Edwards, *The "Miscellanies" [Entry Nos. 833–1152]*, in *The Works of Jonathan Edwards*, vol. 20, ed. A. P. Pauw [New Haven, CT: Yale University Press, 2002], 338–40, no. 1007).

49. For the development of this theological perspective, see John E. Thiel, *God, Evil, and Innocent Suffering: A Theological Reflection* (New York: Crossroad, 2002).

50. Catherine of Genoa, *Purgation and Purgatory*, in *Purgation and Purgatory, The Spiritual Dialogue*, trans. S. Hughes (New York: Paulist Press, 1979), 72.

51. This purgative notion of judgment raises the question of whether a final, eschatological rejection of God is a possibility. The answer, of course, is "yes," not only because the kind of eschatological reflection offered here is speculative but also because, as Karl Rahner has observed, "[i]f this possibility did not exist, then basically there would be no real subjectivity in freedom" (Karl Rahner, *Foundations in Christian Faith: An Introduction to the Idea of Christianity*, trans. W. V. Dych [New York: Seabury Press, 1978], 100). Yet, if we imagine the particular judgment as an encounter with the transforming power of the Beatific Vision, rather than imagine, as the tradition has, the Beatific Vision as the salvational culmination of the particular judgment that typically requires the purgation of sin in purgatory before the Beatific Vision is beheld, then we may be able to imagine a circumstance in which a free will with full integrity, and with the possibility of divine rejection, always in the face of judgment says "yes" to God. In many respects, traditional conceptions of heavenly life, which assume the willful integrity of the blessed dead while yet assuming the impossibility of sin, imagine an analogous circumstance, and not at the cost of heterodoxy. If God's grace and judgment are not the same, and eternal life is not a matter of competition, then we might

very well extend the traditional imaginary of the captivating power of the Beatific Vision over the will of the saints in heaven to those undergoing the particular judgment.

52. This talk of heavenly suspense is an occasion to address directly the issue of heavenly time. I have already noted in chapter 2 that an abiding prejudice against eschatologically thick description is a traditional tendency to conflate heavenly life with God's eternity understood as God's timelessness and so unchangeableness. This conflation is encouraged by traditional tendencies to imagine the heavenly joy of the saints rather statically. Yet, all Christian traditions, even those of the Eastern churches that prefer to imagine salvation as theosis, insist that creatures remain creatures in the resurrected state, and, more, through bodily resurrection remain in some real way the very creaturely persons they were in history. I have argued in chapter 2 that one consequence of the doctrine of bodily resurrection is that to be the selfsame persons in heavenly life that we were in history requires ongoing action on our part that shapes personal character, our very identities. And action, as event, requires time of some sort in order to unfold. Such supernatural time in God's New Creation should not be reduced to historical time, though like all dimensions of creation that share in Christ's resurrection we are obliged to imagine it as radically continuous with historical time and yet radically more than historical time. Thus, heavenly suspense in anticipation of the Last Judgment presumes the existence of supernatural time, as does the ongoing work of eschatological forgiveness on the part of the saints after the Last Judgment.

It is interesting that the International Theological Commission's 1992 text "Some Current Questions in Eschatology" has validated the importance of this conceptualization of a heavenly time in its criticism of the notion of a resurrection at the moment of death: "This community aspect of the final resurrection seems to be dissolved in the theory of resurrection in death, since the latter kind of resurrection would be purely individual. For this reason, some theologians who favour the theory of resurrection in death seek a solution in a so-called *atemporalism*: they say that after death time can in no way exist, and hold that the deaths of people are successive (viewed from the perspective of this world); whereas the resurrection of those people in the life after death, in which there would be no temporal distinctions, is (they think) simultaneous. But this attempted atemporalism, according to which successive individual deaths would coincide with a simultaneous collective resurrection, implies recourse to a philosophy of time quite foreign to biblical thought. The New Testament's way of speaking about the souls of the martyrs does not seem to remove them either from all reality of succession or from all perception of succession (cf. Rev 6:9–11). Similarly, if time should have no meaning after death, not even in some way merely analogous with its terrestrial meaning, it would be difficult to understand why Paul used formulas referring to the future (*anastesontai*) in speaking about their resurrection, when responding to the Thessalonians who were asking about the fate of the dead (cf. 1 Thess 4:13–18). Moreover, a radical denial of any meaning for time in those resurrections, deemed both simultaneous and taking place in the moment of death, does not seem to take sufficiently into account the truly corporeal nature of the resurrection; for a true body cannot be said to exist devoid of all notion of temporality. Even the souls of the blessed, since they are in communion with the Christ who has been raised in a bodily way, cannot be thought of without any connection with time" ("Some Current Questions in Eschatology," 2.2 [http://www.vatican.va/roman_curia/congregations/cfaith/cti_documents/rc _cti_1990_problemi-attuali-escatologia_en.html]).

53. Karl Rahner, "The Concept of Mystery in Catholic Theology," in *Theological Investigations*, vol. 4, trans. K. Smyth (Baltimore: Helicon Press, 1966), 41–42.

54. There are so many good examples, among which are Gustavo Gutiérrez, *A Theology of Liberation*, trans. C. Inda and J. Eagleson (Maryknoll, NY: Orbis Books, 1988); Elizabeth A. Johnson, *She Who Is: The Mystery of God in Feminist Theological Discourse* (New York: Crossroad, 1992); Sallie McFague, *The Body of God: An Ecological Theology* (Minneapolis: Fortress Press, 1993); Kwok Pui-lan, *Postcolonial Imagination and Feminist Theology* (Louisville, KY: Westminster John Knox, 2005); Joerg Rieger, *Christ and Empire: From Paul to Postcolonial Times* (Minneapolis: Fortress Press, 2007); M. Shawn Copeland, *Enfleshing Freedom: Body, Race, and Being* (Minneapolis: Fortress Press, 2010).

55. John Paul II articulates this position in a number of writings, beginning with the Apostolic Exhortation *Reconciliatio et paenitentia* (December 2, 1984), no. 16, and most pointedly in the encyclical *Sollicitudo rei socialis* (December 30, 1987), no. 36. For an illuminating summary of the development of the papal teaching, see Kristen E. Heyer, "Social Sin and Immigration: Good Fences Make Bad Neighbors," *Theological Studies* 71 (June 2010): 415–20.

56. Perhaps von Balthasar's account of eschatological surprise captures something of this suspense that I have suggested continues on in the heavenly kingdom: "In the community that comes into being through the Son's eternal *communio*, everyone is utterly open and available to each other, but this openness is not like the total perspicuity of states or situations: instead we have free persons freely available to each other on the basis of the unfathomable distinctness of each. What is offered to the other is thus always an unexpected and surprising gift" (Hans Urs von Balthasar, *Theo-Drama: Theological Dramatic Theory*, vol. 5: *The Last Act*, trans. G. Harrison [San Francisco: Ignatius Press, 1998], 485–86).

57. Jürgen Moltmann makes a similar distinction between God's judgment and grace in an eschatological context: "The 'Last Judgment' is not a terror. . . . It is a source of endlessly consoling joy to know, not just that the murderers will finally fail to triumph over their victims, but that they cannot in eternity even remain the murderers of their victims. The eschatological doctrine about the restoration of all things has these two sides: *God's Judgment*, which puts things to rights, and *God's kingdom*, which awakens to new life" (Jürgen Moltmann, *The Coming of God: Christian Eschatology*, trans. M. Kohl [Minneapolis: Fortress Press, 1996], 255).

58. This, of course, simply recalls the hope expressed by any number of the ancient Greek fathers. Athanasius may serve as one good example: "but rather let him marvel . . . that by death immortality has reached to all, and that by the Word becoming [human], the universal providence has been known, and its giver and artificer the very Word of God. For he was made [human] that we might be made God" (Athanasius, *On the Incarnation of the Word*, in *Christology of the Later Fathers*, Library of Christian Classics, ed. E. R. Hardy [Philadelphia: Westminster Press, 1954], 107).

Chapter 5. *Forgiveness in the Communion of the Saints*

1. Elizabeth A. Johnson, *Friends of God and Prophets: A Feminist Theological Reading of the Communion of the Saints* (New York: Continuum, 1998), 71–93.

2. *Catechism of the Catholic Church* (New York: Catholic Book Publishing, 1994), 49–50.

3. Few have written as poetically about this paradox as has Hans Urs von Balthasar in his reflection "The Coming of the Light," in *Heart of the World*, trans. E. Leiva (San Francisco: Ignatius Press, 1979), 37–57.

4. Jacques Derrida, "On Forgiveness," in *On Cosmopolitanism and Forgiveness*, trans. M. Dooley and M. Hughes (New York: Routledge, 2001), 32.

5. Ibid., 32–33.

6. Ibid., 45.

7. John Milbank, *Being Reconciled: Ontology and Pardon* (London: Routledge, 2003), 50.

8. Ibid., 51–52.

9. Ibid., 56–57.

10. Ibid., 59.

11. Ibid., 57.

12. Ibid., 58. In the face of these aporias to interhuman forgiveness, it is worth noting that David Konstan has argued that the idea of interhuman forgiveness is a product of the modern period. The virtue of forgiveness, he

claims, did not exist in ancient Greek or Roman culture, and in ancient Jewish and Christian cultures, forgiveness was conceived largely as a divine activity, not as a virtuously obligatory human act. See David Konstan, *Before Forgiveness: The Origins of a Moral Idea* (Cambridge: Cambridge University Press, 2010).

13. Ibid., 62.

14. In this respect, I follow the position of Vladimir Jankélévitch who argues that forgiveness only transpires in a relationship of mutuality between the guilty person forgiven and the forgiving victim. See Vladimir Jankélévitch, *Forgiveness*, trans. A. Kelley (Chicago: University of Chicago Press, 2005), esp. 106–55.

15. Jacques Derrida, *The Gift of Death*, trans. D. Wills (Chicago: University of Chicago Press, 1995).

16. John Milbank, "Can a Gift be Given? Prolegomena to a Future Trinitarian Metaphysic," *Modern Theology* 11 (1995): 137, 154.

17. Milbank, *Being Reconciled*, 57.

18. Sarah Coakley, "Why Gift? Gift, Gender, and Trinitarian Relations in Milbank and Tanner," *Scottish Journal of Theology* 61 (2008): 229.

19. Council of Trent's "Decree on Justification (1546)," in *The Decrees of the Ecumenical Councils*, vol. 2, ed. N. Tanner, S.J. (Washington, DC: Georgetown University Press, 1990), 672.

20. The traditional view of forgiveness understands the unilateral intention of the victim to forgive to be forgiveness itself. Defenders of the traditional view might ask what would the virtue of offering forgiveness, as the defeat of the anger caused by the evil suffered, be called if it is not yet forgiveness? The virtue might be called "serenity," or "magnanimity," or "generosity."

21. Johnson, *Friends of God and Prophets*, 79–85.

22. Ibid., 27–29.

23. A good example, though, is Maria Goretti (1890–1902; canonized 1950), who forgave her attacker and expressed the desire that she share his company in heaven just before she died of the wounds he inflicted.

24. C. S. Lewis offered a counterposition in his literary eschatology *The Great Divorce*. Through conversations between his narrator and a spirit-guide on their otherworldly journey, Lewis decries the notion of universal salvation as an affront to free choice. Lewis's plot unfolds in a supernatural vestibule to heaven in which the guilty dead must recognize their sinfulness and request forgiveness of the blessed dead whom they have wronged before they can enter heaven. But what they must realize is that their past sinfulness matters not at all in light of God's eternity. Forgiveness is not a heavenly activity and heavenly entry presumes a reconciliation already completely achieved.

Typical of the traditional Christian imaginary, Lewis expects the purity of heaven to transcend the effects of sin. See C. S. Lewis, *The Great Divorce: A Dream* (San Francisco: HarperSanFrancisco, 2001), 140–41.

25. Dante Alighieri, *The Divine Comedy*, 6 vols. in 3, trans. C. S. Singleton, Bollingen Series 80 (Princeton, NJ: Princeton University Press, 1970), *Inferno*: part 1, 25 (canto 3, 9).

26. L. Gregory Jones is especially eloquent on this point. See L. Gregory Jones, *Embodying Forgiveness: A Theological Analysis* (Grand Rapids, MI: William B. Eerdmanns Publishing, 1995), 251–62.

27. Anselm of Canterbury, "Why God Became Man," in *A Scholastic Miscellany: Anselm to Ockham*, Library of Christian Classics, ed. E. R. Fairweather (Philadelphia: Westminster Press, 1956), 100–183.

28. A good account of this charge, made by many, can be found in Elizabeth Schüssler Fiorenza, *Jesus: Miriam's Child, Sophia's Prophet: Critical Issues in Feminist Christology* (New York: Continuum, 1995), 98–107.

29. Dante Alighieri, *The Divine Comedy*, 6 vols. in 3, trans. C. S. Singleton, Bollingen Series 80 (Princeton, NJ: Princeton University Press, 1975), *Paradiso*: part 1, 159 (canto 14, 95–108).

30. Dürer's painting is not a unique example of this motif. The Flemish artist Hendrik van Balen (1575–1632) offers an even more striking version in his painting *The Trinity* (c. 1620), which has the heavenly assembly circle a papally vested God the Father, who holds the bloodless body of his crucified Son.

31. There is, of course, a striking difference between the effects of sin in Jesus' heavenly life and the effects of sin in the heavenly lives of all the saints. Jesus is utterly the innocent victim of sin, while all the saints are both innocent victims and guilty perpetrators. Thus, the revision of the traditional understanding of heavenly life I have proposed asks us to imagine that the effects of our innocence and guilt continue throughout eternity in a way that engenders virtuous practice, so that all the saints may contribute to the reconciling fulfillment of grace by the restoration of their broken communion.

32. On this point, I disagree with Miroslav Volf who has argued that final, eschatological redemption requires a forgetting of the guilty burden of sin so that forgiveness may be complete. See Miroslav Volf, *Exclusion and Embrace: A Theological Exploration of Identity, Otherness, and Reconciliation* (Nashville, TN: Abingdon Press, 1996), 131–40. Volf here parses eschatological forgiveness in terms of the traditional Christian imaginary that excludes the effects of sin from heavenly life at all costs. The consequence, though, is an anomalous understanding of resurrection. See also Miroslav Volf, *The End of Memory: Remembering Rightly in a Violent World* (Grand Rapids, MI: William B. Eerdmanns Publishing, 2006).

33. Thomas Aquinas, *The Summa Theologica of St. Thomas Aquinas*, trans. Fathers of the English Dominican Province (London: Burnes Oates & Washbourne, 1942), 107 (ST III [Supplement], 94, 1). This material in the Supplement to the *Summa* is redacted from Aquinas's discussion in his commentary on the *Sentences*. Cf. *Scriptum in IV Sent.*, dist. 50, q. 2, a. 4, q. la. 1.

34. Jonathan Edwards, *The Works of President Edwards*, 10 vols. (New York: G. & C. & H. Carville, 1829–1830), 6.120 (Sermon 11, on Mt 25:46, "The Eternity of Hell Torments").

INDEX

Anselm of Canterbury, 183–85
anticlimax, eschatological, 120–40
    fundamentalist version of,
        131–34, 136–37
    Lutheran and Reformed versions
        of, 120–31, 136
    Roman Catholicism's version of,
        134–35, 137–40
Antony of Egypt, 73–75, 77–78,
    80, 89, 93, 155
anxiety. *See* eschatological anxiety
Ariès, Philippe, 78, 198n18
Aristotelian metaphysics, 31
ascetic(s), 63, 72, 77–78, 80–93, 97,
    107, 155
    ascetical practice, 72–78, 86, 155
    ascetical values, 33–34, 39, 104,
        155–56
Athanasius, 73–75, 77, 80, 212n58
Augustine, 62–63, 79, 98, 193n35,
    197n16

Barnes, Bernadine, 116
Beatific Vision, 33, 35, 37, 40,
    48–49, 54, 57, 94, 96, 107, 117,
    146, 148, 168–69, 171, 179,
    184, 187, 209n51
Bede, 196n4
Benedict XII, 48–49

biology, medieval, 32
blessed dead, 9, 28, 35–38, 41,
    57–58, 147, 149, 151, 176, 179
    distance of, 10
    heavenly life of, 48–55, 146–51,
        169–71, 173–78, 181–82
    Rahner on, 9–12
Bonaventure, 75–77, 80
Boniface, 196n4
Brown, Peter, 68, 80, 82, 197n16,
    198n18
Brunelleschi, Filippo, 112–13
Buber, Martin, 50
Bynum, Caroline Walker, 41, 114

Calvin, John, 99, 131
cannibal thought experiment, 30–31
Catherine of Genoa, 62, 88–91,
    94–96, 146, 200n65
Catherine of Siena, 177
Catholicism, 39
    conservative, 58, 100
    Tridentine, 58, 100
Chalcedon, Council of, 183
Chaunu, Pierre, 78–79
chiliasm, 14, 121
Christianity, Eastern, 205n95
Christology, 51
    John's, 197n14

Tanner, Kathryn, 101–4
Teresa of Calcutta, 177
Tertullian, 198n19
theology
  apologetical, 6
  Barthian, 10
  Catholic, 17
  of the church, 5
  liberal, 10
  liberation, 150
  medieval, 14, 21, 92, 94
  modern, 2–3, 6, 12, 22, 183
  postmodern, 6, 23
  premodern, 6
  Reformation, 121
  speculative, 6
  theological anthropology, 5, 21
  of tradition, 5
Thiel, John E., 194n41, 208n39,
    209n49
Thomas Aquinas, 10, 37, 39–40,
    94, 96, 193n35
  on the heavenly state of
    resurrected bodies, 28–35
  on the joy of the blessed at
    the sight of the damned,
    186–87

time
  in heaven, 210n52
  in purgatory, 107–9, 205n1
  for saintly formation, 77–78,
    80–83, 91, 120
Toledo, Eleventh Council of, 206n13
Tracy, David, 6
tradition, 5, 55, 79, 99–101
Trent, Council of, 79, 98, 104,
    164–66, 179, 208n41
Trinity, 102, 185

universal salvation, 169, 146, 151–52,
    155, 179–83, 186, 213n24

van Balen, Hendrik, 214n30
Vasari, Giorgio, 113
Vatican II, 58, 60, 62, 98–99, 100,
    103, 107, 134–35, 155, 204n93
Volf, Miroslav, 214n32
von Balthasar, Hans Urs, 139
von Keppler, Paul Wilhelm, 95
Vovelle, Michel, 200n57

Weiss, Johannes, 1

Zuccari, Federico, 113

JOHN E. THIEL

is professor of Religious Studies at Fairfield University
and past president of the Catholic Theological Society of America.
He is the author of several books, among which are *Senses of Tradition:
Continuity and Development in Catholic Faith* and *God, Evil, and
Innocent Suffering: A Theological Reflection.*